AF352678

THE RISE OF AMERICANISM IN ITALY, 1888–1919

The Rise of Americanism in Italy, 1888–1919

LUCA COTTINI

UNIVERSITY OF TORONTO PRESS
Toronto Buffalo London

ISBN 978-1-4875-5998-4 (cloth)   ISBN 978-1-4875-6000-3 (EPUB)
                                 ISBN 978-1-4875-5999-1 (PDF)

Toronto Italian Studies

Library and Archives Canada Cataloguing in Publication
Title: The rise of Americanism in Italy, 1888–1919 / Luca Cottini.
Names: Cottini, Luca, author.
Series: Toronto Italian studies.
Description: Series statement: Toronto Italian studies | Includes
    bibliographical references and index.
Identifiers: Canadiana (print) 20240532244 | Canadiana (ebook) 20240532287 |
    ISBN 9781487559984 (cloth) | ISBN 9781487559991 (PDF) |
    ISBN 9781487560003 (EPUB)
Subjects: LCSH: Italy – Civilization – American influences. | LCSH: Italy –
    Relations – United States. | LCSH: United States – Relations – Italy.
Classification: LCC DG450 .C68 2025 | DDC 945/.08 – dc23

Cover design: Val Cooke
Cover image: iStock.com/Dmitr1ch

We wish to acknowledge the land on which the University of Toronto Press
operates. This land is the traditional territory of the Wendat, the Anishnaabeg,
the Haudenosaunee, the Métis, and the Mississaugas of the Credit First Nation.

This book has been published with the assistance of Villanova University.

University of Toronto Press acknowledges the financial support of the
Government of Canada, the Canada Council for the Arts, and the Ontario Arts
Council, an agency of the Government of Ontario, for its publishing activities.

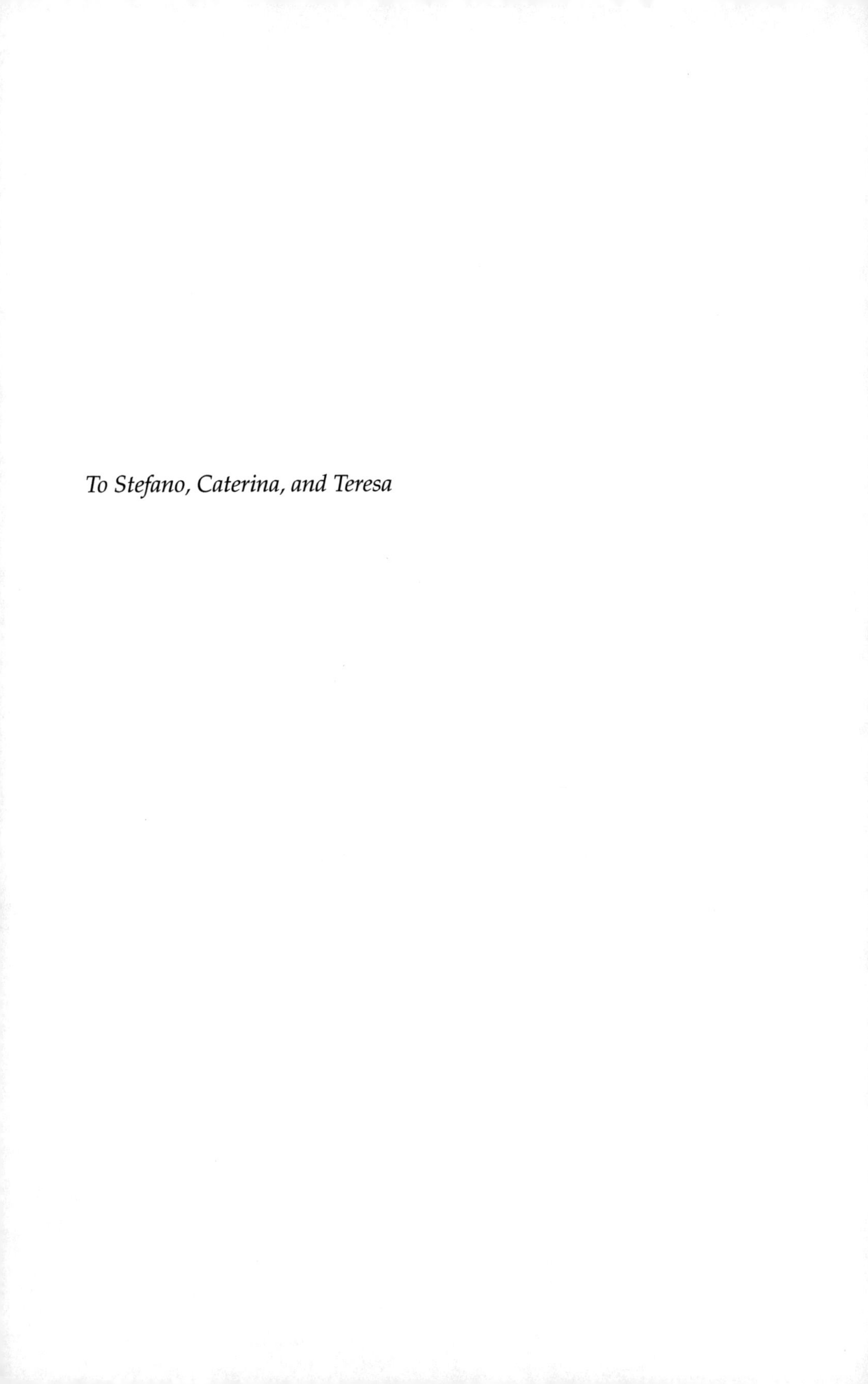

To Stefano, Caterina, and Teresa

Contents

Illustrations

Preface

Americanism is a slippery concept. From the eighteenth century to the present it has referred to a wide variety of ideologies and political agendas. It identified at one time or another with puritanism, republicanism, nativism, imperialism, industrialism, and modernism. It bolstered, on the left, multiculturalism, internationalism, and social reform, and, on the right, the primacy of national community, religious traditions, and local customs. It also embodied a value *in se* or a "creed" above ideologies, as echoed in the common expression "I believe in America" or as summed up in Richard Hofstadter's understanding that "it has been our fate as a nation not to have ideologies but to be one" (qtd. in Kazin and McCartin 1).[1]

In the collection of essays *Americanism: New Perspectives on the History of an Ideal* (2008), scholars Michael Kazin and Joseph McCartin proposed a minimalistic definition of this polyvalent corpus of ideas, reducing it to two core components: first, a descriptive drive to identify what is distinctive about the United States; and second, a political intention to buoy loyalty to the nation's ideals. In their view, these aspects diachronically apply to the diverse set of American self-representations as well as to the historical framework of external opinions about the United States.

The description of America's unique character often paired with the quest for foundational myths. The "quasi-religious ideal" of the nation as a land of mission, dream, and opportunity found legitimation in archetypal figures (e.g., the pilgrims, the Founding Fathers, Christopher Columbus, or the Western pioneers) and overarching visions. From colonial times to the republic, America embodied a "city upon the hill" (in John Winthrop's idea of the settlement as a promised land for a new Christendom), the outcome of a providential design (in John Adams's theorization of the nation's manifest destiny), "an asylum for mankind" (in the words of Thomas Paine), and a new frontier (Kazin and McCartin 2–3). These frameworks shaped a coherent narrative of Americanism, which created an "imagined community" of Americans (in Benedict Anderson's terms) and legitimized America's expansion.

In political terms, Americanism also indicated loyalty to the United States. The term acquired this connotation during the Revolutionary War when it signified support for the settlers' pursuit of independence. In the 1840s, in response to Irish and German Catholic immigration, the concept acquired a more restrictive meaning, designating loyalty to the "native" roots of the nation, identified in white Anglo-Saxon Protestantism. With mass emigration at the turn of the twentieth century, Americanism turned into the object of a lively public debate aimed at defining new forms of allegiance to the United States (since the 1891 introduction of Francis Bellamy's pledge in schools) and informing the integration of immigrants into American society – a process addressed as Americanization.

From an external viewpoint, Americanism concomitantly grew as a European set of projections and reactions to the American experiment. In the eighteenth century, America exemplified a synthesis of Rousseau's ideas on tolerance and natural freedom, a realization of the civil reforms theorized by the Enlightenment, and a utopic anticipation of changes to come,[2] yet also represented an appalling mix of political youthfulness, intellectual immaturity, and natural unpredictability to contemporary French philosophers and scientists (Roger 5–16). The cultural and commercial expansion of the United States throughout the nineteenth century elicited a renewed curiosity towards the nation, confirmed by the publication of Alexis de Tocqueville's report *De la démocratie en Amérique* (*Democracy in America*, 1835–40) and the upsurge of derogatory tropes, stemming from the "cultural snobbery" (Friedman 29) of travellers or the dystopic view of emigrants, and ranging from critique of American industrialism to fear over US global leadership.

The Rise of Americanism in Italy (1888–1919) explores the Italian reactions to the military, cultural, and industrial expansion of the United States at the turn of the twentieth century. Against the backdrop of mass emigration, early industrialization, and the clash with the Holy See (*questione romana*), the Italian view of Americans – in the United States and in Italy – sheds light on Americanism as a global project and documents its unique evolution in the peninsula as a two-way cultural, social, and economic exchange.

The Italian imagination of Americans in the United States illuminates the deep link between emigration and the Americanist debate, transforming the migratory phenomenon from exclusively negative to a strategic, political method of growing Italy's economic influence in America. Following this logic, a comparison of Italian and Vatican sources reveals not just a significant instance of collaboration between the secular state and the Catholic Church, at a time of radical clash, but also their common attempt to empower migrants, their shared endeavour to understand the new US dominance, and their mutual claim of primacy over America (in association with the expansionist ideology of Columbianism).

The Italian view of Americans in Italy documents the early (and often overlooked) phases of Americanization in the peninsula. The varied reactions to American imports (in finance, industry, and culture), their incorporation into the national milieu, and their creative re-elaboration into an endogenous subculture highlight Italy's excited and frightened negotiation of industrial modernity and display the first steps of American penetration in the country, decades before the setting of boots on the ground in 1917. In this sense, the study of Italian Americanism certifies an earlier start of the "American century" and locates its incubation years in the early 1900s.

The Italian outlook on America's new global dominance and penetration in the peninsula aims then to restitute a complex, bilateral view of Americanism in the years between Italy's first emigration law in 1888 and Woodrow Wilson's peace negotiations at Versailles in 1919. Such an inquiry into the diversified meanings of Americanism touches upon a wide variety of materials, sources, and methods and necessarily follows an episodic narration, which, rather than claiming to exhaust research on the selected topics,[3] aims to reconsider this heterogeneous "cloud" of phenomena as a coherent, transnational, and multifocal constellation of factors.

In terms of method, the examination of America's first involvement in Italy's affairs stems from the comparative analysis of Italian, Vatican, and American sources, and the integrated reading of journal debates and their literary or visual counterparts. In examining emigration, I relate fictions to press articles (mainly from the liberal newspaper *Corriere della sera*), and secular reports of Italian travellers to missionary accounts. In considering the evolution of Columbianism into Americanism, from the Columbian centenary celebrations to the Spanish-American War, I observe American and Italian secular texts in dialogue with Pope Leo XIII's documents addressing the US church (as both an Italian and a universal pastor). In surveying US imports in Italy and their Italian re-elaborations, I isolate the most impactful American figures and events in the Italian public opinion, as well as the most relevant American influences in contemporary literature, photography, cinema, and theatre. Lastly, in dealing with Wilsonianism, I investigate Italian and American First World War sources related to common military, sanitary, and entrepreneurial projects.

The chapters are ordered chronologically, even though phenomena often overlap.

In the introductory chapter I offer an overview of the historical meanings of Americanism and Americanization in the United States and consider their implications in Italy at the time of the great emigration.

In chapter 1, I explore the debates surrounding the passing of Italy's first emigration law in 1888 and the diplomatic crisis with the United States following the lynching of "Italians" in New Orleans in 1891. In this context I consider Americanism as a confusing mix of negative and positive reactions towards America (intended then more as a continent than a country) and relate the alternate views of the United States as a land of opportunities or doom to contemporary debates. Such opposition takes form in the secular division of pro- and anti-migration parties (*migrazionisti* versus *anti-migrazionisti*), as well as in the ecclesial contrast between conciliatory and intransigent bishops (*conciliatoristi* versus *intransigentisti*), respectively embracing or rejecting collaboration with the national state.

In chapter 2, focusing on the spreading of Columbianism between 1892 and 1899, I explore the making of Christopher Columbus as an Italian, Vatican, and American hero prior to and following the centenary expositions of Genoa (1892) and Chicago (1893), and I document the transformation of the Columbian myth from a self-legitimizing ideal to an expansionist ideology. With regards to the United States, I observe the reconfiguration of Columbus from a proto-American entrepreneur to a "civilizing conqueror," legitimizing US imperial ambitions over Cuba and the Philippines. With regards to Italy and the Holy See, I consider the reframing of Columbus from a model of faith or primary hero for immigrants into a "betrayed father" in the wake of Spanish defeat in 1898.

In chapter 3, ranging from the ascent of Theodore Roosevelt to the presidency (after the assassination of William McKinley in 1901) to the death in Rome of US financier John Pierpont Morgan in 1913, I explore the early stages of American industrial and cultural expansion in Italian society. I reconstruct the formation of American influence in Italy through mediatic events (e.g., Buffalo Bill's 1906 Italian tour or Wilbur Wright's 1909 first demonstration of flight), the economic impact of American tourists and investors (e.g., Thomas Alva Edison, Theodore Roosevelt, and John Pierpont Morgan), as well as the influence of such artists and intellectuals as the writer Henry James, the painter John

Sargent, the collector Isabella Stewart Gardner, the professor Bernard Berenson, the philosopher William James, and the theosopher Helena Blavatsky. In these experiences I detect the first steps of Italy's Americanization, from the early legitimization process aimed at dislodging Americanism from its negative connection to emigration, to the proactive promotion of the American model as a valid alternative to the pervasive influence of French and German cultures upon the Italian milieu.

In chapter 4, spanning from the 1900 killing of Umberto I to the 1915 Italian entrance into the Great War, I investigate Italian Americanism as a creative re-elaboration of US inputs, as an anti-positivistic philosophy of life, and as an independent ideology of modernization. I trace these perceptions in the development of pictorialism in photography (in dialogue with American master Alfred Stieglitz); the evolution of Italian cinema into an industry (in parallel with the diffusion of American movie theatres); the impact of Buffalo Bill on Italian Western narrations; the spreading of American pragmatism (in the cultural translation of Giovanni Papini's *Leonardo*); the emergence of spiritism and theosophy (in the work of Luigi Pirandello and Antonio Fogazzaro); and the appearance of a new emigration literature, proposing a positive view of America through the eyes of returnees.

In chapter 5, dedicated to the pre-war years and the First World War, I investigate Wilson's transformation of Americanism into a transatlantic platform of international cooperation and reconstruct the first projects of Italian and American exchange, as expressed by Carolina Amari and Maria Montessori in the fields of female entrepreneurship and education, and by Gino Speranza and Fiorello La Guardia in the field of immigrant services. I also explore the role of the Young Men's Christian Association (YMCA) and the American Red Cross (ARC) in reframing the First World War era's Americanism from a logic of expansion and ownership to a paradigm of international leadership and mutual aid. In considering American war propaganda, I reconstruct the phases of Wilson's rise and fall in Italy between 1918 and 1919 and follow the reconfiguration of US Americanism into an isolationist movement and of Italian anti-Wilsonianism into national revanchism.

In the epilogue I trace the evolution of Americanism into nativism in the prohibition era, examine Fascist ambivalence towards America from the countercultural Italianism of the 1920s to the pro-American movements of the 1930s, and observe the war-time formation of anti-Americanism and its legacies from 1945 to the present.

In our age of anti-Americanism, this study of Americanism (seen from Italy and by Italians) aspires to offer a non-English-speaking perspective on the concept and elicit a renewed reflection on the original meanings of the "American creed." May the exploration of this complex bundle of values and beliefs defining American identity or loyalty also provide ground to rethink anti-Americanism and criticism of the United States in less instinctive or partisan terms.

A note on translations: Unless otherwise indicated, all translations from Italian to English are my own.

Acknowledgments

Every book is the synthesis of many voices, inspirations, and contributions. As I complete this new work, I carry with me all the people who supported, fashioned, and informed it – colleagues, students, viewers, and readers, who kept my curiosity alive and gave me the humility and audacity to pursue this scholarly journey. I can't thank all of you individually here but be aware that this volume owes much to your encouragement, inspiration, and even criticism.

I want to express a special token of gratitude to my colleagues in Italian Studies Eugenia Paulicelli, Ara Merjian, Jeffrey Schnapp, Guido Bonsaver, James Kriesel, and Stefano Baldassarri for always enriching my scholarly ventures; to my students at Villanova for turning my research into a space of dialogue; and to my YouTube followers on *Italian Innovators* for pushing me to think outside the box. A particular recognition also goes to Alexandra Ferretti and Angela Wingfield for editing my manuscript and to Mark Thompson for the trust in this project. A final thanks goes to Lisa Tortolani and to Villanova University, which made this publication possible through the Grant for Research for Arts and Sciences Professors.

A long-term project like a book would not take shape without a larger community of people, and I would like to acknowledge my parents, relatives, and friends all over the world. The greatest thank you, however, goes to my children, Stefano, Caterina, and Teresa, who nurture in me the wonder of knowing, and to my wife, Jen, who patiently reminds me that all my academic endeavours are part of a much bigger and even more beautiful Adventure.

THE RISE OF AMERICANISM IN ITALY, 1888–1919

Introduction: The Historical Meanings of Americanism and Americanization

Before the late nineteenth-century debate, *Americanism* was a rarely adopted term and a rather nebulous idea (Shalhope 53). Associated with a quasi-religious doctrine in colonial times, the term assumed a political connotation in the eighteenth and early nineteenth centuries in connection with Thomas Jefferson and republicanism. Jefferson saw "pure Americanism" (Chinard 341) as the expression of America's unique political experiment and, since the Revolutionary War, as the new patriotic allegiance owed to the United States. Republicanism associated it with the principles of self-sufficiency, disentanglement from Europe, and government for and by the people. As *Americanism* gained ground in nineteenth-century vernacular, the term subsumed the meanings of *republicanism*, designating "fervent belief in nationalism, individualism, and free enterprise" (Shalhope 67).

By the early 1840s, Americanism had also acquired an ethnic implication in relation to German and Irish immigration. Rising fears of cultural contamination and Catholic "Romanism" led to the formation of a nativist movement, which claimed Anglo-Saxon Protestantism as the root of American identity. Its political expressions were the Native American Party (which denoted as *native* not the Amerindians but the settlers' offspring) and, starting in the 1850s, the Know-Nothing Party, a semi-secret organization that promoted the nation's original or native values against foreign or Catholic influences. The party emerged on the political scene in 1854, when it elected eight governors, more than one hundred congressmen, the mayors of Boston, Philadelphia, and Chicago, and thousands of local officials (Anbinder ix), but its growth rapidly waned before and during the American Civil War. As ensuing waves of immigrants fuelled the growth of American industry in the post–Reconstruction era, Americanism gradually shifted from the defence of a native heritage to a broader meaning, indicating the debate on what defines American identity within a plural society.

During the same time, Americanism had also emerged in Europe as a cultural framework of projections and reactions about America. The "fever of Americanism" (Kane 50) found ambivalent outlets in eighteenth-century Europe. On the one hand, widespread enthusiasm for Benjamin Franklin stirred the elites' curiosity towards John Locke's *Constitutions of Carolina* or William Penn's legislation on religious tolerance in Pennsylvania.[1] Franklin's presence in France also leveraged support for American independence, as confirmed by King Louis XVI's signing of the first trade agreement recognizing the colonies and by the enthusiasm over the 1782 *Letters from an American Farmer* by the French expatriate Hector St. John de Crévecoeur.[2] On the other hand, persistent suspicion towards the New World continued to appear in contemporary philosophical critiques, iterating the trope of America's psychological and intellectual backwardness, as well as in Comte de Buffon's scientific theory relating the continent's natural, geological, and anthropological newness to the prolonged effects of an "American flood."[3]

The ambiguity towards America continued in the nineteenth century, as discourses on the United States pictured the nation as either a dream of abundance or a demonic land ruled by the mob, Mammon, or the industrial Moloch. While lower-class immigrants saw in it an escape or the promise of a new future, educated European travellers generally assumed a critical attitude towards it, mocking its "artistic sterility" (Roger 36), attacking its dependence on tools and machines, and scorning its democracy, which still tolerated slavery. In exaggerating America's contradictions and in nurturing stereotypes of its vulgarity, their reports promoted an idealized version of Europe "as the aesthetic bulwark against rampant American materialism and industrialism" (O'Connor 13). A similar resentfulness towards the United States also appears in the writings of contemporary Latin American intellectuals who critically addressed Americans as *estadounidenses* and forged a two-hemisphere idea of *panamericanísmo* against the exclusive view of North American hegemony.

Against this backdrop, the introduction investigates the historical emergence of Americanism as a conscious social debate, explores the concept of Americanization as a domestic and global project, and observes the spreading of American ideology from a contemporary Italian viewpoint.

The Debate on Americanism from Roosevelt to Wilson

The centennial exposition of Philadelphia in 1876 and the Columbian exposition of Chicago in 1893 represented two symbolic moments to reassess American identity in the wake of the nation's industrial revolution. The reappropriation of US beginnings (in the Declaration of Independence and Columbus's voyages) ideally framed the ensuing debate on Americanism by establishing a broad narrative, which simultaneously confirmed the "native" stock of settlers and included a cohort of newcomers.

The "deeply engrained belief in the historical uniqueness and originality of the American experience" (Confessore 14) took form as an inward and outward reflection. On the one hand, as several intellectuals tried "to dislodge liberal democracy from its mooring in Anglo-American culture and history and to reestablish it on a civic foundation consistent with cultural pluralism" (Hansen 74), Americanism indicated the push to anchor American loyalty no longer in ethnicity or birthplace but rather in the commitment to a specific set of values (e.g., democracy, freedom, and progress). In this sense, Americanism engendered a process of assimilation and negotiation, which found expression in the call for the Americanization of immigrants and the new foundational narrative of the "melting pot" (in the words of Israel Zangwill's 1908 play). On the other hand, in relation to US territorial and commercial acquisitions (in the Caribbean, Pacific, and European markets), Americanism acquired during the same years an international valency indicating not just the effort to promote American products and way of life abroad but also the fashioning of such expansion as a universal export or civilizing mission (as hypothesized in William Stead's 1901 book *The Americanization of the World*).

The internal debate on Americanism mainly took shape around the diverse political views of presidents Theodore Roosevelt (1901–9) and Woodrow Wilson (1913–21). Theodore Roosevelt first proposed a reflection on the meanings of Americanism in the article "What 'Americanism' Means," which he wrote for *The Forum* in the spring of 1894.[4] Starting from his assessment that the nation "lacked the spirit of 'true Americanism'" (Hansen 73), Roosevelt aimed to dampen public fears over the clash with alien cultures (Morris 37) and to "educate both immigrants and citizens about what it meant to an American" (Dorsey and Harlow 57). By proposing a "broad" notion of Americanism as "a question of spirit, conviction, and purpose, not of creed or birthplace," he called Americans to move beyond the "unwholesome parochial spirit" of little communities, to embrace patriotism as loyalty to the country (and not to the village or previous origin), and to work for the Americanization of newcomers (Roosevelt, "What 'Americanism' Means").[5] Moving from an ethnical/ethical paradigm (rooting American character in "native" values and heritage), he broadly refashioned American identity as a combination of physical strength, moral character, and earned equality (Dorsey 4). At the same time, he promoted the ideal of the "strenuous" or "rugged" life as a path to national reinvigoration, a remedy against immorality and greed, and a formation ground for outsiders to assimilate the country's practices. Roosevelt embodied this new archetype in his military and political career, as well as in his own writings, as exemplified by his six-volume collection *The Winning of the West* (which he published between 1885 and 1894) and *The Rough Riders* (which he published in 1899, following his involvement in the Spanish-American War).

The Winning of the West reframed the story of the early Western settlements from 1763 to 1803 into a new frontier narrative, fuelling the nation's renewed expansion after General Custer's 1876 loss at Little Big Horn. Against the backdrop of his personal experience, Roosevelt portrayed the West as a space of conquest and civilization, equating the efforts of the settlers to the pioneering discoveries of Columbus, and retrieving the doctrine of manifest destiny underlying the first establishment of US colonies. At the same time, he crafted his stories as an all-encompassing narrative, renewing a sense of mission in native-born whites (through civilizing or modernizing settlements) and offering immigrants a character-building experience (allowing them to overcome racial bias and earn the status of "real" Americans).[6]

The Rough Riders iterated the trope of the "rugged" life and extended the notion of "broad" or "earned" Americanism to territories beyond the national borders. In reporting his experience as leader of the First U.S. Volunteer Cavalry Regiment (addressed by the press as the "rough riders"; Samuels 148) and offering an account of his victory in the battle at Kettle Hill (in Cuba on 1 July 1898; Brands 356), Roosevelt framed the Spanish-American War as a continuation of America's civilizing mission to the neighbouring geographies of the Caribbean and the Pacific (after the annexation of Puerto Rico, Hawaii, Guam, and the Philippines). The same framework would apply to his actions as president of the United States, as Roosevelt de facto turned Americanism into an imperialist ideology, advancing American colonization in the Philippines, supporting American investments in Panama, and leveraging US commercial penetration in Europe.

Americanism continued to be a central topic in US public debate at the end of Roosevelt's tenure, in relation to Wilson's political rise and the outbreak of the Great War in 1914. Far from Roosevelt's "civilizing" expansionism, Wilson viewed Americanism as an ideal of cosmopolitan cooperation and mutual aid. His goal to peacefully embolden American leadership in international relations found expression in his support for pan-Americanism and his choice of neutrality during the European war, which aimed at promoting the development of commercial and humanitarian webs of relief and establishing the United States as a global peacemaker.

The outbreak of the First World War marked a radical split with Roosevelt, who rallied for American intervention in Europe by targeting Germans as unloyal to the nation and endorsing a renewed commitment to American values against divided allegiances. In his 1915 speech to the Catholic organization of the Knights of Columbus, Roosevelt reframed the concept of Americanism, as a civilizing mission against "barbaric" Germans (ideally prolonging the missions of Columbus and the Western pioneers) and as a call to abolish old loyalties of hyphenated groups.[7]

Despite common acceptance of the need to assimilate migrants into American society, which was confirmed by Wilson's 1915 proposal "to make the Fourth of July 'Americanization Day'" (Hansen 73), the electoral campaign of 1916 (which eventually led Wilson to a second term) marked a profound division over the concept of Americanism, which indicated either an undefined cloud of narrowly defined "American interests" or a more specific split over the nature and scope of America's expected intervention in Europe.

In one sense, as documented in the essay written by Agnes Repplier for *The Atlantic* in March 1916, "Americanism" defined the delimited interests of different social groups. The writer offered a testimony of its polyvalent implications by commenting on the results of a symposium organized by the *American Journal of Sociology* surveying the opinions of 250 "representative" Americans and mocking the interviewees' inability to look beyond one issue: "the prohibitionist discerned Americanism in prohibition, the equal suffragist in votes for women, the biologist in applied science, the physician in the extirpation of microbes, the philanthropist in playgrounds, the sociologist in eugenism and old-age pensions, and the manufacturer in the revision of taxes" (Repplier, "Americanism").

In another sense, as the debate over America's response to war escalated in early 1917, Americanism acquired a more specific strategic and ideal connotation. Even though Roosevelt obtained authority from Congress to recruit four divisions in March 1917, on the model of his own Rough Riders, Wilson refused to send his volunteers to France,[8] and organized instead a US expeditionary force (Brands 781–4), entrusting General John Pershing with the mission to protect American commercial interests, prolong sanitary assistance in Europe, and lead the Allies towards a peaceful resolution of the conflict. According to this ideal, as Friedman states, "Americans thought of themselves as magnanimously entering a war not only to protect their own interests – to prevent a catastrophic default on loans made to France and Britain, and to defend free passage for neutral shipping, a long-standing principle in the diplomacy of a country that had always depended on international trade – but also to offer European allies a helping hand in the fight and guide them toward the right kind of peace when it was over: 'saving the world' in Wilson's phrase" (70).

The US entrance into war had a double effect on the United States and Europe. At home the conflict rapidly "swamped cosmopolitan patriotism in a wave of jingoism" (Hansen 84). In Europe the United States' late involvement in war and limited engagement in combat appeared, to some, an uplifting aid (in morale, troops, and resources) and, to others, a disingenuous form of commercial penetration.

Despite Wilson's widespread popularity, underlying scepticism towards the United States broke out in the spring of 1919, as European resentment over post-war agreements triggered an upsurge of anti-Americanism and nationalist revanche. Back in the United States the turmoil caused by social unrest, delayed mobilization, and the spreading of the influenza pandemic weakened Wilson's political grasp, reviving fears over a new incoming wave of war refugees from Europe and the moral call to defend the nation's values. Paralleling the start of prohibition (after the 1919 passing of the Eighteenth Amendment), Americanism rapidly shifted from a global peacemaking ideal to an ethical and ethnic marker, in connection with the anti-Communist reaction to Bolshevik Russia, the campaign to restrict emigration, and the rationalization of "segregation as an essential component of the American way of life" (Kazin and McCartin 5).

From Assimilation to Export: Americanization as an Outward Projection of Americanism

As the United States moved from a predominantly agricultural economy to an industrial system of mass production in the second half of the nineteenth century – surpassing Great Britain in the production of steel (1887), iron (1890), and coal (1899) – the word *Americanization* came to reflect a notion of process: of assimilation (for incoming immigrants) and self-discovery (for regular citizens).

Inwardly, such process indicated the intentional effort to complete the nation's transformation from a former colony into a leading world power. Outwardly, the process identified a generic "American advance" (De Grazia xxiv), which US citizens saw in terms of growth, influence, and soft power, and which Europeans saw in terms of challenge, inspiration, or threat. It follows that *Americanization* designated both an explicit American strategy/theory of self-diffusion and a set of European perceptions surrounding US economic, cultural, and military expansion.

In its first meaning, Americanization implied the projection of the American way of life abroad and its manufacturing into a "worldview" (Ellwood 25). Although the 1898 war over Cuba and the 1917 involvement in the European war were visible manifestations of the American project of extraterritorial dominance, US imperialist ambitions found primary expression through the peaceful instruments of "industry, business, inventions, entertainments, and a new kind of man and woman" (Ellwood 27). Whether in the Caribbean, the South Pacific, or Europe, US influence abroad was mostly enlarged through the soft power of comfort culture (extending convenience to the masses), new modern practices (e.g., sports and entertainment), or spellbinding figures (like Buffalo Bill, Wilbur Wright, and the American presidents Theodore Roosevelt and Woodrow Wilson).

As branded consumer goods like Singer sewing machines, Kodak cameras, Gillette razors, Philadelphia cream cheese, Duke cigarettes, Maxwell House instant coffee, Waterman pens, and Edison light bulbs spread in new international markets, they shaped new spheres of American dominance, adding to US established primacy in food export and railway networks (Sassoon 604) and carrying their associated values. Their global diffusion paralleled an aggressive strategy of domestic economic control, attested not only by the contemporary adoption of strict tariff policies for European products but also by the United States' taking over of the Panama Canal project from France.

Exhibitions and mass culture were also key components in the global diffusion of the American lifestyle. Itinerant exhibitions worked as promotional tools, displaying new American practices and recent US history: baseball tours showcased the national sport in the British Isles (in 1874) and the major cities of the world (in 1888–9 and 1913–14);[9] and Buffalo Bill's *Wild West* show first packaged a serial narration of America's westward expansion. Mass culture similarly marketed the nation's association with modernity and progress, from the nineteenth-century growth of America's publishing industry (stirred by education, urbanization, and immigration) to the early twentieth-century development of new forms of communication. The mass-scale evolution of the press not only launched sports but also fashioned emerging technologies (e.g., gramophones and cinematography) into powerful media, empowering the rise of a record market (which spread jazz), and the creation of an entertainment system (later leading to Hollywood's "cinematic invasion of Europe"; Sassoon 816).[10]

The early idea of Americanization as a pragmatic strategy of soft expansion became an explicit political doctrine under Woodrow Wilson. The US president first theorized the "belief that material comforts were an inalienable corollary of the rights to life, liberty, and the pursuit of happiness," openly relating the spreading of America's commodities and values to its "peaceful conquest of the world" (De Grazia 3).[11] As he spoke at the Detroit Convention of Salesmen in the headquarters of the Ford Motor Company on 10 July 1916, Wilson reframed Americanization into an intrinsic necessity, not only to expand Fordism as a manufacturing system, granting low-cost goods and decent wages for workers, but also to extend the American way into a new "Market Empire," conceived as "a great imperium with the outlook of a great emporium" (De Grazia 3). Its foundations lay (and still lie) in a combination of economic development, democratic stability, and global peace, and its realization became the obsession of Wilson's international political actions and war propaganda.

The gradual rise of the United States also contributed a second connotation to Americanization. The French poet Charles Baudelaire first used the verb *to Americanize* to signify the spectre of utilitarianism, the tyranny of public opinion, and the gloomy vision of a new age "marked by the supremacy of America and of industry" (*Painter of Modern Life* 209).[12] His dreadful view of America's civilization framed the later attitude of French public opinion towards the American Civil War, as the press took sides with the Confederacy (despite rejecting slavery) and read the emancipation war as an attempt by the industrialized North to subjugate the South (Roger 79–84). Baudelaire's critique of the United States' "ugly" or anonymous technocracy also informed the spreading of aesthetic anti-Americanism, which later framed European reactions to American military action in Cuba, denounced by the French press as "unaesthetic and inhuman" (Roger 143).

The 1898 Spanish-American War unveiled the "suspended anti-Americanism" of Europeans (Roger 138), who – seeing the American military intervention against Spain as the breaking of a taboo – reacted to it with heightened alert, criticism, and dread and rapidly refashioned America from an object of curiosity to an object of fear. When the United States first set foot on European soil nineteen years later, such pervasive concern over the "American peril" would find a similar, yet less explicit, manifestation in latent scepticism towards belated US intervention, puzzlement over President Wilson's choices, and growing frustration over transatlantic monetary dependence (as Americans became a creditor nation and imposed exchange rates; Ellwood 52–60).

The changing perceptions of Americanization also referred to different understandings of modernity and culture. On the one hand, the American ability to create, produce, and export visions of progress on a mass scale generated great interest, as attested by H.G. Wells's vision of the United States in *The Future in America* (1906) as a source of inspiration for his post-Victorian Britain, and also revamped nineteenth-century intellectual concerns over industrialism and capitalism (perhaps offering "a self-serving alibi, enabling intellectual whiners and moralizers to shift the blame to another nation for the novelties in contemporary life they found distasteful"; Ellwood 32). On the other hand, European reception of American practices and cultural industry related to a diverse understanding of the meanings of culture, which was alternatively seen as either an intellectual endeavour (high) or a business (low). In his monumental work *The Culture of the Europeans*, David Sassoon portends that the rejection or success of Americanization relates to the positioning of American cultural products not in "high culture" (as an elaboration of symbolic values for an educated niche) but rather in the category of "low" or "popular culture" (as a set of media or genres produced for a broader audience), as US imports (books, music, films) easily reached the consumer market, serializing production, formalizing new genres, and targeting diversified segments of the population.

The Italian case is illuminating in this sense. The country's historic diglossia of Latin and Italian, and the separation between high language (written) and low language (dialect) had prevented the creation of a large linguistic base,[13] as confirmed by its limited market for popular or women's literature (Sassoon 166). Faced with the lack of readership (which critic Ruggero Bonghi had debated in his 1855 article series "Perché la letteratura italiana non sia popolare in Italia" ["Why Italian literature is not popular in Italy"]), Italian authors often imitated French models, and Italian publishers generally relied upon proven translations of foreign works. The same *esterofilia* (love of things foreign) appeared in opera, where, despite the national language's status as the international idiom of music, Italian librettists rarely adapted Italian literary works and instead privileged imported models and global settings like Egypt, Japan, or the United States.

The diverse reactions to high or consumer culture mirror the chasm between the intellectual rejection of American modernity (permeated by subtle distaste for emigrating masses and negative accounts of travellers or returnees) and the growing popular acceptance of American idioms and mythologies, as documented in the enthusiasm for Westerns and the successful translation of Louisa May Alcott's *Little Women* in the two volumes *Da un Natale all'altro* (*From One Christmas to Another*) of 1908 and *Tre anni dopo* (*Three Years Later*) of 1911. The US publishing industry developed a strong market in the nineteenth century, publishing major works of high literature (e.g., *Moby Dick*, *The Scarlet Letter*), releasing bestsellers (e.g., *The Last of the Mohicans*, *Uncle Tom's Cabin*), and creating a popular series of "dime novels" (often based on customized genres or real-life heroes like Kit Carson and Davy Crockett). Building on this solid industrial foundation, US cultural production expanded in Italy, intercepting not just the interest in America raised by emigration but also a rising demand for mass entertainment that native writers could not meet (Sassoon 168). As they spread in the peninsula, American books (as later popular cinema or television) gradually created a readership, started social debates in the press, and silently established a new American influence.

Americanism in Italy at the Time of the Great Emigration

The Italian discourse on Americanism at the turn of the twentieth century echoes the impact of American popular culture, which was spreading in the peninsula in parallel with social debates on emigration, journalistic fears of Americanization, and an expanding market of US products.

The great emigration to the United States catalysed Italian anxieties of Americanization (heightened since the 1870s by the agricultural crisis and the growing import of American grain). Reports of Americans' anti-Italian bias, as well as German and French anti-American influences, represented major negative factors on the Italian reading of US expansion, or "Americanismo."

Italian migrants to the United States often experienced cultural criticism or racial prejudice. American stereotypes of Italians were culturally rooted in John Calvin's anti-Catholic writings, William Shakespeare's violence-filled dramas set in Italy, and the dismal accounts of exiles after the fall of the Roman Republic in 1848 (Connell 11–16). Anti-Italian resentment had also risen in response to migrants' seasonal and non-committal habits, their affiliations to anarchism or Catholicism, and the non-transparent management (often bordering on crime) of their labour organizations. At an academic level, the American portrayal of Southern Italians "as racial or cultural others" (Schneider 12)[14] and their association with crime had sprung from social Darwinism and the studies of positivist criminologist Cesare Lombroso, whose popular book *L'uomo delinquente* (*The Criminal Man*, 1876) had "made

race central to the analysis of Southern 'deviancy'" (Gibson 100), vali-
dating the equation of regional origins with a tendency to delinquency
(Luconi 127). The 1891 lynching of Italians in New Orleans sparked
these tensions, detonating a political and diplomatic crisis between
Italy and the United States (see ch. 1).

German presence in Italy's financial institutions and academia, as
well as the French influence on Italian sociology and literature (Mangoni, *Una crisi fine secolo* 62), offered another negative subtext to the
contemporary reading of Americanism. German investors saw the
United States as a competitor, potentially disrupting their financial
stakes in Italy's banks, industry, and infrastructures, and German
Marxists criticized emigration as an individual escape, distancing
militants from the proletariat's cause, or as an illusion, moved by the
empty promises of capitalism.[15] French sociological studies on the
masses – from Gustave Le Bon's *Psychologie des foules* (*The Psychology of
Crowds*) to fin de siècle debates on parliamentarism – implicitly associated rising fears over the participation of crowds in democratic life
with the unruly movements of peoples across the Atlantic. The revival
of religion promoted by Ferdinand Brunetière's *Revue des deux mondes*
as a remedy to the malaise of society and a cure against the unrest of
the masses implicitly validated the official anti-migratory framework
of Pope Leo XIII (see ch. 1).

Under the surface of high culture (whether in political or in academic
debates), Americanism continued to gain popularity in Italy, gradually
evolving from a set of assumptions about the United States to a journalistic narrative, from a repertoire of tropes and caricatures to an independent subculture, re-elaborating US imports in new Italian forms.

At first, Americanism implied an attitude of projection and verification. Contemporary Italian narratives compensated for the scarcity
of information about life in American destinations by dwelling on the
in-between space of the ocean (Dall'Osso 11) or by projecting a vision
of hopeful abundance and tragic disillusion upon "America." Travelling narratives by journalists, politicians, and Vatican nuncios visiting
North America also responded to the need to fill these gaps, certifying
the will to explore American culture and assess the rising dominance
of the United States. Although framed by a formulaic mix of curiosity
and disdain, these narratives nonetheless reveal the emergence of a
new strategic mindset, evaluating the opportunities of emigration and
the elements of convergence between the secular state and the Catholic
Church's missions. The treatises by travellers Egisto Rossi (1884) and
Angelo Mosso (1901) offer insights on American economy and political
institutions. The journalistic reports of parliamentary deputy Edoardo

Arbíb (under the pseudonym of Semplice) and the journalist Ugo Ojetti provide the direct vision of the Columbian exposition of Chicago and of the Spanish-American War. Similarly, the works of Italian missionaries and Vatican nuncios Francesco Satolli and Sebastiano Martinelli document the call to expand Catholic influence in the United States – as outlined in Leo XIII's encyclicals *Quarto saeculo abeunte* (*In the Upcoming Fourth Centenary*, 1892) and *Longiqua oceani* (*Wide Expanse of the Ocean*, 1895) and in his urge to promote papal authority against the spreading of Americanism (a set of doctrines that the pope would formally condemn in the 1899 letter *Testem benevolentiae nostrae* [*Witness to Our Good Will*]). The later address at the Italian chamber (on 22 June 1909) by the criminologist, former director of the Socialist newspaper *Avanti!*, and deputy Enrico Ferri attests to an impactful political shift, presenting emigration as a positive form of *"americanismo."* By reproaching emigrants and the state for their flaws "in practically programming transoceanic life,"[16] Ferri reframed migrations as part of the new global quest for "the conquest of the market,"[17] analysing push factors (e.g., increase in population, mandatory military draft, agrarian crisis) and pull factors (e.g., economic growth, global transportation network, increased labour demand in emerging countries), and presenting the Italian export "of men more than goods" (1239)[18] as an opportunity to expand commercial influence or establish permanent Italian colonies.

At the outbreak of the Spanish-American War, Americanism assumed a new form as a set of journalistic tropes, which replicated the general European disdain for the United States and capitalized on fears and curiosity towards the American nation. The 1898 call for a European union against America by former Italian foreign minister Admiral Canevaro (Ellwood 24) contributed to shifting the characterization of a Yankee from naive or ridiculed to his new portrayal as "the unscrupulous capitalist and the soulless inventor" (Roger 152). The pejorative profiling of American suffragism as a despicable "gynocracy" (Roger 185), and the picturing of the American "type" as predator, expansionist, and imperialist, significantly waned after the US victory. The rapid escalation of American-themed articles in the early 1900s and dedicated editorial sections in the 1910s (e.g., the "Americanate" in *La Domenica del Corriere*) suggests not just a new public craving for American culture but also the visibility that the United States had gained in the Italian imagination. As reported discourses or second-hand accounts were replaced by contextual humour and caricatures, American life gradually moved from an imagined space, seen from afar, to a daily topic of conversation for Italians. The sketching of American leitmotifs reflects an increasing acceptance and recognition of their lifestyle, as well as a lively space of dialogue and negotiation of their own modernity. For instance, Italian debates over the freedom that American women enjoyed in dressing, practising sports, and participating in democratic life outlined a "model of the future woman" (Dall'Osso 65) and promoted social conversations on emancipation and the feminine role in society. The portrayal of the United States as a land of acceleration, speed, and dynamism (brought forth by such American inventions as the telephone, the phonograph, and the aeroplane) matched the vision of Americans as restless and nervous humans and foregrounded the Futurist iconography of urban modernity. The tropes related to American eccentricity iterated the nineteenth-century view of the United States as a "codified, protocolled land of the unusual" (Dall'Osso 105) through the caricatures of American extravaganza (the so-called *americanate*). At the same time, the exaggeration or deformation of millionaires like Cornelius Vanderbilt, Andrew Carnegie, John Pierpont Morgan, and John Rockefeller also reflected a subtle critique of American materialism, greed, and seemingly endless cash liquidity.

As Americanism found fertile ground in Italy, the concept also applied at last to the Italian reconfiguration of US imports into an independent ideology or corpus of works. The emergence of mass tourism, the impact of American intellectuals on the Italian milieu, and US financial and technical investments in the peninsula heavily contributed to reframing anti-American discourses and promoting the American ideals of modernization, democracy, and work. Italians saw in such American imports an alternative entrepreneurial philosophy and anti-positivistic thought. In one way, the introduction of new American models of production and consumption (e.g., the adoption of Taylor's assembly line at Fiat and Olivetti in the early twentieth century, or Buffalo Bill's *Wild West* show) coincided with the dissemination of industry as a new entrepreneurial mindset and of culture as a mass-product. In another way, the spreading of American poetry, philosophy, photography, and religious experiences in Italy (e.g., in the diffusion of James's pragmatism, the success of Stieglitz's pictorialism, or the spreading of theosophy) connoted Americanism as a spiritual or pragmatic reaction against the perceived preponderance of positivistic thought. The more US consumer culture entered Italian society, the more *americanismo* gradually took the form of an original emulation, appropriation, and reinvention of American themes. At first the cultural momentum coming from the United States represented the dynamism of industrial modernity (as a new mindset, a novel energy of growth, or a new philosophy of life). During the war it became a platform of mutual help, as expressed in dialogue with the American Red Cross and the YMCA. Lastly, as Wilson chose to downplay Italy's Adriatic claims in April 1919, Americanism become a negative identity builder (anti-Americanism), fuelling the oppositional rise of Fascist "Italianism."

1 The Emigration Debate and the Spreading of Anti-Americanism in Italy (1888–1891)

The Italian debate on mass emigration was primarily formed domestically. In its initial phase, from the first published record of departures in 1876 to the first emigration law of 1888, migrations were broadly considered "a safety valve" or "a means to get rid of undesirable and disgruntled Italians" (Cinel 70). After the 1888 bill made departures legal, emigration shifted from a matter of national security or social order to a cultural and economic problem, stirring a lively debate between those who saw it as a social plight and those who considered it an enriching opportunity. After the Zanardelli law of 1901 had established the Commissariato Generale dell'Emigrazione (General Commissariat of Emigration) and relocated migratory issues from the Ministry of the Interior (e.g., policing, permits, passports) to the Ministry of Foreign Affairs, the phenomenon gained diplomatic and economic recognition from commercial penetration overseas and the impact of remittances on the country's growth.

While considering this overall trajectory, this chapter investigates the years surrounding Italy's first emigration law of 1888 – from the economic depression of 1887 to the diplomatic crisis of 1891 – from a broader Atlantic perspective, relating the early spike of Italian migrations to the United States since the late 1880s to the cultural and economic context of post-unification Italy. By examining the impact of global commercial wars on the Italian philosophy of emigration, the double-edged approach of the Catholic Church towards Italians travelling to North America, and the formation of a specifically anti-American discourse in contemporary literary and pictorial sources, I argue that Italy's domestic approach to emigration is intrinsically linked to a larger oppositional framework, informing both Italy's negative characterization of the commercial, industrial, and political expansion of the United States and the parallel growth of Americanism in North America.

The Post-Risorgimento Crisis and the Development of the Atlantic Route

Financial difficulties and prolonged warfare marred Italy's post-unification years. The new nation was "burdened by seemingly unsolvable economic problems" (Cinel 37), as it had to face reparation fees for the independence wars against Austria,[1] expenses for repressing the internal insurgency of brigands in the South (a guerrilla war that produced about 200,000 casualties between 1862 and 1865), and costs for the military campaigns of 1866 and 1870 (adding Venice and Rome to the national territory).

The 1866 adoption of forced currency (abolishing the lira's equivalence to the gold standard) covered the accumulated debt from the independence wars but partially limited imports and isolated Italy's trade in Europe (Coppa 162). The grist tax, approved in 1869, provided relief to public finances, eventually leading to the squaring of the national debt in 1875, but also contributed to the closing of small mills, rising wheat prices, and increasing social discontent. Although foreign investments provided capital for infrastructures and the building of a national railroad system, they also tied the country to pricey obligations, external liquidity, and international contingencies. An example of the Italian dependence on foreign capital or external factors was the rerouting to Marseille, Genoa, and Trieste of a proposed train route that would have connected Calais to the Apulian port of Brindisi, after the 1869 opening of the Suez Canal, which represented a major economic blow for the South and substantially affected its later isolation.

The global economic crisis of 1873 made Italy's financial instability even more manifest. Heavy reliance on foreign sources led to limited industrial development. In addition, crop failure and natural catastrophes (like the disastrous flooding of the Po River in 1872) considerably curtailed domestic agricultural production. Coinciding with the agrarian crisis, low-priced American grains and cheaper Indian rice coming from the Suez route gained ground in the Italian market. Soaring dependency on foreign suppliers led to a sudden drop in the price of grain, corn, wine, and olive oil,[2] and the loss of competitiveness exposed the Southern economy's fragility. As the South gradually shifted from its traditional role as a primary exporter of wheat (since the opening of the Atlantic route in 1492) to an import economy, its social and political structures also went into crisis. The aristocracy of landowners, producing for foreign markets and maintaining local control through self-referential baronies and geographical isolation, contributed to limited investments in roads; to *campanilismo*, as an endemic resistance against any form of state intervention or change in the production chain; and to a culture of powerlessness, fatalism, and coping, centred around the sole durable bonds of family, friendship, and religion (Cinel 60–9).

Against this backdrop another powerful trigger for the later formation of a new Atlantic route for Italian labourers came from the passing of Italy's first protectionist laws in 1878. While the imposition of custom duties marked the first step of Italian industrialism, it also caused the commercial and political rupture with France, Italy's best trade partner – a breach that would manifest in a diplomatic war for the possession of Tunisia (ending with the creation of a French protectorate in 1881) and Italy's subsequent joining of the Triple Alliance with Austria and Prussia in 1882. The protectionist measures also isolated the nation in the North Atlantic system, as seen in declining exports and in the failure to contain the penetration of American wheat in the Italian market.

Faced with aggressive American expansion, the Italian government sent the economist Egisto Rossi as an envoy to the United States, commissioning him to a study, which was later published in 1884, *Gli Stati Uniti e la concorrenza americana: Studi di agricoltura, industria e commercio* (*The United States and American Competition: Studies on Agriculture, Industry, and Trade*). In his first-hand report Rossi singled out the ingredients of American agrarian success (e.g., abundant fertile land, mechanization, efficient and relatively inexpensive transportation, willingness to experiment, taxes promoting accumulation of capital, and the absence of a large army) and predicted an ever-greater flow of capital from Europe to the United States. Paralleling the rising demand of a workforce in Argentina and the abolition of slavery in Brazil (with the Golden Law of 1888),[3] Rossi's study had a crucial impact on the Italian government's shifting attitude towards emigration, as the phenomenon gradually moved from desertion (Franzina, "Conclusione" 617) or a temporary relief for a struggling domestic economy (thanks to the extra income granted to peasants by reversed seasons)[4] to the potential opportunity of commercial expansion.

To feed the growing demands produced by the Atlantic economy (Nugent 619) and to ensure movement of Italian labourers, foreign companies began to invest in Italian routes and navigation infrastructures. The British lines Prince, Dominion, Cunard, Anchor, and White Star, as well as the German lines Hamburg America and Lloyd Bremen, started to cover Italian harbours (Molinari 238), and German banks backed the formation of two Italian lines: Navigazione generale Italia (Italian General Navigation) in 1881, out of the merger between the Sicilian Florio and the Genoese Rubattino,[5] and La veloce (Speedy) in 1887. The harbour cities of Genoa, Naples, and Palermo grew in traffic volume and acquired significant wealth, as attested by the 1889 opening of the Neapolitan department store Mele, one of the largest in Europe; the 1891 exposition of Palermo (launching the Liberty style in Sicily); and the 1892 international regatta organized in Genoa to celebrate the fourth centenary of Columbus's first voyage to the New World. The growth in naval production – in Genoa, around the steel manufacturer Ansaldo, and later in Palermo with the Florio shipyards (established in 1897) – followed the increasing demand for quicker, stronger, and safer fleets of liners over steamers (especially after the 1891 sinking of the Anchor Line *Utopia* in Gibraltar). Despite the effort to streamline the required passport and hygienic protocols, navigation companies did not adapt terminals (e.g., tiers, lodging, facilities) to the increasing traffic. Faced with inadequate or overcrowded boarding and welcoming structures (Molinari 248) or with a plethora of unregistered travel agents, the Italian government gradually defined more immediate control over travel logistics and a clearer approach to departures.

The Italian Political Philosophy towards Emigration

By the time of unification, 100,000 Italians were fleeing Italy annually (Gabaccia 21), and by 1871, when the first *Censimento degli italiani all'estero* (*Survey of Italians Living Abroad*) was published, about 555,000 Italians were already living outside the peninsula.[6] Jurisdiction over emigration pertained to mayors and prefects and was restricted to police orders (*circolari*) that tolerated departures without incentivizing them, as seen in the Circolare Lanza (18 January 1873) requiring mandatory verification that departing citizens could provide for the return, and in the Circolare Nicotera (28 April 1876) allowing travels only if they were not supported by state economic aid.

The first parliamentary debate over emigration took place in 1873 regarding the specific issue of child trafficking (*tratta dei fanciulli*). The approved law "forbidding employment of boys and girls in wandering professions" (*proibizione dell'impiego di fanciulli d'ambo i sessi in professioni girovaghe*; n. 1733, 21 December 1873) unanimously condemned the migration or trading of vagabond minors outside of Italy (a phenomenon known since the 1850s). The issue, however, offered the first occasion for a complex analysis of adult emigration, specifically focusing on two causes: illiteracy and the agrarian crisis. In response to illiteracy, Parliament approved the Coppino law (n. 3961) on 15 July 1877, imposing mandatory elementary education on all Italian citizens. In response to the agriculture crisis, Parliament approved the publication on 26 March 1877 of the first statistics on emigrating peasants (relative to 1876), and, from 1878, of the additional record on migrants' professions to track the flow of departing workforces.

The sharp decline of small farming and the practice of seasonal migrations on the Atlantic route led to a rise of departures in the 1880s and a new political view of emigration as a vent for the labour market, a remedy to the agrarian crisis, and a stimulus for infrastructural development. Beyond its aid to a struggling economy, emigration also started to appear as an opportunity for trade penetration abroad, the formation of national enclaves or agrarian settlements, and even demographic colonization, as confirmed by Deputy Diomede Pantaleo's January 1883 parliamentary proposal to occupy Libya as an outlet for Italian farmers (Montevecchi 606).

The philosophy of temporary economic relief that characterized the early Italian approach to migrations formally moved from a matter of national security to a full-fledged political issue in 1887, coinciding with the global recession, Italy's colonial failure in the Eritrean outpost of Dogali, and the death of Prime Minister Agostino Depretis.

The international financial crisis forced Italy to pass a second set of protectionist tariffs, which caused a second trade standstill with France,[7] followed by the short-term French retaliation against Italian products and the long-term withdrawal of French investors from Italian banks (eventually leading to the collapse of the Italian financial system in 1893). Migratory movements on the Atlantic route and foreign remittances consequently represented a "positive factor in regulating the workforce market" (Soresina 724) and a remedy to the nation's lack of liquidity.[8]

The halt of the colonial enterprise in Eritrea reconfigured emigration into a viable substitute for military conquest, as seen in the theorized models of the Phoenician enclave (Incisa di Camerana 464), supporting commercial penetration in foreign markets or in demographic colonies annexed to the national territory. The plan of a "greater Italy in Latin America" (Cinel 89), modelled on the ancient Great Greece in Southern Italy, gained ground in the increased presence of Italians in Argentina and Brazil, following those countries' unprecedented growth. In the case of Argentina, an 1887 act aimed to block Italy's "free colonies" (Devoto 35) and rebalance the migrant population (which was 70 per cent Genoese and Piedmontese), through the deliberate exclusion of Italians from the country's program of travel benefits and tax incentives for foreign labourers.[9] Brazil's abolition of slavery in 1888 led the country to subsidize Italian emigration as a way to support *fazendas* (where most former slaves worked) and populate with white settlers a vast territory mostly controlled by *indios*. Federal laws covering travel expenses and granting migrants free lodging, fiscal exemptions, and low-cost land acquisition made Brazil a key destination for Italians; 900,000 arrived between 1888 and 1901 (when Italy banned travel benefits; Trento 3–5).

Against this backdrop, Prime Minister Francesco Crispi, who succeeded Agostino Depretis after his sudden death, started off his new cabinet with a proposed bill for assisted emigration. After a year-long political debate and a six-day parliamentary discussion (5–11 December 1888), Italy's first emigration law (n. 5866) was approved in the chamber with a 162–44 vote (on 12 December), and in the senate with a 73–6 vote (on 27 December). The bill and its ensuing debate constituted a crucial watershed moment, both in Italy's internal approach to emigration and in the later evolution of Italian transatlantic travel.

Domestically, the law ratified a person's freedom to move, implicitly recognizing emigration as an economic opportunity, but also followed the repressive tone of previous *circolari* (Ostuni 310). From a practical point of view, the law set basic protocols against financial offsets or human trafficking by establishing stricter navigation standards and requiring that travellers sign a mandatory contract (confirming their ability to provide for their own expenses). Reflecting the condemnation of definitive emigration as unpatriotic or immoral (a condemnation shared by the secular press and the Catholic Church) and the aspiration to prevent economic and social destabilization, the law discouraged permanent settlement abroad, obligating migrants and their children to serve in the national army and punishing renitence to the military draft.

Internationally, the 1888 law powerfully stimulated transatlantic travel. While Argentina's restrictions made Brazil a key destination for Italian peasants in South America, declining fares to New York, rising American salaries, and the commercial war with France also made the United States a coveted destination (Clementi 200); from 1888 to the end of the century, 800,000 Italians arrived, and the numbed spiked to 3.5 million after 1901 (Vecoli 56). The law's assumption that emigration was temporary or seasonal subsequently made transatlantic travel an experience of continuous return (as confirmed by the 50 per cent return rate) and failed integration (due to cultural stigma or unsuccessful assimilation). Returnees significantly affected Southern agriculture and Northern industrialization through remittances (Clementi 206),[10] but they often failed to reintegrate into their original communities. Failed returnees permanently settled overseas but lost Italian citizenship when they or their children skipped the draft or were naturalized in another country.[11]

Starting in the late 1880s, Italian labourers increasingly travelled to the United States as workforce for public construction in the northeast or agriculture in the south, but their inherently seasonal mindset stymied their assimilation into society. Seeing emigration as a temporary remedy to poverty through winter income or as a long-term investment eventually leading to economic independence, Italians worked to maximize their US wages by minimizing cost of living, rent (through overcrowded lodging), and clothing expenditures. At the same time, in the return logic mandated by the emigration law, Italians were often reluctant to learn English and opposed naturalization (Vecoli 56–7). Americans saw this attitude with a dual lens: of convenience, as Italians replaced Irish emigrants in urban construction, railway maintenance, or mine digging (Vecoli 57–8); and of suspicion, as the Italian refusal to settle was observed as an act of disregard for the American economy and exceptionality (Cinel 98).[12] This outlook was also induced by racial prejudice, especially in the South, where Sicilians occupied a transitory space as "not totally 'white' but […] not 'black' foreign workers and voters" (Barbata Jackson 2). In the rest of the United States, Southern Italians were also associated with crime, in connection with the negative framing of Italy's post-unification war against Southern banditry (known as the Brigands War), and the widely known studies by Italian positivists Giuseppe Sergi, Cesare Lombroso, and Alfredo Niceforo, who openly tied their ethnic, racial, and anthropological traits to moral deviance.[13]

In this context, the Italian debate between *migrazionisti* and *antimigrazionisti*, envisioning emigration as either a resource or a loss, a valve or an escape, evolved in the aftermath of the 1888 law into a parallel controversy opposing *americanisti* and *anti-americanisti*, similarly contrasting a vision of the United States as a land of either opportunity or alienation. The anti-Americanism surrounding and following the debate on the emigration law is documented in ecclesial sources on the migratory phenomenon, as well as in secular literature and painting.

The Ecclesial Approach to Italian Migrations

Despite receiving limited attention in both Catholic and migration studies,[14] the ecclesial debate on emigration represents a valuable source to reconstruct the Italian political debate of the late 1880s and the parallel growth of an anti-American bias in Italy.

The loss of temporal power was a key factor in propelling the Church's novel approach to migratory movements. Before the Italian seizure of Rome, the Catholic Church in fact did not approve migrations, and, after Pope Clement VIII formally rejected them in 1596, Propaganda Fide actively monitored Catholic enclaves in Protestant Europe or the New World. During the nineteenth century the Church suspiciously viewed Italian migrants' adherence to Mazzini's anti-clerical philosophy (*Mazzinianesimo*), Risorgimento political ideals, and the anti-Catholic predication by the former Barnabite Alessandro Gavazzi (1809–89). To counter these influences, it entrusted the order of Vincenzo Pallotti (the so-called Pallottini) with the mission to keep migrants faithful and supported the 1844 opening of Saint Peter in Clerkenwell, the first Italian church in London (Sanfilippo, "Breve storia"). With the 1870 reconfiguration of Rome as the secular state's capital, the Church lost its Italian aspect and acquired a more prominent international dimension. Consequently, the growing transatlantic movement of Polish, Irish, and Italian migrants was then reconfigured from being a phenomenon to control to being a missionary occasion of evangelization, a political instrument for a new Vatican influence in global affairs, and a diplomatic tool exerting international pressure on Italy in support of a hoped for, yet never accomplished, papal restoration in Rome (see ch. 2). After the pontificate of Pius IX (1846–78), his successor, Leo XIII (1878–1903), shaped the Church's new focus on emigration in two ways. First, in conjunction with the Catholic rejection of Risorgimento and the non-committal attitude towards the political life of unified Italy (as stated in the papal *non expedit* of 1874), Leo XIII negatively portrayed emigration as the national state's failure. Secondly, considering the Church's new global role and expansion, Leo XIII operated in favour of Catholic migrants, supporting the creation of national parishes as enclaves against anti-clerical or anti-Catholic influences.

The global and national crisis of 1887 represented a crucial contingence for the formation of a Vatican policy on Italian emigration to the United States. Leo XIII approved the Propaganda Fide's request to establish national parishes in the country (on 11 April 1887) and the opening of the first seminary, Istituto Cristoforo Colombo (Christopher Columbus Institute), for the formation of priests assigned to Italian communities in North America (on 25 November 1887).

Following the pope's approval of the institute, its founder, Giovanni Battista Scalabrini, bishop of Piacenza, became a prominent figure in the emigration debate. His public interventions shaped the ecclesial position on the phenomenon, and his highly regarded work made him an ideal mediator with the national state, at a moment of radical clash between the Vatican and the new, anti-clerical prime minister Francesco Crispi.[15] Scalabrini's booklet *L'emigrazione italiana in America: Osservazioni di un vescovo* (*Italian Emigration to America: Observations of a Bishop*, 1887) influenced the ecclesial *conciliatorismo* (aimed at softening a radical *non expedit* into a conciliatory attitude of collaboration with the state) as well as the political debate on Crispi's emigration bill. The text framed emigration as a providential fact and a human right,[16] and urged the state to legislate on departures, to reform the consular system, and to support the existing network of private Catholic associations caring for migrants. Its approach also informed the sixty-page open letter *Il disegno di legge della emigrazione italiana* (*The Law Proposal on Italian Emigration*), which Scalabrini published in November 1888, anticipating the parliamentary discussion in December. The letter, published both in the Vatican newspaper *Osservatore Romano* (on 9 November) and in the secular *Corriere della sera* (on 23 November), was addressed to Scalabrini's high-school classmate, leftist deputy, and undersecretary of finances Paolo Carcano. Confirming general support for the emigration bill, Scalabrini indicated his institute as a platform of collaboration between church and state (as missionaries also served as cultural ambassadors and civil officers for Italian migrants)[17] and invited deputies to change the expression "freedom to emigrate" into "protected freedom to migrate." His proposed change was not included in the law (even though it appeared in the subsequent 1901 emigration law), but his venture into Italian politics marked a significant moment of conciliation between church and state, later confirmed not only in the praises for his work in the secular press[18] but also in the 1889 creation of the San Raffaele society of assistance (partly funded by the state; Perotti 74–8). Scalabrini's recognized leadership also anticipated the Church's renewed involvement with social issues (*questione sociale*), later confirmed by Leo XIII's first dedicated encyclical *Rerum novarum* (*Of New Things*) of 1891.

In addition to Scalabrini, Pope Leo XIII intervened in the emigration debate by releasing the encyclical letter *Quam aerumnosa* (*How Pitiful*) on 10 December 1888 (coinciding with the Italian parliamentary debate). The letter, written from an Italian perspective but addressed to American bishops, provides a double-edged view on emigration and Italian migrants in the United States. Without explicitly mentioning parliamentary deliberations, Leo XIII negatively depicts emigration and the migrants' dire travelling conditions to enact his polemical stand towards the Italian state. In contrast with the liberal press, which framed emigration as the outcome of a bad yet not irreversible economic contingency,[19] the pope presented the migratory phenomenon as a symptom of the Italian state's inability to provide citizens with adequate means to survive. At the same time, paralleling the contemporary novel *Sull'oceano* (1888) by Edmondo De Amicis (*On Blue Waters*),

Leo XIII decried the human tragedy of migrants, unmasking the mirage of American wealth (thereby impoverishing Italian society), denouncing the perils of transatlantic travels, and condemning human trafficking, depraved habits, and new enslavement.[20] As a sign of his care for migrants, Leo XIII announced both the approval of Scalabrini's Istituto Cristoforo Colombo and his intention to "send from Italy to that land many priests to console their countrymen in their own tongue" (*Quam aerumnosa*, sec. 3), and explicitly urged American bishops to accommodate his fellow Italians in their new land with pastoral attention and without prejudices.

Quam aerumnosa warns against the perils of modernity, coming either from Italy's secular state (unscrupulously dealing with the phenomenon of emigration) or from US influence (separating church and state and forcing migrants to drop their heritage). The migrant's victimization, which follows the tropes of contemporary representations in literature and art, deliberately enacts an oppositional narration, targeting Italy and the United States to reassess papal primacy and the Church's role in global society. In this context, the two different readerships of the document highlight two different perspectives on the migratory phenomenon.

From an Italian standpoint, the value of the document consisted not in its effects on the parliamentary debate but rather in its affirmation of the Church's position towards emigration. The negative view of emigration, polemically exposing the inadequacies of the liberal state and Crispi's cabinet, functionally stressed the concrete role played by Catholics in addressing the migrants' needs. While endorsing Scalabrini's publications and missionary work, Leo XIII's emphasis on the Church's evangelizing mission also affirmed the positive impact of a Catholic global network in the linguistic, cultural, material, and spiritual support of migrants. Against this backdrop, the final address to American bishops appeared to Italian readers as an implicit confirmation of the pope's growing involvement with the United States – an interest that had moved the secular press to gossip about Cardinal James Gibbons as the pope's possible successor. In this context, it is significant that the journalist Fra Pacomio of the liberal *Corriere della sera* dedicated his editorial "Note Vaticane" ("Vatican News") of 15–16 December 1888 neither to the parliamentary debate on emigration nor to Leo XIII's *Quam aerumnosa* but rather to the American church's financial impact on Rome, a hypothetical American pope, and the suitability of Cardinal Gibbons as a potential remedy against the stall of cardinals.[21] While iterating the strategy to delegitimize Leo XIII as an aged man obsessed with fear and money, the article documents growing concerns over America's influence on Italy, even in ecclesial affairs.

From an American standpoint, *Quam aerumnosa* expressed the ambivalent relationship of the Holy See with the US hierarchy. On the one hand, the papal dispatch of Italian missionaries and the establishment of national parishes expressed a genuine endorsement of migrants and support for the evangelization of the United States – a direct participation in American affairs that had also been confirmed by Leo XIII's 1887 approval of Cardinal Gibbons as chancellor of the newly founded Catholic University of America and praise for Monsignor John Ireland's vowed support for migrant Italians (Scalabrini, *L'emigrazione italiana* 227). On the other hand, the papal request to accommodate Italian migrants was met with hesitancy by the American hierarchy, given Italian anticlerical views, perceived unwillingness to assimilate, lack of commitment to local parishes, insensibility towards Protestants or other Catholic immigrants, and even immoral behavior (Sanfilippo, "La chiesa cattolica" 482–3). The papal intervention in national affairs then highlighted a broader controversy over the relationship of Catholics with Rome and the US government, which dated back to the Baltimore council of American bishops organized by Gibbons in 1883. Leo XIII's endorsement of national parishes appeared to stifle not just the assimilation model then promoted by American bishops but also the autonomous development of the US church. Against this backdrop, the American bishops' reaction of due obedience and silent annoyance mirrored the divergences of the *questione romana*, opposing in Italy the *intransigentisti* (those who were inflexible on the *non expedit* stance) to the *conciliatoristi* (those who were open to dialogue with the state). In the same way, the papal encyclical exposed two factions among American bishops: those who claimed unwavering fidelity to the pope in endorsing the Catholic heritage of migrants and rejecting the US separation of church and state; and those, guided by Saint Paul's bishop John Ireland, who called for a dialogic attitude with the US government and an American reconfiguration of the Catholic Church – a position that would be later labelled as "Americanism."

Italian Anti-Americanism in the Representation of Migration

A key source to contextualize the parliamentary and ecclesial debate on emigration and reconstruct the evolution of an anti-American imagination in Italy is offered by De Amicis's book *Sull'oceano* (*On Blue Waters*), published in 1888 by Treves and reprinted in 1890 with illustrations by Arnaldo Ferraguti.[22] Based on the writer's own travel to Argentina in 1884, *Sull'oceano* is both an activist report and a fictional depiction of the migrants' journey across the Atlantic Ocean, providing not just a masterful synthesis of Italian emigration literature but also a powerful visual framework for its later pictorial renderings.[23]

While following the typical depiction of emigration as a mournful event, a traumatic loss, or equivalent to death (Martelli 435), the socialist writer De Amicis formalized its narrative pattern by overlapping reticence (over benefits) and heightened emotionality (over the trauma of departure), silence (on causes) and denunciation (of effects), perceived peril (at destination) and recalled safety (back at home). By his unprecedented vision of transatlantic travel, De Amicis allows the reader for the first time to see the space in between of "Italy aboard," polemically rejecting a law that permissively let Italians depart without establishing a clear path home and dramatically tracking them in the attempt to bring them back. The opening and closing visions of harbours (Genoa and Montevideo) frame the travel around a dialectics of fullness and emptiness, relating departure to intensified drama (e.g., crowd-filled tier, emotional boarding, and moving goodbyes) and arrival to solitude, anonymity, or unfathomability. The journalistic or pathetic exhibition of harbours (and of the travellers' conditions in between) is intertwined with the narrative strategy of concealment. While aimed at stirring social awareness or an immediate call to action, the emotional display of effects at departure serves to purposefully omit reasons for emigration. Conversely, silence on destination, expressed through direct omissions, generic allusions, or demonizing narratives of enslavement and peril, is implicitly related to a narration of intervention and self-defence, aimed at reclaiming Italy's role and position within the global commercial wars.

The opening description of Genoa's harbour exemplifies De Amicis's exhibition strategy, in a crafty mix of denunciation and drama, veristic report, and heightened emotionality:

Quando arrivai, verso sera, l'imbarco degli emigranti era già cominciato da un'ora. Il *Galileo*, congiunto alla calata da un piccolo ponte mobile, continuava a insaccar miseria: una processione interminabile di gente che usciva a gruppi dall'edifizio dirimpetto, dove un delegato della Questura esaminava i passaporti. La maggior parte, avendo passato una o due notti all'aria aperta, accucciati come cani per le strade di Genova, erano stanchi e pieni di sonno. (De Amicis, *Sull'oceano* 5)

[It was towards evening when I reached the wharf. The embarkation of the emigrants had been going on for an hour; and there lay the *Galileo* filling up with misery as there passed over her gangplank an interminable procession of people, coming in groups out of the building opposite where the police official was examining passports. The greater part, having passed a night or two in the open air, lying about like dogs in the streets of Genoa, were tired and drowsy.] (De Amicis, *On Blue Waters* 1)

The journalistic report of the lengthy boarding process (an hour), the unstructured groups of people between the passport office and the boat, and the overcrowded tier purposefully connects the book to the emigration debate, as the writer immediately alludes to the shortcomings of the law (e.g., the lack of organization in port authority controls and the underdeveloped terminals of Italian harbours). Likewise, by referring to the migrant's lack of lodging in the city and sleepless nights on the streets, he criticizes the missing infrastructural investment in the key harbour cities after the legalization of departures (Molinari 248). The denunciation parallels a pathetic element, as the writer depicts the boarding line as a "procession" and compares the migrants to sleepless dogs. The image of the procession refers to his own previous poem "Gli emigranti" ("Emigrants," 1882), which equally staged migrant boarding as a parade of mourners,[24] "betrayed by false merchants" (traditi da un mercante menzognero; line 26) and "unaware of everything" (ignari di tutto; line 31),[25] boarding the ship as though mounting the stage of death (ascendono la nave / come s'ascende il palco de la morte; lines 4–5). The animal comparison dramatizes the indistinct misery of migrants, as seen in the subsequent mention of a ram herd processing into the ship, confusing bellows with the noises of loading machines or the screams of seamen and porters. A similar image of a "sad procession" (triste processione; De Amicis, *Sull'oceano* 248), of a "crowd as cattle" (folla come d'armento; 248), reappears in the closing chapter, where De Amicis likens the anonymous counting of people at their destination to a modern replacement of the slave trade (after its last abolition in Brazil).[26]

The same tension to report and dramatize applies to the liner, which "bags" their miseries (insaccando miserie; De Amicis, *Sull'oceano* 5) scattered over the wharf (e.g., the passengers' luggage and bags). Two additional metaphors characterize the boat: the floating piazza and the biting whale. Following the author's realistic vein, the steamer appears as a "crowded piazza" (piazza affollata; 6), gathering peoples, faces, and costumes from every part of Italy and social class: "workmen, peasants, women with children at the breast" but also "gentlemen in natty dusters, priests, ladies in plumed hats, leading a lapdog, or carrying a satchel, or perhaps a parcel of French novels of the well-known Lévy edition" (*On Blue Waters* 1–2).[27] The boat then represents the floating nation, ideally persisting undivided to the Americas and evoking a "floating part of my country" (lembo natante del mio paese; *Sull'oceano* 257) in the author's farewell to the *Galileo* at the book's conclusion. Heightening the dramatic vision of travel as a haemorrhage of Italians, the reporter compares the immobile ship to "an enormous cetacean biting the shore" (un cetaceo enorme che addentasse la riva; 6), which "kept drawing Italian blood" (succhiava ancora sangue italiano; 6). While foreseeing in this monster the dangers of the new land, the image of the ship as a whale is intrinsically related not only to the hope of preserving unity in its belly before the conclusive entrusting of Italy's "wandering children to their new mother"[28] but also to the impulse to "rescue" them. As in the story of his character Marco, protagonist of the famous chapter of *Cuore* (*Heart*, 1886), "Dagli Apennini alle Ande" ("From Apennines to Andes"), who crosses the Atlantic in search of his emigrant mother, De Amicis's own voyage in *Sull'oceano* similarly attempts to rescue the motherland abroad, to follow lost Italian blood, and to invite migrants to return (also attested in his poem "Emigranti," wishing travellers to "cross again those seas" and "return to their humble and dear villages"[29] where their loved ones still await with open arms).

De Amicis's juxtaposition of activist denunciation and pathetic emphasis in the depiction of harbours and ships frames a recurring pattern in subsequent pictorial and literary depictions of departures and returns. The harbour is a key setting in the illustration of departure, as seen in the two paintings *Emigranti (Emigrants)* by Raffaello Gambogi (1894; fig. 1.1) and Angiolo Tommasi (1896; fig. 1.2). Gambogi mirrors the opening of *Sull'oceano* by coupling the veristic depiction of cluttered bags on the dock and the random flow of people towards the boats, to the pathetic farewell of a father to his baby girl, as his wife and older daughter cannot look at him. Tommasi similarly stages departure through the denouncing vision of the overcrowded tier, filled with luggage and groups of travellers, paired with the melodramatic figure of a woman in the foreground, looking at us, stirring the viewer's emotional response and visualizing an implicit call to action.[30]

The emphasis on return, from De Amicis's "rescuing mission" to painting, mirrors not only the understanding of migrations as a seasonal movement and the active call for tighter control over departure (and a more organized consular network) but also the recurring narrative contrasting Italy as the *focolare* (hearth, fullness) to America as the land of doom (desolation, emptiness). Egisto Ferroni's depiction of a mother and a daughter welcoming back an emigrant man in *Torna il babbo* (*Dad Returns*, 1883; fig. 1.3) reinforces the idealized vision of a warm homecoming and confirms emigration as a primarily male experience. Such stylized image conceals the difficulty of contemporary

Figure 1.1. Raffaello Gambogi, *Emigranti* (1894). © Museo Civico Giovanni Fattori, Livorno.

Figure 1.2. Angiolo Tommasi, *Emigranti* (1896). © Galleria Nazionale d'Arte Moderna e Contemporanea, Rome.

Figure 1.3. Egisto Ferroni, *Torna il babbo* (1883). © Galleria Nazionale d'Arte Moderna e Contemporanea, Rome.

painting to represent the alienation of returnees and foresees a poetic trope, epitomized in Giovanni Pascoli's story of Molly in his 1903 poem "Italy" – a little girl from Ohio returns to her parents' Italian village and finds her grandparents unfailingly expecting her.

The sad return of the emigrant is represented in Giovanni Segantini's *Ritorno al paese natio* (*Return to the Home Village*, 1895; fig. 1.4), where the painter stages a dead returnee being pulled in a cart, with a weeping woman alongside, in a procession to his home village in the mountains.[31] In this visual representation, return coincides with the pain of absence, a trauma that Pirandello will turn into folly in his later short story "L'altro figlio" ("The Other Son," 1909), featuring a Sicilian mother's obsession over her departed son.[32]

In contrast with these visual representations, the conclusion of *Sull'oceano* identifies the literary and pictorial trope of emigration in

Figure 1.4. Giovanni Segantini, *Ritorno al paese natio* (*Rückkehr zur Heimat*, 1895). © Staatliche Museen zu Berlin, Nationalgalerie (Jörg P. Anders).

relation to silence and omission. De Amicis's report presents America as both a sorrowful unknown and an upside-down world, as symbolically staged in the passing of the equator, or the discovery prior to arrival (in dialogue with the ship commander) that the American night corresponds to the Italian morning because of time differences.[33]

The negative association of emigration to a mournful unknown, leading to sickness, folly, disgrace, or ruin (Martelli 436) finds poetic expression in the recurring motif of the shipwreck. As anticipated in the image of the ship as a swallowing cetacean, emblematically foreseeing the fear of disappearance inherent to every departure and the implicit projection of America as a devouring monster, literary shipwrecks manifest the secular and religious fears of losing everything forever (e.g., fears held by workers or the faithful; Magnani 263) and the prefiguration of destination as hell. In this sense shipwreck surely staged a pathetic element, mirroring contemporary tragedies like the sinking of the liner *Utopia* off the coast of Gibraltar (which killed 576 Italian migrants on 17 March 1891), but also a practical narrative tool, justifying a missing account on life after the Atlantic crossing, and allowing the writer, in the absence of other information, to negatively characterize or even demonize destination.

It follows that the practical removal of America is implicitly related to an oppositional tone. In reference to the United States, a deliberate anti-Americanist stance found expression in the explicit depiction of the country in terms of greed, materialism, and reckless industrialization.

While the omission of American stories from Italian literary sources deterred departing migrants and dispelled the idea of emigration as an opportunity, the anti-migratory stance of Italian writers and playwrights (which also manifested in the anti-American stereotypes portrayed by Italian journalists travelling to America)[34] also silenced the accounts and impact of returnees in breaking the cycle of hunger and poverty (Teti 582). Lastly, the negative portrayal of the United States was also related to a political strategy of soft aggression (deliberately constructing the "other" as an enemy) and to commercial antagonism, opposing Italy's anti-industrial stance and different production model to American modernization, seen as a frightening materialistic, mechanical, and immoral society (Martelli 435).

The New Orleans Lynching and the Diplomatic War with America

Despite these negative depictions of emigration, the Italian emigration law of 1888 and the American higher demand for workforce engendered a spike in departures towards North America and led to a more capillary organization of Italian communities in the United States.

From a secular perspective, the legalization of emigration was preceded by the 1887 institution of the first Italy-America chamber of commerce in New York and followed by the 1889 foundation of the Dante Alighieri Society for the protection of Italian language. The establishment of state-assisted or community-driven associations of mutual aid,[35] the formation of Little Italies, and the rising number of periodicals published in Italian (seventeen in the United States as of 1893; Deschamps 317)[36] signalled the growing network of Italian communities. Although the state funded institutions in New York City like the Italian Home (in July 1890) and the Labor Bureau (in June 1891) to provide seasonal workers with professional services, the presence of Italians abroad was never organized around a coherent national project. Its village-minded model of associationism ("associazionismo campanilistico"; Bugiardini 560) focused instead on providing migrants with temporary arrangements, economic and psychological support, a job-placement system (often run by the Black Hand or structured around a padrone system), and a replica of the loyalties or rivalries from their home villages. From a religious perspective, Italian communities developed around local parishes, supported by Scalabrini's priests after the missionary call of *Quam aerumnosa*, or around the network of the Missionary Sisters of the Sacred Heart of Jesus, who not only developed schools, services, and orphanages for Italian migrants after the arrival in New York of their founder, Frances

Cabrini, in March 1889, but also founded the first Columbus Hospital of Manhattan in 1892.

The increasing arrivals and the formation of such communities after 1888 were received by American society with a certain degree of diffidence. From a legal standpoint, Americans questioned the commitment of Italians to their land, considering both the economic practice of remittances (which diverted money from the US economy) and the Italian law's imposition of military duties, which forced migrants to report back to their homeland. In terms of US legislation, Italian immigration was neither promoted (as it had been incentivized for Slavic, Scandinavian, and German workers in the years following the civil war) nor banned (as in the case of Asian and Chinese migrants, who were formally excluded by the Page Act of 1875 and the Chinese Exclusion Act of 1882). Like all other groups, Italians were subject to the Immigration Act of 1882, which gave port authorities expulsion or admission preclusion rights solely against "any convict, lunatic, idiot, or any person unable to take care of him or herself without becoming a public charge" (Immigration Act).[37]

From a social standpoint, the isolation of Italian communities enhanced the fear of their growing influence (as in the Italian settlements in Argentina) or of their criminal actions, in connection with the Black Hand or anarchist enclaves (in Barre, Vermont; Paterson, New Jersey; or Braintree, Massachusetts). The American ecclesial hierarchy also viewed Italian migrants uneasily because of their religious folklore (often bordering on paganism), their limited involvement in local churches, their prolonged division (even among national parishes; Bugiardini 562), or, at times, their priests' licentious behaviour (Vecoli 64). Based on these social perceptions, the press forged a stereotypical portrait of Italians, relating their temporary living arrangements to hygienic and moral degradation, their religious practices to superstition, and their social organization to a violent racket. In many cases, as seen in the 7 September 1888 vignette in the New Orleans paper *The Mascot* (fig. 1.5) that featured ways to dispose of Italians, migrant communities were targeted with expressions of open racism and, in a few cases, even with the practice of lynching (Salvetti XIII).

Preceded by several episodes – in Eureka, Nevada (1879); Vicksburg, Mississippi (1886); and Louisville, Kentucky (1889) – the 1891 lynching in New Orleans ignited the latent antagonism between Italy and the United States (Pierantoni 51), exposing internal "socio-economic dualism" in Italy (Patriarca 87) and the racial hierarchization of "Italians" in the American South.

Figure 1.5. "Regarding the Italian Population," vignette for the New Orleans newspaper *The Mascot*, 7 September 1888. Wikimedia Commons.

The Sicilian community had grown in Louisiana during the 1880s, thanks to the opening of the Palermo–New Orleans route after the creation of a French protectorate in Tunisia in 1881. Sicilians were prompted to migrate by the rising labour demand for US agricultural production and the agrarian crisis at home, worsened by the estate owners' fierce opposition to land sale. Sicilian returnees who had generated cash to buy land were denied this right and started a protest in Catania to force estate owners to reconsider their position. This early upheaval of 1891 developed into the movement of the Fasci siciliani (Sicilian Fasces), which Crispi would repress militarily in 1894. Sicilian settlers, who had formed a Louisiana colony of about thirty thousand people and who were perceived as a threat to the local economy, came under fire in 1890 after the murder of the head of New Orleans police, David Hennessy. The resentment over Italian influence found expression in the imputation of the death to Italian immigrants and was largely stirred not only by the later acquittal of nine men indicted in Hennessy's murder but also by the widespread suspicions of bribery, as the jury failed to agree on the verdicts of three charges. Enraged by these resolutions and moved by the ambition to curb an ever-growing Sicilian influence in the city,[38] the mob broke into the jail where the men were being held prisoner and lynched eleven of them on 14 March 1891.

The event led to legal contention over the status of the Italian victims, as some were naturalized American citizens who had already voted in local elections, and others were planning to return to their homeland. Italy claimed them as "Italians," assimilating their racial distinction as Sicilians into a new pan-Italian identity for the sake of expanding the "Italian colony in Louisiana" (Barbata Jackson 41). Conversely, the United States treated the victims as naturalized "Americans," introducing a "performative" or act-based idea of citizenship and initiating a political campaign to officially recognize a Southern Italian ethnicity – a change that would take place in 1899 when the U.S. Bureau of Immigration began to record "Southern Italians" separately from "Italians."[39]

The lynching of New Orleans also had a political repercussion, as it opened a diplomatic rift between Italy and the United States. Two weeks after the fact, on 31 March, Italy broke diplomatic relations with the United States in response to the unanswered request for clarification by the Italian ambassador Fava to Louisiana governor Francis T. Nicholls, and even threatened a military intervention. The silence of the American government after Italy's recalling of Ambassador Fava was followed by an aggressive anti-Italian campaign in the press, exemplified on 12 April by the derogatory vignette on the cover of the *Philadelphia Inquirer*, which openly ridiculed Italy's prime minister, Di Rudinì, King Umberto, and Fava himself. When the grand jury acquitted the lynch mob on 5 May (justifying it as an accepted racially based form of self-justice), the controversy further amplified, as the Italian communities' demand for justice clashed against the American assumption that an entire city could not be put on trial.

At this time, Italy formally presented a motion to the US government, requesting it to make lynching a crime and to modify the constitution on the matter of federal and state laws on emigration (Salvetti 11). The Italian bid – the first and only petition from a foreign nation to amend the American constitution – exposed the unsolved issue over the migrants' jurisdiction. Despite the bilateral agreement signed by Italy and the United States on 26 February 1871, which bound the nations to protect foreign citizens reciprocally and treat them equally to their own, the US government could not in fact interfere with each state's constitutional right to rule autonomously. The disconnect between federal international law and local legislation was confirmed by President Harrison's nine-month delay in acknowledging and condemning the lynching, on 9 December 1891.

The constitutional amendment proposed by Italy, deferring the autonomy of states to the federal government in the matter of lynching foreigners, did not move forward and, despite McKinley's later interest, would be finally dropped by Roosevelt. Despite his failed attempt to criminalize lynching at a federal level (a ruling that would become law only in 2022 with the passing of the Emmett Till Antilynching Act), Harrison nonetheless approved Italy's call for a punishment to the perpetrators and granted federal indemnity in support of the victims' families, thus opening the path for the return of Ambassador Fava to Washington on 23 May 1892. After the alleged mobbing of Seattle on 17 June 1892 (a fact that risked jeopardizing the pacification), the reinstatement of diplomatic ties was staged on 19 May 1893, with the official establishment of the Italian embassy in Washington, DC.

The New Orleans episode did not end attacks on Italians, as seen in the brutal murder of Daniele Arata in Denver in 1893, and the later lynchings in Tallulah, Louisiana (1899); Erwin, Mississippi (1901); and Tampa, Florida (1910; see Salvetti). However, three impactful consequences rose from the gravest diplomatic crisis between Italy and the United States.

Politically, the Italian push to grant citizens stronger diplomatic protection led to a strengthening of the consular network and the implicit recognition of migration as a permanent phenomenon.[40] Commercially, the New Orleans lynching led to the Italian refusal to send an official delegation or pavilion at the Columbian exposition of Chicago in 1893, confirming the trade war between Italy's soft expansion via emigration and the national interests of hosting nations.[41] Culturally, the indignation following the New Orleans case enflamed the anti-Americanism of Italian sources, further nurturing their negative view of America as a land of disillusion and tragedy.

2 From Columbianism to Americanism:
Italian, Vatican, and American Perceptions
of the United States from the Columbian
Expositions to the Spanish-American War
(1892–1899)

The 1892 celebrations for the fourth centenary of the Western discovery of the New World coincided with a time of historical and cultural reappraisal of Christopher Columbus. Two main expositions honoured the anniversary: the Esposizione Italo-Americana of Genoa (Italian-American Exposition; 10 July–4 December 1892) and the Columbian exposition of Chicago (1 May–30 October 1893). On both occasions Columbus was extolled as a universal figure and a national hero. Italians portrayed him as a visionary anticipator of the Risorgimento, and Americans as a proto-founder of the United States. Even Pope Leo XIII joined the celebrations in 1892 with a dedicated encyclical letter that pointed to Columbus as a model of Christian virtue and faith, and in 1893 through the dispatch of his personal envoy to Chicago.

In exploring the expositions of Genoa and Chicago as laboratories of a global Columbian spirit, this chapter examines the formation of Columbus as a national or transnational myth of self-legitimization and cultural expansion. Moving from the accounts of two Italian journalists in the United States – Semplice at the Columbian exposition of Chicago (1893) and Ugo Ojetti in the aftermath of the Spanish-American War (1898) – this study reconstructs the makeover of the early Columbian excitement, or Columbianism, into the imperialist project and heresy of Americanism.

The Columbian Expositions of Genoa (1892) and Chicago (1893)

The expositions of Genoa and Chicago offered favourable occasions to collect materials on Christopher Columbus from all over the world and construct a universalist narrative around him. At the same time, they also shaped his figure into a malleable prototype, as Columbus was turned respectively into an Italian, Catholic, or American hero.

The Esposizione Italo-Americana of Genoa, organized by the Società Ginnastica Ligure Cristoforo Colombo (Christopher Columbus Ligurian Gymnastics Society) under the patronage of the Savoia monarchy, gathered a significant cross-section of Italian society to celebrate the city's native explorer. Among its 808,572 visitors were King Umberto (who visited Genoa for the universal regatta); the nation's leading industrialists (who praised the Genoese Ansaldo as Italy's greatest manufacturer of parts for railways and navigation); intellectuals (who convened at the Teatro Carlo Felice on 6 October 1892 for the premiere of Alberto Franchetti's opera *Cristoforo Colombo*); union leaders and workers (who benefited from reduced train prices to meet on 14–15 August 1892 and founded the Italian Socialist Party); and Catholics (who first assembled objects related to Columbus in the Exhibit of Catholic Missions).[1]

The Columbian anniversary offered Italy a pretext to showcase its place among modern industrialized nations and affirm its universal primacy. Mesmerizing attractions like the funicular cable railway, the hot-air balloon, the egg-shaped restaurant Uovo di Colombo (Columbus's egg) and roller coasters (first introduced in the country) displayed Italy's commitment to modernity and progress. The celebratory regatta of 3 August 1892, which assembled British, French, Austrian, German, American, Spanish, and Australian ships in Genoa's harbour, visibly united Columbus's *italianità* with Italy's ensuing universal leadership and pacifying mission. *Corriere della sera* explicitly stressed this symbolism on 3–4 August 1892 by claiming Columbus as a universal hero who "belongs to Europe, the world, mankind" (appartiene all'Europa, al mondo, all'umanità), yet also as an immortal Italian, to whom all nations owe "the tribute of their admiration and gratitude" (il tributo della loro ammirazione e della loro riconoscenza; "La visita del re").[2]

The official exposition posters visually enforced this narrative, promoting the idea of America as an Italian offspring to implicitly call for better treatment of Italians after the events in New Orleans. Adolfo Feragutti Visconti's poster advertising Alberto Franchetti's opera *Cristoforo Colombo* (fig. 2.1) stages the sailor's gesture of unveiling the new land for his mariners (and the whole world) as an alluded sign of ownership. The official poster of the exhibition (fig. 2.2) manifested the civilizing rhetoric of Columbus's voyage, in the visual transition from the city's iconic lighthouse (on the top left) to the Caribbean shores (on the top right), as well as in the centre-left embrace of two women, one bare chested and one dressed in a white garment (adorned with a Genoese flag), signifying the passage from a "native" to a "civilized" condition.

In addition to a primacy narrative, Columbus offered the secular state a powerful myth of self-legitimization, fashioning him as a prophet of

Figure 2.1. Adolfo Feragutti Visconti, poster advertising Alberto Franchetti's opera *Cristoforo Colombo* (1892). © Comune di Milano, Raccolta delle stampe "Achille Bertarelli" (Castello Sforzesco). All rights reserved.

unified Italy and a forerunner of Risorgimento. Such depiction dated back to early nineteenth-century Romantic literature, from Leopardi's fictional "Dialogo di Cristoforo Colombo e Pietro Gutierrez" ("Dialogue of Christopher Columbus and Pietro Gutierrez"; *Operette morali* [*Small Moral Works*], 1824), portraying Columbus as a doubtful, yet forward-looking hero, to Manzoni's novel *I promessi sposi* (*The Betrothed*), where the naming of Fra Cristoforo is related to the character's concluding vision of "salvation, resurrection, and Risorgimento" for Renzo and Lucia (Watt 169). The fame of Columbus had grown over the century

Figure 2.2. Official poster of the Esposizione Italo-Americana of Genoa (1892).
BnF (Bibliothèque Nationale de France).

in connection with the war hero Giuseppe Garibaldi (who had admired
him since his sailing apprenticeship years) and the patriotic intellectual Giuseppe Mazzini (as poetically stressed by Giosuè Carducci). In
the sonnet "Mazzini" ("Mazzini," *Giambi ed epodi [Iambics and Epodes]*,
1882) Carducci in fact equated the Risorgimento thinker to Columbus
by way of their common birthplace in Genoa and their similar ability to
see beyond the horizon, as confirmed by the philosopher's positioning
on the "rocks from which the child Columbus saw new worlds appear
in the sea" (da quelli scogli, onde Colombo infante / nuovi pe 'l mar

vedea mondi spuntare; lines 5–6). Carducci's vision of the sailor as a prophet of Italy's resurgence was confirmed in the rhetoric of *Corriere della sera* at the time of King Umberto's visit to Genoa. On 8 September 1892 the newspaper presented the monarch as the embodiment of Columbus's vision of freedom and unity (or the visible manifestation of Italy's rise after centuries of subjugation), and the sailor as an unsung Italian, forced to look for patronage elsewhere and still in search of his lost glory.[3] A comparative vision of Columbus's unrecognized dignity and unclaimed Italian-ness also appears in Cesare Pascarella's contemporary collection of Romanesque poems, *La scoperta de l'America* (*The Discovery of America*, 1893–5), praised by Carducci and organized around a series of dialogues at a Roman inn. In sonnet 47, Pascarella openly linked the trope of Columbus's concealed glory to the appropriation of his Italian identity,[4] as stated in the concluding verses: "but the story of the sane world / – History is history – / is that Cristopher Columbus was Italian" (ma la storia de tutto er monno sano… / eh! La storia, percristo! è sempre storia …? / Cristofero Colombo era italiano!; lines 12–14).

Alongside the Italian narrative, the Catholic Church upheld an "anniversary version" of Columbus, which instead extolled the explorer as a true Christian hero. Pope Leo XIII released the encyclical letter *Quarto abeunte saeculo* (*In the Upcoming Fourth Centenary*) on 16 July 1892. Addressed to the bishops of Italy, Spain, and the Americas, the letter praised Columbus as the author of a remarkable human feat ("the greatest and most marvellous of all that were seen in the order of human things"; *Quarto abeunte saeculo*, sec. 1),[5] which had caused the unexpected advance of communications and science and the passage of millions of creatures from oblivion, barbarism, and paganism to light, civilization, and salvation. By claiming Columbus as "our man" (uomo nostro; sec. 2) and portraying him as a Christian hero, Leo XIII endorsed the contemporary effort to canonize him and legitimized the Catholic involvement in the secular celebrations of Genoa (through the Esposizione delle missioni cattoliche [Exposition of Catholic Missions] and the Salesian journal *Cristoforo Colombo*).[6] Mirroring the secular state's strategy, the pope laid out a primacy argument around Columbus, portraying the Catholic Church as the agent of the New World's discovery and a civilizing institution towards which "the world owes much" (tutto il genere umano ha obbligo non lieve; sec. 2).

Quarto abeunte saeculo inspired divergent responses in Italy and the United States. In the weeks following the letter, the Italian press mounted a public controversy over a procession to the bust of Columbus at Pincio Hill in Rome that had devolved into a riot on 8 August

1892, opposing the clerical association La Romanina and a group of secular citizens. The episode rekindled the tensions that had arisen months earlier over the placement of Giordano Bruno's statue in Piazza Campo de' Fiori, and revamped the internal Catholic debate – a division between the intransigent "guardians of orthodox papacy" (custodi del papato ortodosso; *Corriere della sera*, "Una cagnara," 10–11 August 1892), who rejected any compromise with the Italian state, and those who favoured collaboration and had a conciliatory approach on such social issues as labour and emigration.

In the American context, the Columbian letter of the pope, which expanded on the themes of *Quam aerumnosa* (see ch. 1), offered instead cultural relief for Italian migrants distressed over the New Orleans lynching. The praise of Columbus in *Quarto abeunte saeculo* provided a powerful primacy argument against any prejudice towards Italians and gave the Church self-legitimization, capitalizing on the growing Columbian spirit in the United States. In the years preceding the centenary celebrations, Columbus had already become a key figure, as seen in the creation of societies (e.g., the Knights of Columbus in 1882), in the erection of statues (e.g., the Ohio Statehouse in Columbus in 1891), in the dedication of public spaces or buildings (Columbus square and the Columbus hospital in Manhattan in 1892), and in President Harrison's institution of a celebratory day in 1892 (later reconfigured as Columbus Day).

The Chicago World's Fair of 1893 gave this Columbian momentum its highest cultural expression, as documented in the pavilions of the White City in Jackson Park, by the monumental statue of Columbus overlooking the central pond (symbolizing the Atlantic Ocean), the real-size replica of the caravels, and the reconstruction of the Spanish friary of La Rabida, where the explorer had resided before his first travel.

Like Genoa, the Chicago exposition extolled Columbus as "a man of great vision whose mission was to bring about the unification of all mankind" (Badger 125) and prolonged the narrative of Columbus as a symbol of unity among nations and cultures. Such universalistic tone found correspondence in two occasions: on 1 May 1893, at the inauguration of the fair, with the opening of an exhibition that showcased the first coordinated collection of American, Vatican, and Spanish sources on the sailor's voyages; and on 11–27 September 1893, during the so-called Parliament of Religions, experimentally gathering world representatives from all creeds.[7]

Paralleling this globalist narrative, the Chicago World's Fair also promoted a national portrayal of Columbus as "the original prototype of the American adventurer/hero" (Badger 43) and constructed

Columbianism as an ideological support system to uphold the new plot line of America as a prime, non-colonial, or non-European formation. Its two key elements – Columbus's autonomy from Spain and the New World's endogenous development – had already appeared in the early nineteenth-century representations of Joel Barlow's *The Columbiad* (1807) and Washington Irving's *History of the Life and Voyages of Christopher Columbus* (1828). Such foundational versions of Columbus took visual form in Chicago in the theatrical performance of Buffalo Bill's *Wild West* show, which featured a parade of nations and included an episode dedicated to the fifteenth-century "Pilot of the Ocean," refashioning the sailor into a proto-pioneer, a forerunner of America's progress, and a relentless entrepreneur.[8] By associating Columbus with the conquest of the West, the show visually related America's adventurous beginnings to its present expansion as a way to proudly assert its cultural and political differences from Europe and inaugurate "the age of America's rise to industrial supremacy among the nations of the world" (Burg 6). In this sense, the personification of Columbus as the archetype of the American pioneer functionally supported the cultural endeavour to construct the United States as a self-defined culture and not just as a melting pot of heterogeneous European imports – an attempt that found expression in the new "commercial style" of Chicago architecture and the influence of native and African American musical traditions on Antonin Dvořák's 1893 *Symphony of the New World*. Such Columbian ideology, which preceded and followed the exposition, formed the basis for the later evolution of Americanism (see the introduction).

An Italian View of American Columbianism

The Columbian expositions of Genoa and Chicago came at a time of diplomatic rupture between Italy and the United States. Even if the crisis was resolved by 1893, Italy did not send a formal delegation or build a national pavilion at Chicago World's Fair but did allow individual companies, scientists, and journalists to travel to the exposition at their own expenses. Among them was the pasta manufacturer Filippo De Cecco, who won the prize of excellence in the macaroni exhibit; the young engineer Camillo Olivetti, who attended the International Electrical Congress as a translator for the Italian physicist Galileo Ferraris; and the chamber representative Edoardo Arbìb, who joined the opening ceremonies with President Cleveland and wrote the column "Lettere dall'America" ("Letters from America") for *Corriere della sera* under the pseudonym of Semplice (The Simple One).[9]

Semplice's letters offer insights into the post-crisis state of relations between Italy and the United States. Arbìb was no random journalist but rather a former patriot in Garibaldi's Expedition of the Thousand, war correspondent in the second and third independence wars, and founder of the Roman newspaper *La libertà* in 1870. Moreover, as an elected representative in the Italian parliament (from 1879 until 1895; Di Peio),[10] he was a key political ambassador and economic observer. His "Lettere dall'America" superficially followed a familiar pattern, from the presentation of his trip to the exposition as an excuse to visit and know more about America to the configuration of stages (e.g., the liner, New York, Chicago, Philadelphia, Connecticut, return) into episodes of a larger narration on the American life of both Americans and Italians in the United States.[11] At a deeper level, beyond the anecdotal value, his testimony provided a live assessment of the emerging political and cultural power of the United States, updates on the state of Italian migrants, economic considerations on Italian-American trade, and an evaluation of the diplomatic impact of the Vatican mission in Chicago.

Responding to his readers' curiosities about the emerging global role of the United States, Semplice isolates the distinguishing features of the original American way of life, implicitly outlining the pillars of the Columbian (later Americanist) ideology. In his reading, three elements form the base of America's expansion: the acceptable relationship between finance and politics (8–9 May 1893); the recognized impact of industrial production and advertising (or "réclame"; 6–7 May 1893) on daily matters (2–3 August 1893);[12] and the direct participation of citizens in public life, as attested by his piece of 18–19 May 1893, which described his personal meeting with President Cleveland at the fair's inauguration. Semplice's astonishment at how easily he "got close to the Head of State" (a fact that he saw as "emblematic of this inimitable country's political organism") acquires diplomatic significance, in reinforcing the renewed ties between the nations and promoting a positive vision of Italy's American partner. In Semplice's view, the American financial, industrial, and political mindset was manifested in Cleveland's honest and clear understanding "that his office is only temporary, and that in four years, if they don't re-elect him […] he will return to be a citizen like all others" (*Corriere della sera*, 18–19 May 1893).[13] In contrast to America's successful interplay of finance, politics and industry, Semplice's visit to America became the occasion to lament Italy's lack of a goal-setting attitude (23–24 April 1893),[14] its missed opportunity in Chicago, and its reluctance to improve commercial relations and national reputation abroad, as bluntly stated on 18–19 August 1893: "no one worked for Italy, for its decorum and its interest" (per l'Italia, pel suo decoro e pel suo interesse, non lavorò nessuno).[15]

Paralleling his assessment of Italy's belatedness in international trade, Arbìb also gives valuable insights into the long-debated issue of emigration. His first-hand account of Italian migrants aimed to remedy a general lack of information on their American life and to correct myths that still circulated after the debate on emigration law. In line with *Corriere della sera*'s support for the 1888 bill, Semplice presents a positive image of migration, indicating it as an opportunity and rejecting its daunting connotations. Semplice's piece from the liner (23–24 April 1893) displays his documentary interest in tracking the origin, class, and routine of travelling migrants, mirroring the opening of De Amicis's novel *Sull'oceano*.[16] Unlike the socialist writer, however, Semplice presents life aboard as one of communal fun and enjoyment[17] in the attempt to dispel "all the whimpering against emigration that people used to take in Italy, especially if directed to the United States."[18] Following a traditionally liberal approach, his support for emigration is grounded in the awareness that "since we cannot ensure a pacific and well nurtured existence to many creatures, holding them in Italy would be proof of fierce selfishness towards them and little affection to the homeland" (23–24 April 1893).[19] He will later confirm a vision of emigration as a genuine advantage in his report of success stories by Italians in America (as in the case of Italians in Philadelphia),[20] and his systematic dismissal of the negative myths constructed around customs and American life in general. In the piece of 2–3 May 1893, dedicated to his arrival in New York, he compares the view from the Hudson to the majestic gulf of Naples, minimizes the difficulties at customs, and downplays the city's high prices.[21] In the subsequent letter of 6–7 May, he goes so far as to dismiss the stereotype of American eccentricity as a European exaggeration.[22]

In addition, Semplice's report offers valuable diplomatic insights into the mission of the Holy See at the Columbian exposition. In his piece of 8–9 July 1893 he turns the visit of apostolic delegate Francesco Satolli to the Catholic Educational Exhibit and the Columbian friary of La Rabida into a pretext to observe the politics of the Holy See towards the United States, from both an Italian and an American perspective. As an Italian, Semplice saw the positive value in the American mission of a fellow Italian. Along the lines of his colleague Fra Pacomio, who had once praised Scalabrini as a model of charitable assistance for migrants and promotion of Italian language and culture,[23] Semplice approved the papal choice of Satolli as his first apostolic delegate (after the establishment of the Vatican *nunziatura* in Washington, DC, in 1892) and observed his presence in the United States as positively supporting the development of an Italian strategic partnership with the Holy See for the protection of migrants. From his conciliarist position, Semplice pointed to the United States as a model of collaborative attitude between the Italian state and the Catholic Church and offered his testimony of the American "perfect harmony between religious and national feeling" (perfetta Concordia fra il sentimento religioso ed il sentimento nazionale) to validate his claims.

From his American standpoint, however, Semplice documented the lukewarm reactions of the US bishops to the appointment of Satolli and presented the divisions in the American hierarchy between "Americanists" and "papists" along the same lines as the Italian opposition between *conciliatoristi* and *intransigentisti*. In this sense, he confirmed the vision that his colleague Fra Pacomio had previously outlined on 8–9 February 1893, in the *Corriere della sera* op-ed "L'America, il Vaticano e la missione di Monsignor Satolli" ("America, the Vatican, and Monsignor Satolli's Mission"). Fra Pacomio presented the American hierarchy's negative response to the papal appointment of Satolli as a consequence of his Italian nationality (in reaction to *Quam aerumnosa*) and his previous involvement with the Catholic Church in the United States. At the Third Council of American Bishops in Baltimore in 1884 Satolli had opposed the idea of opening Catholic schools to non-Catholics, and at the inauguration of the Catholic University of America in 1889 he had enforced papal authority by personally reading Leo XIII's letter *Magni gaudii nostri* (*Of Our Great Joy*), written for the occasion, in which the pope explicitly mandated that "no other institution of this nature shall be undertaken by anyone without consulting the Apostolic See" (sec. 7). In this context Fra Pacomio depicted Satolli's appointment as an ecclesial statement aimed at legitimizing the Church at Columbian celebrations and aligning American bishops to papal authority on such issues as confessional schools, the presence of Catholics in American politics, the rejection of secret societies, and the separation of church and state.[24]

In the same way his colleague Fra Pacomio did, Semplice reported Satolli's visit to the exposition and the participation of Monsignor Ireland and Cardinal Gibbons in the Parliament of Religions as serious moments of friction between the Vatican and American Catholicism. In his first-hand account he spelled out for his Italian readership the two opposing factions in the US hierarchy. On the one side, he listed Ireland and Gibbons as the bishops championing active engagement in society, ecumenical dialogue, and the development of an English-speaking American church. On the other, he named Archbishop Corrigan of New

York and Delegate Satolli as representing those who remained sceptical towards ecumenism, promoted schools for Catholics only, disengaged from civil society, and encouraged different groups to retain their own church traditions and language.

From Columbian Americanism to Imperial Americanism (1893–8)

From Semplice's assessment – on contemporary American culture as well as on the Italian and Vatican presence in the United States – Columbianism appears as an ideology of self-assertion, cultural influence, and complex dialogue with the times. In the aftermath of the Chicago World's Fair, Columbianism continued as a strong ideology, even during the financial crisis that shook international markets from 1893 to 1897. During this time of incubation the Catholic Church, the Italian state, and the United States developed their different Columbian constructions in three different forms of "Americanism."

For the Holy See, Columbus remained a positive figure, grounding the Catholic primacy over the New World. In Pope Leo XIII's encyclical letter *Longiqua oceani* (*The Wide Expanse of Ocean*), addressed in 1895 to American bishops to assess the situation of the Catholic Church in the United States, the initial mention of *Quarto abeunte saeculo* laid the groundwork for an iterated celebration of Columbus. By stressing the sailor's missions "to open a pathway for the Christian faith into new lands and new seas" and "plant upon the shore the sacred emblem of the cross" (*Longiqua oceani*, sec. 2),[25] Leo XIII once again pointed to Columbus as a model for American Catholics (in spreading Christianity across North America) and Italian migrants (in maintaining relationships with the Church of Rome), and as a hero expressing the Catholicism of those who kept loyal to their mother country and of those who worked for the Americanization of immigrants. After reviewing the historic ties between the Apostolic See and the United States, from the sailor and the first missionaries to Bishop Carroll and his friendship with "the Great Washington," Leo XIII then identified his delegate Satolli as the continuator of such history, as the "one who should represent Our person" (*Longiqua oceani*, sec. 2).

This historical genealogy of the nation as a Columbian offspring and a fertile land of mission offered the pope a lens for observing ecclesial divisions as well as the country's social and political challenges. On the one hand, Leo XIII defended his appointee Satolli, confirming *Quam aerumnosa*'s line of care towards national affiliations and passive approach to secular society (Reuter 23–4). On the other, he outlined the Church's impact on US society (in education, associations of mutual aid, relief for the poor, and care for African and Native Americans),[26] reiterating the message of his first social encyclical *Rerum novarum* of 1891, which was inspired by Cardinal Gibbons and promoted active involvement in political life.

Starting from awe for the growing reality of Catholicism in America and personal commitment to the evangelization of the United States, Pope Leo XIII articulated his vision of Catholic Americanism as directly affirming Christianity's primary role both in the life of emigrants and in the defence of democracy. The pope's enthusiasm for America was manifested in his admiration and personal involvement with American society. While praising the fact that the Catholic Church in the United States was "free to live and act without hindrance," and exhorting Catholics to "share in" and "help to bring about, this [the nation's'] prospective greatness" (*Longiqua oceani*, sec.13),[27] Leo XIII also called American authorities to promote the positive fruits of religion in perfecting society (sec. 5). While extending his blessings to the nation's growth, he also warned against the effects of the separation of church and state and made explicit that "it would be very erroneous to draw the conclusion that in America is to be sought the type of the most desirable status of the Church, or that it would be universally lawful or expedient for state and church to be, as in America, dissevered and divorced" (sec. 6).

Building on the ecclesial weight of the Italian nuncio Satolli and the recognized missionary work of Scalabrini, Columbus offered a suitable narrative for implementing the collaboration between the Italian state and the Catholic Church on the issue of emigration. After the exposition at Genoa, the Italian state continued to invest in Columbus as a fundamental reference for grounding and legitimizing the nation's migratory presence in the United States. The Columbian primacy represented – for the state as for the church – not only a shared argument to bolster the ties of migrants with Italy and Rome but also a key structure in reverting a common perception of (religious or colonial) subalternity. After Mother Frances Cabrini had opened an Italian school in New Orleans in 1892, Italian authorities increasingly supported Roman Catholicism "as a key element of *italianità*" (Choate 129) and openly accepted missionaries as cultural and linguistic ambassadors of the nation. After Italy's colonial defeat at Adwa in 1896, the explicit theorization of a "new, American colonialism" (Choate 48) reframed emigration from an internal haemorrhage into a strategy of international expansion (59), replacing a lost power (whether colonial or temporal) through cultural, economic, or social influence abroad. The theory of "emigrant colonialism" (59) was further confirmed in 1901, when the Italian state approved a law that moved emigration from the interior ministry to the foreign ministry and aimed to track migrants in the endeavour to maintain their ties to the motherland and turn them into potential settlers. In this context, the papal interest in Italian migrants and the pope's attempt to establish a more consistent Roman authority (through Satolli or the Italian priests sent to the United States who "reported directly to the orders in Rome"; Choate 134) offered the Italian state a favourable convergence of interests and a common vision of emigration as an opportunity for expansion.

While the Vatican and Italian Americanism mirrored an expansionist and cautious approach to the United States, the Columbian spirit of independence and self-assertion of the early 1890s gave rise to a distinctive Americanism in the United States, which found expression both in religious and secular contexts. In religious terms, the criticism of Roman intrusions matured into the conceptual attempt to forge an endogenous and experimental Catholicism, originally synthesizing Christian faith and modernity. Many American Catholics, who laboured "to define themselves as Americans, not alien imports," had seen the papal support for Italian migrants in *Quam aerumnosa* or his appointment of Satolli as "unnecessary and undesirable" (Choate 133) and had embraced the preaching of Bishop John Ireland of Saint Paul, Minnesota, who publicly endorsed a freestanding model of American Catholicism. In his collection of sermons *The Church and Modern Society* of 1897, Ireland developed the Columbian rhetoric of the Chicago exposition into a doctrine of American exceptionality,[28] envisioning through it two providential missions for the US church: "to make America Catholic" (73), and to open in the upcoming century a "new season of grace" (130) ultimately aimed at reconciling "the Church and the age" (126), or, in other terms, "Rome and America" (126). In contrast to the papal letter *Longiqua oceani*, Ireland indicated the US separation of church and state as a favourable situation for American Catholics and called them to honour the constitution and the flag,[29] and not to reject US society, culture, and politics but to get involved with it. Ireland's insistence that the American Catholic Church "must be American" (91) confronted the mounting frustration of some bishops towards the perceived weakness or "appearance of foreignism" (Reuter 25) of Catholic national churches. Building on the growing discomfort over the pope's "Italianism" or "Romanism" (Reuter 28), Ireland's push for a more American Catholicism matured from an ecclesial current into a full-fledged theology, initially defined as "Irelandism" (Sanfilippo, "Chiesa, ordini religiosi" 64) and later identified as "Americanism."

The same word, *Americanism*, acquired a political meaning, coinciding with the Cuban crisis. From Josè Martí's uprising of 25 February

1895, which the Spanish general Arsenio Martinez de Campo repressed four months later, to the military conflict with Spain in 1898, the early emancipatory tone of Columbianism turned into an ideological support for both the Monroe Doctrine and American imperialism. Although Cleveland maintained neutrality over Cuba during his second term as president (1893–7), the new McKinley administration assumed a more aggressive stance on the issue, sending the USS *Maine* battleship to Havana in December 1897 to defend the island's bid for independence (and the growing American stakes in the Caribbean sugar trade). Following the sinking of the USS *Maine* on 15 February 1898, Americanism became an ideology of military aggression.

In contrast with the Spanish assessment that the explosion had been fortuitous, an American investigation determined on 21 March 1898 that a Spanish submarine had sunk the battleship, killing 266 Americans. During a month-long period of negotiations, the American press aggressively rallied for American military intervention under the slogan "Remember the Maine" to vindicate the sinking and support Cuba's thrust for freedom. In this context, Americanism evolved from an escalating outcry of public opinion to an interventionist and imperialist ideology, which led to Congress's approval of war on 11 April and military action on 25 April 1898.

The New American Hegemony: From Fear to Recognition

The Italian press attentively covered the diplomatic crisis and the unfolding of military operations. As the war rapidly progressed, *Corriere della sera* gradually shifted from an initial tone of fear and self-defence to the final acknowledgment of a new American hegemony, offering an invaluable source for reconstructing Italian reactions to US industrial and political expansion before and after the war with Spain.

In the op-ed of 28–29 March 1898, "Alla vigilia della guerra" ("On the Eve of the Conflict"), the newspaper saw a possible war between Spain and the United States as an "absolute unknown" (un'incognita assoluta) from both a financial and a military perspective. At the conclusion of the American inquiry into the sinking of the USS *Maine*, the piece examined the tragic repercussions of an interruption to Atlantic trade on industry (when the United States had already accrued 30 per cent of the world's production; Fiorentino 12) and on financial markets (after the depression that had struck the global economy between 1893 and 1897).[30] Pondering the likely scenario of a global battlefield, the article analysed each side's political, military, and economic readiness for war. While maintaining a Eurocentric annoyance at the United

States,[31] the editorial scrutinized the weaknesses and strengths of the two nations involved in the crisis, countering the considerable size of Spain's navy with the alleged weakness of America's army and the painstaking Spanish attempt to gain support from other European nations with the solidity of American financial backing.[32]

Right before the outbreak of war, the perceived fears of the unknown, American hegemony, and another colonial defeat by a European nation (after the 1896 Italian loss at Adwa) found expression in the op-ed of 21–22 April, "Europa contro America" ("Europe versus America"), which portrayed the conflict as an inevitable clash of civilizations. At this time *Corriere della sera* started to indirectly characterize Americans as enemies. In the 28–29 April op-ed "Aspettando" ("Waiting"), the newspaper assumed a sarcastic tone towards the American lifestyle and bluntly presented Americans as "the seething people of *time-money*, of 'acting early,' of 'getting there first,' the people of *raids, records, express trains*, and train wreckages" (il bollente popolo del *time-money*, del 'far presto,' del 'giunger primi,' il popolo dei *raids*, dei *records*, degli *express*, e degli scontri ferroviari). A few days earlier, in the op-ed "L'inevitabile" ("The Inevitable") of 23–24 April, the circumstances of a geographic congress in Florence in honour of Amerigo Vespucci gave the newspaper the pretext to connect the "inevitable" war to the alleged American "ingratitude" towards Columbus, characterized as the discovered nation's "treason" towards its discovering "homeland":

> É singolare veramente che gli americani colgano proprio questo momento sentimentale per muover guerra alla nazione scuopritrice, la quale sola sostenne e sospinse sulla via ignota il Divinatore, alunno del Torricelli e precursor del Vespucci. Ma non fecero essi stupire già una volta il mondo con la ingratitudine loro verso la madre-patria? (*Corriere della sera*, 23–24 April 1898)

> [It is quite singular that Americans take this very sentimental moment to wage war against the discovering nation, which only lifted and took towards the unknown way the Diviner, student of Torricelli and precursor of Vespucci. But haven't they already astonished the world once with their ingratitude towards their homeland?]

The piece's subsequent debasement of the US military's might, and mockery of the US president's subservience to public opinion, further confirmed the readership's widespread confidence, loyalty, or alignment with Spain.

Notwithstanding European comradeship, a latent anxiety towards the real strength of Spain surfaced in the newspaper's coverage of the papal mediation between Madrid and Washington and the Vatican's separate negotiation with the McKinley administration to ward off the war. After the Italian nuncio Sebastiano Martinelli (who had succeeded Satolli in 1896) was replaced by the American bishop John Ireland (who was friends with McKinley), reports on diplomatic relations became more ambiguous, and scattered updates were increasingly filtered by pre-existing prejudices or cultural misrepresentations. Ireland met with McKinley on 1 April 1898, reporting to the Vatican secretary of state, Cardinal Rampolla, that the president was ready to accept "either a proposal to purchase Cuba or an armistice leading to Cuban-Spanish negotiations" (Trask 48). Spain was ready to accept these conditions, under the mediation of the pope, "provided that the United States withdrew its naval forces from the Caribbean area, as a way of showing that the United States did not support the insurrection" (Trask 48). Despite the promise, the mediation failed a few days later, officially because of the "lateness of the Pope's offer" (Reuter 9) but more likely because of the indignation of the American press towards the release of a Vatican dispatch urging US Catholics not to fight Spain. The mounting "rumors of Catholic disloyalty" (Reuter 10) and annoyance towards a perceived papal intrusion in the nation's affairs were confirmed in an interview with an undisclosed American diplomat that *Corriere della sera* published on 9–10 April, suggesting that Leo XIII's intervention represented a breach of the US separation of church and state.[33]

As the conflict started in late April, Italy was immediately hit by its economic and political repercussions. In early May, while Turin was opening its national exposition, the news of the rising prices of American grain from custom duties created sudden turmoil across several Italian cities, as reported in the op-ed "La prima conseguenza della guerra" ("The First Consequence of War") on 6–7 May 1898.[34] Between 5 and 9 May, the city of Milan became the epicentre of social unrest and the theatre of a dramatic urban warfront. Anarchist protests over the price of bread spread through the city until military intervention suffocated them. Under the orders of General Bava Beccaris, the army opened fire on crowds, killing about 80, wounding 450, and arresting 1,500. The riots of Milan destabilized the government, leading to a constitutional crisis, the resignation of Prime Minister Antonio Di Rudinì in July 1898, the subsequent military cabinet of Luigi Pelloux, and the closing of Parliament for three months in 1899. The Milan uprisings also inspired the killing of King Umberto I on 29 July 1900; the murder, which was set in place by the anarchist and returned Italian migrant

Gaetano Bresci, was presented by him as a vendetta for Bava Beccaris's massacre.[35]

After Americans won a battle in Manila, advancing claims over the Philippines, newspapers changed their tone and started to foresee, against all expectations, an upcoming Spanish defeat. The Vatican press reacted to these events with fear: first, of a renewed liberal influence on the American hierarchy (as American Catholics saw the conquest as an occasion to gain political favour with McKinley and debunk the Eurocentrism of the Holy See;[36] Confessore 71); and, second, of a debasement of papal temporal power (as the American separation of church and state applied to the former Catholic colonies of Spain; Rossini 21). The Italian secular press swiftly abandoned the pre-war anti-American tone, embracing the American victory as a fait accompli and transforming the war into an episodic narration a posteriori. In the article series "Guerra ispano-americana" ("Spanish-American War"), *Corriere della sera* started to reassemble the conflict as an adventurous feuilleton, relating it through situational chapters: "Intermezzo" ("Interlude," 13–14 May 1898); "La sorpresa" ("Surprise," 18–19 May); "La caccia" ("The Hunt," 21–22 May); "La trappola" ("The Trap," 29–30 May); "Perché ritarda?" ("Why Delay?," 27–28 June); "Il suicidio" ("Suicide," 8–9 July); and "L'onore" ("Honour," 21–22 July). Over the same time, the publisher Treves released the serial collection of volumes *Guerra Ispano-Americana* (*Spanish-American War*) to recollect the main facts of the war through a similar episodic structure.

With the final negotiations over the armistice taking place in July 1898, *Corriere della sera* opted to send its top journalist Ugo Ojetti as a correspondent to the United States, with the dual tasks to re-narrate the war from a US viewpoint (to revert its previous Eurocentric tone) and to document American life after the victory (along the lines of Semplice's diary of the Columbian Exposition of Chicago).

In his quasi-daily column "Lettere dall'America" ("Letters from America"), published from 19–20 July to 22–23 October 1898, Ojetti provided an American account of the war, offering updates on military operations, internal parliamentary debates, and external negotiations with Spain. Meanwhile, as he toured the United States, he met with and interviewed key American figures, including President McKinley and the two prelates Monsignor Ireland and Cardinal Gibbons. In conversation with McKinley on 29–30 July 1898, Ojetti quoted the president defining himself as a defender of the same cause of freedom that had moved the Italian Risorgimento and as a "Christian" desiring immediate peace.[37] In dialogue with Ireland on 19–20 August, Ojetti depicted him as a savvy politician able to turn the Vatican's criticism of his failed negotiation into a profitable opportunity for the American church to evangelize new territories. In conversation with Gibbons on 21–22 August, he presented the bishop not just as "one of the most beloved and revered figures in all America" (uno dei personaggi più amati e venerati in tutta l'America) but also as a member, along with John Ireland and John Keane (first rector of the Catholic University of America), of that "apostolic trinity to which is owed the diffusion of Catholicism over the last few years" (trinità apostolica cui si deve l'enorme diffusione del cattolicismo in questi ultimi anni).

These two "ecclesial" interviews came after the piece "Epilogo" ("Epilogue") of 18–19 August, in which Ojetti had announced the end of the conflict, recapitulating its main facts in light of a new proclaimed allegiance to the United States and declaring a posteriori that "the disproportion of nautical and, above all, economic forces *did not leave any doubt* on the outcome and the duration of the unequal fight" (la sproporzione delle forze nautiche e più ancora delle economiche *non permetteva alcun dubbio* sull'esito e sulla durata della impari lotta; my italics).[38] After the piece proclaiming American victory, Ojetti abandoned the war theme and concluded his mission by relating his visits to the main attractions of the United States, writing from Mount Vernon (16–17 August), Annapolis (27–28 August), Boston (31 August–1 September), Harvard (8–9 September), Niagara Falls (23–24 September), Chicago (26–27 September), and aboard a liner going to Santiago in Cuba (22–23 October).

Ojetti's testimony offers a powerful witness to the radical shift in Europe's perception of the United States during the Spanish-American War. At the same time, his report anticipates the later awareness, fully expressed during his 1904 visit to the Saint Louis World's Fair, that the new American emergence had turned Italy into "the museum of Europe" (il museo d'Europa; 28 June 1904)[39] and that "all Europe is ready to follow the destiny of Spain in 1898" (tutta l'Europa è pronta a seguire le sorti della Spagna nel '98; 3 October 1904).[40]

Americanism as Ecclesial Heresy

Ugo Ojetti's interviews with Ireland and Gibbons captured a significant moment of transition in the relations between America and the Holy See, detailing the early seeds of the "Americanist" case, which rapidly shifted from a political project into an ecclesial heresy.

From an American perspective, the war had offered Catholics a moment of unification (as different groups coalesced around a common national consciousness)[41] and of self-affirmation (as the task to evangelize Cuba or the Philippines moved from the Spanish to the US episcopate). From a European perspective, the growing influence of the American church and the transition of the United States from a land of mission to an evangelizing agent was instead viewed with great anxiety.

The Italian secular press had pondered the American church's economic impact on the Vatican since the late 1880s and early 1890s. In the 28–29 July 1892 op-ed for *Corriere della sera*, "Che cosa diventerebbe il papato in mano agli americani?" ("What Would the Papacy Become in the Hands of Americans?"), Fra Pacomio even conjectured the possibility of an American pope,[42] imagining the Holy See transferring from Rome to Baltimore and the new posture of the pontiff as an entrepreneurial leader of an industrial company.

The ecclesial fears of American influence escalated in the mid-1890s around the figure of Monsignor John Ireland, whose advocacy for a self-defining American church was rapidly expanding from the United States to Europe. As it reached France, Ireland's Americanism appeared as a form of Gallicanism (the call for an independent national church). As it reached Italy, it represented a form of Italianism and identified with the more proactive Italian current of *conciliatorismo*.

The French reception of Ireland's Americanism related to a theological dispute that followed Félix Klein's 1897 translation (*Vie du Père Hecker*) of Walter Elliott's biography *The Life of Father Hecker*. The book, prefaced by John Ireland, was dedicated to the American founder of the Paulist congregation, Isaac Hecker, but Klein's translation significantly altered the original, emphasizing points like the separation of church and state or the Catholic Church's relationship to Darwinism with the goal of advancing the agenda of Gallicanism or evolutionism. Based on this text, the scholar Charles Maignen wrote a review for the journal *Etudes sur l'americanisme* (*Studies on Americanism*) entitled "Le P. Hecker est-il un Saint?" ("Is Father Hecker a Saint?"), in which he attacked Elliott's book, rebuked Hecker's positions on ecumenism or evolution, raised doctrinal concerns over their relation to Ireland's ideas,[43] and openly indicted the American church as schismatic. The American hierarchy, led by Cardinal Gibbons, immediately reacted to the controversy raised by the review by rejecting false doctrinal "Americanism" (based on the flawed French reading of Hecker's life), and by defending instead true political "Americanism" (as the one preached by Monsignor Ireland), rooted in the loyalty due to America and its constitution.

Ireland's ideas had been known in Italy since 1894, when a similar theological dispute opposed the journals *Rassegna nazionale* and *Civiltà*

Cattolica, separating the former's praise for his work of conciliation between church and the age (Vitali 809–25) from the latter's affirmation of "the unreconcilability of modern society and the religious institution" (Confessore 30). The Italian translation of Ireland's *The Church and Modern Society* (*La chiesa e la società moderna*) by Sabina di Parravicino di Revel appeared in 1898, revamping the fame of the American bishop. Ireland inspired the liberal Catholic writer Antonio Fogazzaro, who had met him through their mutual friend Bishop Geremia Bonomelli of Cremona. In 1899 Fogazzaro published his essay collection *Ascensioni umane* (*Human Ascents*), which similarly aspired to synthesize Catholicism, social sciences, and evolutionary theory, and in 1905 he would model the protagonist of his novel *Il santo* (*The Saint*) after Father Hecker.[44]

Moving beyond theological disputes, popular opinion mostly depicted Monsignor Ireland as an example of a conciliatory approach between the Catholic Church and the liberal state. As outlined by Ojetti, Italian readers saw in Ireland and Gibbons the American counterparts of bishops Scalabrini and Bonomelli, who had distinguished themselves by their involvement with social issues and emigration. In this scenario, Ireland's Americanism positively appeared as a model of a wished-for "*italianismo*," as outlined in the *Corriere della sera* op-ed "Due pastori" ("Two Pastors") of 22–23 May 1898, commenting on the ecclesial reactions to Milan's anarchist turmoil. By remarking on the "intransigent" tone of Milan's Cardinal Ferrari, who had rebuked the uprising as an anti-clerical attack (also enforced in Pope Leo XIII's later letter of support, *Non poteva* [*We Could Not*]), the piece departed from the news of the Italian translation of Ireland's *The Church and Modern Society*[45] to uphold a conciliatory attitude towards the same event.[46] The mention of the American ecclesial debate was a way to legitimize diverse voices in the Italian episcopate ("certain tendencies that are typical of American episcopate exist also in Italian prelates"; certe tendenze spiccatamente caratteristiche dell'episcopato americano esistono anche in prelati italiani) and to appraise the work of Bishop Bonomelli as an expression of a "profoundly Christian yearning of renewal that comes to us from young America" (grido rinnovatore, profondamente Cristiano, che ci arriva dalla giovane America).

Associating Ireland's Americanism with Bonomelli's *conciliatorismo* or, more broadly, with a path to doctrinal renewal, is a key element in deciphering the Italian reading of the US bishop's negotiation with McKinley and his political involvement in the Americanization of Cuba and the Philippines. Ireland's support for the broader involvement of US Catholics in problems of the age (e.g., education, ecumenism, culture) was uneasily viewed by intransigent Catholicism in light of his suspicious friendship with Bonomelli, who had been under the mark of heresy since his anonymous critique of the *non expedit* in *Rassegna nazionale* in 1889 (followed by a public apology).[47] Bonomelli's later pastoral letter "La chiesa e i tempi nuovi" ("The Church and the New Times," 1905), arguing in favour of the French separation of church and state, would be condemned to the Index of Forbidden Books. The Holy See then attributed Ireland's failed negotiation to his duelling loyalties, as he operated for the pope under the alleged promise of promotion to cardinal but considered himself an "Americanist" from both an ecclesial and political standpoint. In this light, his support for American expansion in Catholic Cuba and the Philippines was then seen as an affront to the traditional evangelizing role of Spain.

While pre-existing misconceptions, ecclesial internal glitches, and delayed dispatches from America influenced the Italian narration of the "Ireland case," in the American context the failed negotiation over the Cuban war appeared instead as a clear-cut rejection of the pope's mediation. At its roots were the traditional anti-papism of Protestants, the mounting anti-Romanism of liberal Catholics, and the "mal d'Italia" (Monsagrati 79) of a large part of society, which was increasingly reluctant towards Italian emigration.[48]

In this context, the war then represented for American Catholics the "first basic clash of interests" (Reuter ix) between the Church and their country. In one way, the war challenged their allegiance to the United States, their commitment to the American separation of church and state, and their willingness to defend the Monroe Doctrine even against another Catholic nation. In another way, the war became an occasion to overcome internal divisions or national partisanships and organize a more unified presence in society through a greater involvement with McKinley. As Washington expanded its influence and the US separation of church and state over former Spanish colonies, the militaristic Americanism of the pre-war campaigns rapidly changed connotations. In political terms, it shifted from a self-affirming ideology into an imperial project. In ecclesial terms, it moved from a missionary impulse into a heresy, as Ireland's call for the Americanization of Catholicism and his vision of a new era of American influence clashed against the pope's intransigent position on the separation between church and state.

In this political and theological scenario Pope Leo XIII addressed the apostolic letter *Testem benevolentiae nostrae* (*Witness to Our Good Will*), with the English subtitle *Concerning New Opinions, Virtue, Nature and Grace; With Regard to Americanism*, to Cardinal Gibbons on 22 January 1899. On the same lines as Gibbons's clarification of the French theological dispute over Monsignor Ireland, the letter condemned doctrinal "Americanism" as a heresy but did not express any judgment on the American war or on the political alignment of a part of the American hierarchy. Considering Ireland's diplomatic failures in Washington and the new imperial power of the United States, however, the letter indirectly served doctrinal and ecclesial purposes.

From a doctrinal perspective, the initial mention of the dispute surrounding the French translation of Fr Hecker's life constituted a pretext to reassess new doctrines allegedly coming from America and thus reconfigure the American church's relationship with Rome after the US military victory. While affirming a "renewed expression of that good will [towards the United States] which we have not failed during the course of our pontificate to manifest frequently," the letter aimed at correcting the "lovers of novelty" (a key expression in Leo XIII's writings, from *Aeterni patris* to *Rerum novarum*) who wanted to shape the teachings of the Church "more in accord with the spirit of the age" and "make some concessions to new opinions." In keeping with *Longiqua oceani*, the stated need to not reject "everything that modern industry and study has produced" is paired with the urgency to safeguard the "divine deposit" and with the call to reassert papal authority over a set of false doctrines (e.g., on natural virtue, religious vows, and ecumenical dialogue).

From an ecclesial perspective, the letter achieved a double result. With regards to the United States, the document struck the liberal front of the US hierarchy and realigned the American episcopate to Rome. Despite the initial reaction of bewilderment and denial by some bishops, the "Roman" conversion of Monsignor Ireland offered him a way out of his diplomatic fiasco.[49] Three years later, in his last letter to the American church, *In amplissimo* (*In the Broadest Sense*), Leo XIII returned to this circumstance, stressing the success of the measures taken "to enlighten dissidents and to draw them to the truth" (sec. 4), and fully reappropriating the motive of his love for the United States ("by reason of the increase of Catholicity among you" and the "liberality with which your people are endeavouring to contribute by their offerings to relieve the penury of the Holy See"; sec. 5). With regards to Europe, the letter indirectly attacked Gallicanism through the isolation of French "Heckerism," and downsized Italian "Irelandism" through the reduction of the bishop's thought to a philosophical heresy (similar to that of Rosminianism).[50] Such underlying politics of the letter are also confirmed by the fact that, after its release, Leo XIII neither included the unfaithful translation of Elliott's *The Life of Father Hecker* in the Index of Forbidden Books,[51] nor condemned Hecker or his congregation, the

Paulist fathers, which he had previously extolled as a model of evangelization for non-Catholics in a note to Satolli on 18 September 1895.[52]

Notwithstanding its contingent nature, the impact of *Testem benevolentiae* extended beyond Leo XIII's death. From a doctrinal perspective, the letter constituted a practical prelude to Pius X's broader condemnation of modernism in the 1907 encyclical *Pascendi Dominici Gregis (Feeding the Lord's Flock).*[53] From a cultural perspective, the letter expressed the complex evolution of Americanism from a Columbian renaissance to an imperial ideology, offering one of the earliest acknowledgments of the effects of the new American hegemony.

3 Americanizing Italy: The New American Presence in Italian Industry and Culture (1901–1913)

Victory in the Spanish-American War accelerated the industrial and cultural ascent of the United States, marking its transformation from a rural, isolationist society to a leading presence on the world stage (Traxel xii). The rise of Theodore Roosevelt after the 1901 assassination of President McKinley fostered a new era of American imperialism and fuelled the rapid diffusion of US products, investments, artefacts, philosophies, and trends throughout Europe. The ideology of Americanism supported this moment of growth and propelled different forms of Americanization in foreign markets.

The development of faster routes and the growing traffic across the Atlantic Ocean made industrial and cultural exchanges between Italy and the United States more accessible and frequent. In tandem with migrants, Italian visitors travelled to the United States to observe and study the country's economic model. Middle-class, wealthy Americans likewise increasingly travelled to Italy, spreading with their presence a less-filtered knowledge of America and different models of thought regarding industrial development, cultural perspectives, and scholarly approaches.

Whether permanent or temporary, visitors like the US president Theodore Roosevelt (at the end of his term), the financier John Pierpont Morgan, the writer Henry James, the painter John Sargent, the collector Isabella Stewart Gardner, the professor Bernard Berenson, the philosopher William James, and the theosopher Helena Blavatska embodied such American influence, manifesting various facets of Americanism to Italian society. Two events specifically catalysed Italy's new positive attention towards the United States: Buffalo Bill's peninsula tour of the *Wild West* show in 1906 and Wilbur Wright's first demonstration of flight in Rome on 15 April 1909.

In observing the impact of US tourists, intellectuals, and entrepreneurs in Italy at the turn of the twentieth century, this chapter investigates the formation of a new American presence in the Italian economic, financial, and cultural systems – a presence that would actively assert itself during the First World War and the 1920s. At a time of French and German influence in Italian culture, industry, and politics, the early Americanization of Italy took shape in two distinct ways: as a legitimization process, aimed at loosening the anti-Americanist narrative associated with emigration; and as a proactive moment, aimed at promoting new models in Italian literature, painting, sculpture, and academic culture.

Americanization as Commercial, Financial, and Industrial Penetration

The US penetration of Italy began in the 1870s when cheaper American wheat first entered the peninsula and heightened the Southern Italian agrarian economic crisis (see ch. 1). The impact of American grain imports was critical during the Spanish-American War when the temporary interruption of transatlantic trade in 1898 led to a sudden spike of bread prices in Italy and the subsequent reaction of social turmoil across many Italian cities (see ch. 2). Paralleling agriculture, American technologies and capital began to emerge on the Italian market during the last two decades of the nineteenth century.

Two impactful American exports were telephones and phonographs. The first Italian telephonic line, connecting Varese and Gallarate, was established in 1877, a year after Bell's patent and a year before the technology's official introduction at the 1878 universal exposition of Paris. Increasingly appearing in contemporary advertisements, telephones became widely adopted in the country starting in the 1880s. Recorded sound developed in Italy during the late 1880s (Gelatt 101), after Edison's 1888 promotional European tour to record the voices of Gladstone, Bismarck, and Brahms. Phonography moved from an American export to an independent national industry in the early 1900s with the formation of the Anglo-Italian Commerce Company (AICC) in 1901 and Fonotipia in 1904.

Beyond these technologies the most significant American exports at this time related to industrialization itself. The American leadership in the production of utensils or "machines to manufacture machinery" (Giannetti 399) and the establishment of electrical power – with the opening in Milan of Edison's first European plant in 1883[1] – were two major catalysts for Italy's industrial conversion in the early 1880s.

Electric energy represented a powerful stimulus for industrialization. Edison's alternative power source lowered Italian dependence on imported coal (which, at the time, was three times the cost of England's; Toninelli 393) and drove the expansion of mass-scale manufacturing.[2] Electricity first appeared in Italian social life at the national exposition of Milan in 1881 when the inaugural display of urban illumination from Piazza Duomo to La Scala (across the Galleria Vittorio Emanuele II) found symbolic expression in the theatre's ballet *Excelsior*. Luigi Manzotti and Romualdo Marenco's choreography sumptuously staged the victory of light and progress over darkness and obscurantism, as the ballet's allegorical plot celebrated the scientific and technological accomplishments of the age, including the steam engine, the Brooklyn Bridge, electricity, telegraphy, the Suez Canal, and the Fréjus tunnel, which connects Italy and France across the Alps. After premiering at La Scala Theatre on 11 January 1881, the show enjoyed global acclaim until Manzotti's death in 1905 (Adamo 158). After its Parisian success at the Eden theatre the American theatre manager Bolossy Kiralfy brought *Excelsior* to the Niblo's Garden Theatre of New York City in 1883, where he partnered with Edison to introduce electrical lights on stage (Tenneriello 102–3).

While advancing commercial expansion and fuelling industrial growth, Americans also began to exert influence on the Italian financial system. Junius Morgan participated "in a £14.6 million loan to the Italian government" in 1881 ("History of JP Morgan Chase"), and his son John Pierpont Morgan had an impact on various levels of the Italian economy at the turn of the twentieth century. Personal friends with King Victor Emmanuel III and Pope Pius X, J.P. Morgan founded the American Academy of Rome in 1894 in conjunction with Andrew Carnegie, John D. Rockefeller, Jr., William K. Vanderbilt, and Henry Clay Frick. In 1904 he earned international recognition for returning an ecclesiastical cope to the Italian government after acquiring it from a dealer in Paris – an art object later discovered to have been stolen from the cathedral of Ascoli. *The New York Times* celebrated the fact on 4 November 1904, and in a ceremony at the Quirinal Palace the Italian king conferred on Morgan the decoration of the Grand Officer Order of Saints Maurizio and Lazzaro (Carosso and Carosso 451). In 1911 the Italian state also acknowledged Morgan's decisive role in relieving the global financial panic of 1907, triggered by the failure of the Knickerbocker Trust Company, by nominating him honorary president of the foreign committee preparing the fiftieth anniversary of Italy's unification (Cingolani).

At that time, Morgan also secretly bid £450,000 in a public auction to acquire the memorabilia of Milan's La Scala Theatre. After the public lobbying of three Milanese artists (Lodovico Pogliaghi, Ettore Modigliani, and Arrigo Boito), Morgan withdrew the offer, and the items became the core collection of the Museum of the La Scala Theatre, which was founded in Milan in 1913 ("History of the Museum"). In that same year, Morgan unexpectedly died while in Rome, and, prior to the return of his body to the United States, official state ceremonies and a papal blessing were conferred upon him in the Italian capital.[3]

Around the same time, US president Theodore Roosevelt had also gained popularity in Italy, thanks to his dispatching of capital, skilled workers, and trained Navy personnel to aid Sicily after the Messina earthquake of 28 December 1908. On 23 March 1909, as he was embarking on a journey to Africa at the end of his presidential term, the Italian Chamber of Commerce of New York recognized his relief efforts by conferring upon him a bronze tablet in the city's harbour. After Roosevelt had crossed the ocean, Italians paid him cheerful homage in Naples and Messina, where he saw the ruins, spent time with the US relief forces, and met with Italian king Victor Emmanuel III on board the battleship *Re Umberto*. On his way back from Africa in 1910, Roosevelt returned to Italy, briefly visiting Rome (where Mayor Ernesto Nathan welcomed him as a modern equivalent of Roman emperor Marcus Aurelius), and travelling to the Ligurian city of Porto Maurizio (the site of his honeymoon with his second wife, Edith), where he was proclaimed an honorary citizen. Commenting on these facts on 3 April 1910, *The New York Times* wrote: "the great hunter is now a more popular man in Italy than any other foreigner has ever been and can be compared only with some of the great heroes of the National epoch" (Praino).[4]

In addition to American capital and resources, new models of production started to emerge in Italy in the first decade of the twentieth century, in connection with Frederick Winslow Taylor's philosophy of scientific management (later known as Taylorism). In 1900 the American mechanical engineer first presented in Paris the theory that he later compiled in the 1911 volume *The Principles of Scientific Management*. The early impact of his manufacturing system is documented in the organization of partial assembly lines by the Italian companies Olivetti (since 1908) and Alfa Romeo (since 1910). The first full application of Taylor's principles in Italy, however, belongs to Fiat, which completely line-assembled both the model Zero (Italy's first accessible car) in 1912 and its production during the First World War (Accornero).

While neither Taylorism nor later Fordism fully developed a volume of production in Italy comparative to that of the United States (Bigazzi

899), their manufacturing philosophies and organization models had an impact on Italian social debate, as attested in the a posteriori reflections on Americanism by Antonio Gramsci (see the epilogue). In his notes, elaborated in the *Prison Notebooks* and posthumously released in the self-standing volume *Americanismo e fordismo* (*Americanism and Fordism*, 1950), the Marxist thinker equated Americanism to industrialization, characterizing it as the cynical realization of

> un processo ininterrotto, spesso doloroso e sanguinoso, di soggiogamento degli istinti (naturali, cioè animaleschi e primitivi) a sempre nuove, più complesse e rigide norme e abitudini di ordine, di esattezza, di precisione che rendano possibili le forme sempre più complesse di vita collettiva che sono la conseguenza necessaria dello sviluppo dell'industrialismo. (Gramsci, *Americanismo e fordismo* 36)

> [uninterrupted process (often painful and bloody) of subjugation of (natural, that is animal or primitive) instincts to ever newer, ever more complex or rigid norms or habits of order, exactitude, and precision which might enable ever more complex forms of collective life, as necessary consequences of the development of industrialism.]

In Gramsci's view of American culture as "an organic prolongation and intensification of European life" (si tratta di un prolungamento organico e di una intensificazione della vita europea; *Americanismo e fordismo* 65), Taylor's model represents the key difference between European and American capitalism, exemplifying a method that successfully produced more effective results, neutralized violence, and overcame national affiliations.[5]

Gramsci's notion of Americanism as mere "difference" in execution – and not as the expression of an independent culture – relates to the cultural framework of nineteenth-century Italian travellers to the United States. Italian observers of the age considered Americanism a prolongation or intensification of European culture and defined the difference of US products, funds, and ideas only by way of their dissimilarity from European counterparts.[6]

In his *Lettere americane* (*American Letters*) of 1893 (later published in 1968), the young entrepreneur Camillo Olivetti singled out two elements of American difference in the country's "construction and management economy" and in its "pragmatic spirit of simplification" (see Bigazzi 911–12). In his trip to the 1893 Chicago exposition Olivetti documented these principles through unsystematic, on-site observations. He reported his encounter with Edison, praised the power of the electricity-fuelled plant, assessed the impact of telephony on social life (Olivetti 11), visited the Pulman wagon plant near Chicago (19), highlighted the efficiency of the library system (31), and stressed the role of strong-willed women workers (54) upon American society.

Paralleling private letters and individual testimonies, contemporary publications for the broader public gradually veered from cultural stereotyping and travel reports (as epitomized in Giuseppe Giacosa's *Impressioni d'America* [*Impressions of America*], 1898) to more elaborate studies on the social, economic, and anthropological difference between Italy and the United States. Moving away from the exclusive focus on migration, these publications certainly contributed to fashioning a new Italian perception of American contemporary culture.

The most important anthropological inquiry into American "otherness" is the 1901 book *La democrazia nella religione e nella scienza: Studi sull'America* (*Democracy in Religion and Science: Studies on America*) by Angelo Mosso, physiologist, promoter of physical education, and inventor of the first neuroimaging technique. A contemporary American review of the book significantly presented Mosso's text as a work that "purports to be a résumé of impressions gathered on his visit to this country in 1899" but "goes quite beyond the scope of a journal of travel," offering "a very suggestive survey of some of the most characteristic aspects of American life" (Tosti 293). In his essays Mosso presents a scholarly investigation into the anthropological differences between the Latin and American "races" and studies such issues as the expansion of Catholicism in the United States, Protestant universities, modern tendencies in education, and lastly Americanism (presenting it as a controversy between the Roman Curia and the representatives of US Catholicism). In his analysis Mosso identifies the two greatest American contributions to modern life as the mechanization of agriculture[7] and the separation of church and state.[8] At the level of collective psychology, Mosso connects Americanism to two key characteristics in the American mindset: the "work fever" (febbre del lavoro; 47), expressed in the cult of "rush" (fretta; 24); and a heightened patriotism (in its connection to democracy). Echoing Roosevelt's ideals, Mosso reads Americanism as the American pervasive love and appreciation for the country, as expressed in the following passage:

L'entusiasmo degli americani per il loro paese trapela da ogni atto e da ogni parola e lo si vede specialmente nei giornali che fanno continuamente appello al vero americanismo: *true americanism, thorough americanism, intense americanism,* come se fosse questo il sentimento più nobile e la corda che vibra più intensamente nel cuore di ogni cittadino dell'America. (Mosso, *La democrazia* 65)

[The enthusiasm of Americans for their country exudes from every act or work and is specially visible in newspapers that continuously appeal to the true Americanism – *"true americanism, thorough americanism, intense americanism"* – as if this were the noblest sentiment and the chord that vibrates more intensely in the heart of every American citizen.]

Ugo Ojetti also saw American patriotic pride as a major feature distinguishing the United States from other countries. The journalist returned to the United States in 1904 to cover the universal exposition of Saint Louis for *Corriere della sera* and collected his reflections in the 1905 volume *L'America e l'avvenire* (*America and the Future*). Expressing his enthusiasm for American energy and vigour, Ojetti defines the "ideal that everyone all over the world today calls American" (l'ideale che oggi in tutto il mondo si chiama americano; 19) in relation to the primacy of work (as "the goal of individual and social life" and not as "a means towards rest")[9] and the influence of patriotism on public opinion and democratic institutions.[10] While expressing his admiration for the United States and inviting his readers to evaluate it with different criteria than the ones used for European states,[11] Ojetti, however, ultimately maintains a sense of distance from the nation. In a way, he avoids pointing out its failures, as confirmed by his silence regarding the flop of the Olympic games of Saint Louis in 1904 (marred by scarce attendance and the blatant display of racism during the so-called Anthropology Days).[12] In another way, he remains openly sceptical about US expansion, indicating that "Americans don't have the sense of eternity that we Mediterraneans have," and cynically suggesting that the "imperialist fever will slowly fade in front of reality" (36).[13]

Paralleling journalistic scepticism and the fascinated reception of American imports, Italy's negotiation of the United States' rising dominance manifests during the same years in new ideas of tourism and new models of American presence in Italy.

The Development of Atlantic Tourism

The opening of tunnels across the Alps – Fréjus (1871), Gotthard (1882), and Simplon (1906) – made Italy more accessible from continental Europe. The expansion of the railroad system, the development of harbours, and the growth of the Italian navigation lines Rubattino and Florio also made it easier for travellers to cross the peninsula or reach it from the Mediterranean. Lastly, the investment in roads and the creation of grand hotels – in Stresa (Grand Hotel des Iles Borromées, 1863), Sanremo (Grand Hotel de Londres, 1861, and Grand Hotel des Anglais, 1888), Venice Lido (Grand Hotel des Bains, 1900), Rimini (Grand Hotel Rimini, 1908), and Varese (Grande Albergo Campo dei Fiori, 1911) – supported a new form of tourism, replacing the old tradition of a humanistic Grand Tour with the recreational exploration and discovery of contemporary Italy.

In addition to British, French, and German tourists, middle-class Americans and educated professionals increasingly travelled to Italy during this period for social prestige, artistic or scholarly interests, or leisure. The growing number of transatlantic liners and reprints of Baedeker guides to Italy confirm this trend.

To capture the growing market of American travellers, passenger ships competed to provide clients with shorter navigation time across the Atlantic Ocean and extravagant first-class spaces, mirroring the comforts of grand hotels and replicating the grandeur of European architecture. For example, the Cunard Line's ship *Mauretania* gained notoriety for its record-beating transatlantic crossing of 1907 (five days, five hours, and ten minutes) and its on-board attractions, which included a smoking room shaped like a late-Renaissance Italian palazzo and a dining saloon inspired by a mid-sixteenth-century French chateau ("Ocean crossings").[14]

The many reprints of the three-volume Baedeker English guide to Italy (fourteen editions between 1867 and 1903) testify to increased Anglo-Saxon traffic towards the Italian peninsula.[15] For American or British travellers who did not speak Italian or French, the guides offered useful tips (regarding currency, safety against bandits and beggars, passport requirements, and hotels) as a way to remedy "many a trial of temper," given that, as explicitly noted in the preface of the Baedeker guide, "there is probably no country in Europe where the patience is more severely taxed than in some parts of Italy" (*Italy*, vol. 1 v).

As mobility increased and new travelling modes emerged, a new American perspective on Italy also took shape – an inquisitive outlook that focused less on a romantic quest for ruins or Gothic atmospheres and more on contemporary aspects. American travellers had been visiting the Italian peninsula since the eighteenth and nineteenth centuries, as attested by Thomas Jefferson's 1787 travels to Northern Italy or the testimonies of nineteenth-century American writers. Herman Melville wrote his poem "Naples at the Time of Bomba" (1857) during his stay in Bourbon-ruled Naples. Nathaniel Hawthorne's novel *The Marble Faun* (1860) mirrored his year-long experience in Rome between

1858 and 1859. Mark Twain based chapters 17–31 of his novel *The Innocents Abroad* (1869) on his 1867 visit to Genoa. These testimonies, which now provide a meaningful image of the country prior to or immediately after its unification, mostly followed traditional iconography of Italy, focused on its attractions, ruins, or landscapes, and predefined humanistic templates or tropes. Edgar Allan Poe's poem "The Coliseum" (1833) or his short story "The Assignation" (1834) shows that the literary vision of Italian monuments or cities (e.g., Rome or Venice) was often not even based on actual on-site visits.

Against this backdrop the gradual formation of mass tourism and the evolution of travelling from a humanistic journey to luxurious, educational, or recreational trips significantly changed American perception or understanding of Italy. A symbolic marker in this passage from an aesthetic to a more interactive or critical vision of Italy can be found in a collection of essays by Henry James, written in different trips over four decades and published in 1909 as *Italian Hours*.

The book depicts a new modern tour of Italy, creating a novel space of interaction between the idealized and the actual country as attested by the author's transparent dialogue between American cultural imagination and Italian contemporary society. The book also stages a new intellectual posture towards Italy, which is summed up by James's sophisticated admiration for the country, made simultaneously of daring exploration and of critical observation. The writer purposely bypasses the "Baedeker's polyglot estimate of […] recommendations" (229), assuming instead the position of a "fearless explorer" (H. James 229), visiting the country's less beaten territories – as seen in his descriptions of Narni and the space between Assisi and Perugia, of the Alpine path from Chambéry to Turin through the Fréjus tunnel, or of the area between Como and Bellinzona in Swiss Ticino. While preserving his unshakable awe for what he defined in the book's conclusion as the "luxury of loving Italy" (364), James nonetheless also examined the nation's current state, moving beyond picturesque stereotypes or preformatted descriptions of attractions and amenities, and offering instead poignant commentary on its contemporary situation with a singular mix of critical and nostalgic attitude.

In one way, his enthusiasm for Italy's marvels parallels his regret over its transformation into a modern nation. James in fact sees modernization as the cause of Italy's lost charm, as expressed in a memorable statement of his essay "A Roman Holiday": "now that Italy is made the Carnival is unmade" (H. James 133). In another way, as seen in the opening chapter on Venice, James aspires to move beyond the immobilization of Italy's attractions and ruins. With sarcasm, he scorns trite depictions of Venice by stating that "there is notoriously nothing more to be said on the subject" and that "every one has been there, and every one has brought back a collection of photographs" (1). Conversely, he then introduces a new outlook on the actual city by dwelling on its unexplored corners, by pondering the "misery" (3) of its paralysis and impossibility of novelty, and by considering the living conditions of its inhabitants (whose "habitations are decayed; […] taxes heavy; […] pockets light; […] opportunities few"; 3).

In the essay "Italy Revisited," James lays bare for the reader the "frequent perplexity to the observer of actual Italian life" (H. James 110), by stressing the stark "contrast between the fecundity of the great artistic period and the vulgarity there of the genius of to-day" (110). Looking at contemporary buildings, James outlines Italy's "accomplished schism between the old order and the new" (112) and denounces this paradoxical break where "the old has become more and more a museum, preserved and perpetuated in the midst of the new, but without any further relation to it" (112). Such ambiguous perception of Italy as a nation that was altered "both for the better and for worse" (133) also finds exemplary expression in reference to train lines, which simplified travelling but also constrained the vision of the landscape to fixed routes. Another example comes from the city of La Spezia, which "since it has become more prosperous […] has grown ugly" (119). Despite the new functionality of its harbour, turned into the operative "headquarters of the Italian fleet" (118), James laments the loss of attractiveness of Spezia's gulf, which, in his words, has acquired the "look of monstrous, of more than far-western newness which distinguishes all the creations of the young Italian state" (119).

Henry James's admirative yet disenchanted gaze reflects the formation in the US traveller of a novel gaze towards Italy. His *Italian Hours* likewise configures a new American posture of active dialogue and interaction with the actual country. In addition to James, other American intellectuals visited the nation during the same years, enacting a non-conformist and external perspective in the Italian milieu, reinventing its heritage and introducing new cultural models in painting, sculpture, scholarship, philosophy, religion, and photography.

A New American Presence: Spreading American Art and Thought in Italy

The most influential American painter who visited Italy was John Singer Sargent. Between 1898 and the outbreak of the First World War he spent time almost annually in Sicily, Rome, Florence, and for the most part Venice, where he painted about 150 watercolours and served as a reference point for the American and British expatriates attending the artistic centre at Palazzo Barbaro (including, among others, the collector Isabella Stewart Gardner; McCauley). Similar to Henry James, Sargent moved away from preformatted views (*vedute*) of the city's attractions and instead observed Venice with a contemporary outlook, characterized by a comparable mix of fascination and inquisitiveness. Sargent captured the essence of the city, more than its external façade, by depicting its life behind the scenes (e.g., a hidden backstreet in *Venice*; fig. 3.1), original details (e.g., the undulated mosaics in the *Pavement of Saint Mark*; fig. 3.2), unexpected views (e.g., a secret passageway seen from a canal, in *Venetian Passageway*; fig. 3.3), and revealing moments or atmospheres (Hirshler).

While Sargent's Italian work visually reflects Henry James's intellectual curiosity towards uncharted spaces, many other American painters aligned instead with the writer's critical disenchantment, regretfully scorning Italy's modernization as a force depriving the country of its original charm and attractiveness. American painters in fact mourned the Italian attempt to remodel the nation "on what it presumed to be an

Figure 3.1. John Singer Sargent, *Venice* (1880–2). © The Metropolitan Museum of Art. Image source from the Art Resource, NY.

Figure 3.2. John Singer Sargent, *Pavement of Saint Mark* (1898). Wikimedia Commons.

American model" and later viewed as disincentivizing factors both the Futurists' endeavour "to Americanize Italy" (Licht 133) and Marinetti's aggressive nationalism or outspoken xenophobia.[16]

Unlike painters, however, American sculptors maintained a lively interest in Italy for at least three reasons. Politically, Italy was seen as a nation that highly regarded public sculpture, vis-à-vis the latent American hostility towards monumental art.[17] Historically, Italy had a primacy in sculpting, as attested in its long tradition of excellence and the contemporary impact of Italian sculptors on American government buildings. Economically, the marble ateliers of Carrara and Pietrasanta were international leaders in the industry, offering a "thriving catalogue-order business" of statues, and shipping products all over the world (Licht 135). In this context, the American Academy of Rome represented an ideal site for American sculptors, both for training purposes and for cultural enrichment. Among many, two important artists were formed there: Paul Manship (1885–1966), who studied in Rome between 1909 and 1912 and sculpted *Prometheus* in New York City's Rockefeller Center (1934); and the Norwegian American Hendrik Christian Andersen

Figure 3.3. John Singer Sargent, *Venetian Passageway* (1905). © The Metropolitan Museum of Art. Image source from the Art Resource, NY.

(1872–1949), who moved to Rome in 1893, met Henry James there in 1899, and worked in the city until his death. In collaboration with the architect Ernest Michel Hébrard, Andersen developed his laboratory at Villa Hélène Andersen as an international gathering centre for the world's leading intellectuals and scientists. His studio later became a museum hosting the collection of his monumental statues. Andersen's "insidious blend of erotic impulses with utopian socio-political ideals" would influence the official governmental style of Italian monuments, as seen first in the reliefs of Giuseppe Sacconi's monument to Vittorio Emanuele II in Rome and later in Fascist public sculpture (Licht 137).

Paralleling these artists, two important American travellers of the period – the philanthropist and art collector Isabella Stewart Gardner and the Renaissance scholar Bernard Berenson – profoundly influenced Italian contemporary culture. Stewart Gardner repeatedly travelled to

Venice, where she spent time at Palazzo Barbaro (the site of her famous portrait immortalized by the Swedish painter Anders Zorn in 1894). With the aid of Berenson, who accompanied her as an art dealer, she acquired numerous antiques and paintings that would later form the core of her collection. The inspiration for the project of her house-museum in Boston came from her first trip to Italy, in 1857, after the visit to the art house of Gian Giacomo Poldi Pezzoli in Milan. Berenson – an art critic and collector – had established his Italian base in the out-skirts of Florence, in a seventeenth-century farmhouse that he had been renting in Settignano since the late nineteenth century. Between 1894 and 1903 he composed his five scholarly masterpieces there and earned an international reputation for both his successful method of attribu-tion and his systematic survey of Italy's Renaissance paintings.[18] The art critic Heinrich Wölfflin praised his essay on Lorenzo Lotto, and William James commended his application of psychology to art interpretation in *Florentine Painters of the Renaissance* (1896). After purchasing the Set-tignano farmhouse in 1907, Berenson reconfigured it in the years pre-ceding the First World War as an Anglo-Italian Renaissance villa with garden (Villa I Tatti) and, most importantly, as an international aca-demic centre aimed at providing scholars with a quiet environment to develop new ideas slowly. After his death, Berenson's villa became the Harvard Center for Renaissance Studies, prolonging its founder's mis-sion of enabling academics to pursue knowledge beyond set degrees or curricula in a slow-paced collaborative setting.

As for permanent or recurring travellers, occasional American visi-tors also left an imprint on Italian society, spreading contemporary expressions of American culture through conferences, congresses, or exhibits. The Russian medium Helena Blavatsky and the American lawyer Henry Olcott, who founded the Theosophical Society of New York City in 1875, frequently visited Italy at the turn of the twentieth century, spreading their new occult religion through lectures in Venice, Trieste, Bologna, Florence, Rome, Bari, and Naples ("Teosofia in Ita-lia"). The American philosopher William James, brother of Henry and founder of pragmatism, visited Rome in 1905 for the Fifth International Congress of Psychology (Maddalena and Tuzet 4) and established his first direct connection with Giovanni Papini, who had been promoting his philosophy from his journal *Leonardo* since 1903. The presentation of American artist and dealer Alfred Stieglitz's photographic work at the 1902 Exposition of Modern Decorative Arts in Turin also left an indirect impression on Italian culture, legitimizing photography as an aesthetic language and inspiring the subsequent development of the Italian Pic-torialist school.

The novelty and success of Stieglitz's photographs strengthened the photographic momentum that Turin had previously generated with the photographic congress of 1898 and the foundation of the Società Fotografica Subalpina (Subalpine Photographic Society) in 1899. The organizers of the 1902 exposition – former mayor of Turin Edoardo di Sambuy and the honorary president of the Società Fotografica Subalpina Luigi di Savoia, Duke of Abruzzi – hoped to give Italian photography an opportunity to transcend its national horizon, offering visitors "a large field of observations and opportune comparisons" and an introduction to a new transnational "branch of photography, cultivated only for a few years and logically inspired by Modern Art" (*Esposizione internazionale* 9).[19] The president of the American committee for the 1902 exposition was Luigi Palma di Cesnola, former general of the so-called Garibaldi Guard (the Thirty-Ninth Italian regiment) during the American Civil War and the first director of the Metropolitan Museum of Art in New York. Palma di Cesnola contacted Alfred Stieglitz, the American photographer, gallerist, and founder of the journal *Camera Notes* in 1897, and convinced him to exhibit the work of his Photo Secession group, which promoted a new form of photography aimed at "seceding" from the accepted rules of contemporary camera clubs. The group of photographs that Stieglitz arranged to send to Turin by way of Palma di Cesnola was awarded the "diploma of honour," and the additional collection of American pictorial photographs was awarded the "King's Prize."

Such cultural expressions coming from the United States (e.g., theosophy, pragmatism, and pictorialism) promoted the idea of Americanism as a form of anti-positivist thought among Italians (see ch. 4). In the same way, the new sensibility brought by American tourists, artists, and writers associated Americanism with an alternative, different, or nonconformist trend. Against the backdrop of individual interactions, two contemporary events fed the mass curiosity about the United States, constructing Americanism as a serialized culture or a pioneering mindset. One was the Italian tour of Buffalo Bill's *Wild West* show in 1906. The other was Wilbur Wright's demonstrative flight in Rome in 1909.

Americanism as a Mass-Product: The Case of Buffalo Bill's *Wild West*

In 1906, Buffalo Bill (William Frederick Cody) visited Italy for the second time. His first Italian tour was in 1890, when the *Wild West* show was performed in Milan, Bologna, Florence, Rome, and Naples. At the time, Cody's "display of American exoticism" (Rydell and Kroes 111) in his theatrical circus helped create a positive vibe towards the United States vis-à-vis the heated Italian debate on emigration. With skilful entrepreneurial spirit Cody had managed to win over the masses, the press, and intellectuals by pairing the show with galvanizing attractions (as seen in Bologna when popcorn was first introduced in Italy),[20] interviews in local newspapers, and promotional events, like the wild-horse-taming race with local peasants at Cisterna di Latina or the presentation of his "Indians" in Saint Peter's Square for the blessing of Pope Leo XIII (Bussoni 80). After attending the Milanese performance, the composer Giacomo Puccini also shared his excitement for the show, as seen in a letter to his brother on 24 April 1890:

> C'è stato qui Buffalo Bill che mi piacque. Buffalo Bill è accompagnato da una compagnia di americani del Nord, con una quantità di indiani pellirosse e di bufali, che fanno dei giuochi di tiro splendidi e riproducono al vero delle scene successe alla Frontiera. (Bussoni 90)

> [Buffalo Bill was here, and I liked him. Buffalo Bill is accompanied by a company of Northern Americans, together with a number of redskin Indians and buffalos, who perform marvellous games of target shooting and reproduce live scenes that happened on the Frontier.]

Later in his career Cody's performance would inspire his Italian re-elaboration of the West in the 1910 opera *La fanciulla del West* (*The Girl of the Golden West*; see Cottini, "Buffalo Bill" 97–9).

When Buffalo Bill brought his show back to Italy in 1906, his context was different, not only because of America's novel dominance after the war with Spain but also because of Italy's ongoing industrial transformation, launched by Prime Minister Giolitti and symbolically staged in the international Esposizione del Sempione (Simplon Exposition) hosted by Milan that same year.

In about a hundred performances,[21] the 1906 show capitalized on Italy's new enthusiasm for America, giving rise to a real "buffalomania," as it was known at the time. Two contemporary testimonies confirm the excitement surrounding Cody's performances: one by the cinema pioneer Filoteo Alberini, who filmed Buffalo Bill's arrival in Rome for the newly founded cinematographic company Cines; and the other by the journalist Emilio Salgari, who reported for the newspaper *L'arena* his own experience at the Verona performance, when Cody invited him on stage as a volunteer for a robbery scene.

A description of the actual spectacle can be found in the program of the Milan performance, conserved in the archives of the Buffalo Bill

Center of the West in Wyoming. In its opening remarks the booklet presents the show as an "exhibit" (*mostra*), an "educational show" (*spettacolo istruttivo*), and a "real impression" (*impressione reale*) of the West, arguing that William Cody was "not just a banal impresario, but rather [...] the most original scene director of true history of bold and heroic war deeds" (non è un impresario banale, ma bensì il più originale direttore di scena della storia vera di fatti d'armi audaci ed eroici; "Wild West" 11). The ensuing program is now a valuable source to reconstruct the show's complex juxtaposition of multiple dimensions and its crafty mix of clichéd and customizable scenes. The *Wild West* was in fact at once a circus of animals and attractions, a histrionic one-man show, an itinerant museum, and a live re-enactment of America's recent history. At the same time, as a self-proclaimed "Drama of Civilization," its five acts[22] revolved around a combination of fixed scenes related to the West (e.g., robbery, unexpected attacks on coaches, slaughters, the American loss to the Sioux in the 1876 battle of Little Big Horn, Cody's scalping of Yellow Hair) and circumstantial episodes occasionally included depending on the performance's location.[23] In the Milan performance of 1906, for instance, the added scenes related to other ethnic groups (e.g., Mexicans, Russians, Arabs, Japanese) in dialogue with the ongoing international exposition, and to Italian emigrants in an attempt to reframe contemporary migration from a necessity into a form of world exploration.

Like the ballet *Excelsior*, which transfigured national events into a universal story for broader international audiences and absorbed elements coming from current news or different world traditions within a rigid yet malleable structure, Buffalo Bill's *Wild West* celebrated the victory of progress and civilization over darkness and barbarism, through the transfiguration of Cody's biography and stereotypical American tropes into a universal narrative.

In this light, the frontier – site of Cody's adventures – symbolized the border between wilderness and civilization, parting the "barbaric" genuineness of the natives from the "advancement" of Western pioneers. The prairie, the arena for Cody's hunting prowess, constituted an ideal background for his own personification of Western civilization's relentless exploration of space (at the very end of the age of discoveries, after the nineteenth-century completion of the earth's mapping). Buffalos and wild horses prolonged the romanticized trope of a pure state of nature in their wild force and thoroughbred race and drove a latent narrative of wilderness and domestication, which subtly enforced the vision of Roosevelt's *Winning of the West* (see introduction) and equated the taming of animals with the colonial act of subjugating/"civilizing"

Indigenous populations. Lastly, the train, the symbol of the imperialist expansion of the United States – funded by financial capital (as seen in Wells Fargo agents), imposed by military force (as seen in Buffalo Bill achieving justice for the dead soldiers of Little Big Horn), carried forth by pioneers, and materially completed by emigrants – was also transfigured into a universal symbol of human progress.

Against the backdrop of this ambivalent imagery, of marvel and violence, myth and history, wilderness and civilizing conquest, Cody's Italian success related to a prepackaged Americanism, which iterated the colonial framework of European nations and skilfully stylized a cultural representation into a malleable mass-product for global export. Cody's "*mostra*" (show, exhibit, exposure, display) of the new American civilization and its pioneering heroes also established a long-lasting cultural template of the Old West that powerfully shaped Italian imagination, as seen in early twentieth-century Italian reinterpretations of the theme by Emilio Salgari, Giacomo Puccini, and F.T. Marinetti (see ch. 4) and in the genre's success in Italian cinematography after the Second World War.

Wilbur Wright in Rome and the Start of Italian Aviation

Wilbur Wright's 1909 visit to Rome was another significant moment of American influence in Italy, triggering the later birth and evolution of the Italian aviation industry.

After the first experiments in flight of 1903, in which the Wright brothers were able "to successfully combine a suitable airframe and an internal combustion engine to create a controllable airplane" (Niccoli 38), their invention had been struggling to emerge on the American market. By 1908 the Wrights had started to tour their invention in Europe, organizing flying performances in France and Italy to sell their products and promote heavier-than-air flight over the more common airships or dirigible balloons.[24]

The flying performance of the Wright brothers in Le Mans in August 1908 resonated in the Italian press, as attested by an interview of Luigi Barzini, Sr., with Orville Wright in *Corriere della sera* on 4 October 1908. In the interview, the first in an Italian newspaper, the renowned Italian journalist commended the "simplicity and modesty of this man who had realized the most ancient and daring dream of humanity" and presented the Wright brothers as the "missionaries of aviation" who "discovered a marvellous truth and want to convert mankind to this new religion of theirs."[25] Building on such an aura of mysticism and legend surrounding their technology, the Wright brothers rapidly gained notoriety in Italy. The apex of their growing fame coincided with Wilbur's visit to Rome between 1 and 27 April 1909 (only weeks after Roosevelt's visit to Italy).

Other pilots had previously attempted engine-operated flights in Italy,[26] and a few months earlier, on 13 January, the triplane that Italian engineer Aristide Faccioli had assembled for the Società Piemontese Automobili (Piedmontese Automobile Society) and briefly flown over the Turin airport of Venaria Reale, had crashed in its landing phase. In this context, the success of Wilbur Wright's demonstrative flight in Rome marked a momentous watershed in Italian aviation, not only for the proven effectiveness of his biplanes as viable alternatives to dirigibles but also for the feat's impact on public opinion.

The flight of Wilbur's *Flyer* at the Roman airport of Centocelle on 15 April 1909 was the first to ever be completed in Italy. The Italian military officer (and later senator) Maurizio Moris had invited Wright; King Victor Emmanuel III, the Queen Mother Margherita, and Sydney Sonnino (who later in the year would become prime minister) were in attendance. During the following days Wright performed and completed sixty-seven other instructional flights, selling one of his aeroplanes for £25,000 and receiving a £25,000 honorarium for training the two members of the Italian Aeroclub Mario Calderara and Umberto Savoja (Mancuso 25–8).

Wilbur Wright's feat sparked an immediate enthusiasm for aeroplanes, which led that same year to the organization of the first international aerial circuit in Montichiari in September and of the first exposition of Italian aviation at the Hotel Corso of Milan in November. The two events, respectively promoted by the newspapers *Corriere della sera* and *La gazzetta dello sport*, captured the momentum generated by Wright and contributed to the launch of the Italian aviation industry.

The aerial contest of Montichiari took place between 9 and 20 September 1909. It was the first aviation race in Italy and the second in Europe, following a similar event organized in Reims in August 1909. The competitors, some of them coming directly from Reims, included two French pilots – Louis Blériot, who had flown across the English Channel, and Henri Rougier, who would beat the height record in Montichiari (flying at 198.50 metres) – the American motorcyclist Glenn Curtiss, who was developing flight engines for Alexander Graham Bell,[27] and the Italian Mario Calderara, who had just been trained by Wilbur Wright. Other attendees at the race included the poet Gabriele D'Annunzio (who flew with Calderara and Curtiss), the composer Giacomo Puccini, the director of *Corriere della sera* Luigi Albertini, and the young writer Franz Kafka (who would later report his experience for the Prague newspaper *Bohemia*). This extraordinary event had a major impact on the Italian press, stimulating the evolution of industrial production and literary imagination alike.

On the one hand, the flying contest displayed the potential of biplanes over airships. In 1907 two Milanese companies had started producing dirigibles in Italy: Fabbrica Italiana Aerostati Milano (FIAM; Italian Aerostat Factory Milan) and Enrico Forlanini's Società Anonima Leonardo da Vinci (Public Limited Company Leonardo da Vinci; Curami 13–42).[28] In 1910, after Montichiari, Gianni Caproni started his aviation business at the Malpensa airport, near Milan, producing both biplanes and dirigibles. Caproni, who would later become one of the leading innovators in global aviation, was the first to promote his products for military use. In 1911, during the Italo-Turkish War, the Italian army would be the first to ever conduct aerial bombings, as also reported in Marinetti's war diary *La battaglia di Tripoli* (*The Battle of Tripoli*, 1911).

On the other hand, the Montichiari circuit stimulated literary imagination in unprecedented ways. The event inspired D'Annunzio's first aviation novel, *Forse che sì forse che no* (*Maybe Yes, Maybe No*, 1910), similarly featuring an aeroplane contest and the attainment of a height record. The novel also included the new word *velivolo* for aeroplane, a neologism that first appeared in a preview of the novel published by *Corriere della sera* on 28 November 1909. Equally inspired by Montichiari, the playwright Paolo Buzzi released his new poetic collection *Aeroplani: Canti Alati* (*Airplanes: Winged Songs*) in October 1909 for the Futurist Edizioni di Poesia, which featured Marinetti's second Futurist text after the Manifesto "Uccidiamo il chiaro di luna" ("Let's kill off the moonlight"). Buzzi's collection became the first Futurist work to embrace the aeroplane theme, anticipating and modelling the movement's later iconography of flight, as displayed in Marinetti's *Le monoplane du Pape* (*The Pope's Monoplane*, 1912, published in Italian in 1914 as *L'aeroplano del papa*), Pratella's *L'aviatore Dro* (*The Aviator Dro*, 1915), Azari's *Il teatro aereo futurista* (*Futurist Aerial Theatre*, 1919), and, in the 1920s and 1930s, Marinetti's manifesto of aerial painting, the *First Italian Aerial Dictionary* (*Primo dizionario aereo italiano*), and *L'aeropoema del golfo della Spezia* (*Aeropoem of La Spezia's Gulf*).[29]

A couple months after Montichiari, the aviation exposition of November 1909 continued and reinforced industrial and intellectual momentum over aeroplanes. On that occasion, Milan's industrialists founded the Società italiana di aviazione (Italian Aviation Society) and organized two inaugural events for the following year: the international aerial circuit of Milan and the challenge to cross the Alps in flight from Ried-Brig to Domodossola (Domański). The Peruvian aviator Jorge

(Geo) Chavez undertook the challenge and flew over the Alps on 23 September 1910, but his monoplane Blériot crashed near Domodossola, eventually causing his death four days later. The event stirred a collective outpouring of emotion in the Italian press, which was echoed in contemporary literature, as seen in the poem "A Chavez" ("To Chavez") by Paolo Buzzi (now in *Versi liberi* [*Free Verses*]) and the ode "Chavez" by Giovanni Pascoli (November 1910). Pascoli's fictional representation of the bald eagles' estrangement in front of the "winged man" (uomo alato; "Chavez," line 33) would be further transfigured in Luigi Capuana's 1911 short story "Il domatore di aquile" ("The Tamer of Bald Eagles"), which sarcastically portrayed the figure of an entrepreneur who pursues flight by taming and riding eagles and ends up tragically victimized by the birds.

Considering these evolutions, Wilbur Wright's visit to Rome marks not just the beginning of Italian aviation (Mancuso 27) but also the long-lasting association of Americanism with an attitude of entrepreneurial and ground-breaking audacity.

4 Italian Americanism: Italianizing the United States (1900–1915)

The gradual emergence of a tourist, intellectual, or mass-mediated American presence in Italy generated positive momentum for the United States at the turn of the twentieth century.

In keeping with the absorption of transatlantic thought and artefacts on the national side, the contemporary emulation, appropriation, and reinvention of US cultural imports in early Italian industrial society powerfully documents American incubation in Italy before its full-fledged influence starting in the late 1910s. After surveying US Americanism, this chapter reconstructs the formation of Italian Americanism as a widespread and endogenous trend, which permeated in various ways the nation's visual, theatrical, literary, philosophical, and religious imagination in the years preceding the First World War.

Following Stieglitz's impact on photography and the diffusion of the new American model of permanent movie theatres, this chapter examines the formation of pictorialism in Italy and the evolution of Italian cinematography from itinerant attraction to organized industry. Likewise, starting from the success of the *Wild West* show, this research tracks Buffalo Bill's influence on the theatrical performances of Marinetti and contemporary recreations of the West in literary fictions by Emilio Salgari and musical works by Giacomo Puccini. In contrast with the standard imagery of emigration literature, this study explores the singular case of Luigi Capuana's novel *Gli "Americani" di Ràbbato* (*The "Americans" of Ràbbato*, 1912), which staged a new Americanized vision of Italy through the eyes of Sicilian returnees in the village of Ràbbato. Lastly, observing the spreading of American philosophy and new religious experiences, this chapter reconstructs the formation of an Italian version of American pragmatism, around the experience of the journal *Leonardo*, and the impact of Blavatsky and Olcott's theosophy on Maria Montessori and contemporary Italian writers like Antonio Fogazzaro and Luigi Pirandello.

American Influence on the New Photographic and Cinematographic Imagination

American photography profoundly affected the Italian market starting in the late nineteenth century. The 1888 release of the first-ever portable camera (Kodak n.1) introduced a new model for producing photographic images, which separated the act of taking pictures from their development (as advertised in the famous campaign "You press the button. We do the rest"). As photography started appearing in the previously unexplored realms of fashion, leisure, and travel, George Eastman's innovation reconfigured cameras into accessible tools for entertainment, and photographic images moved from the practice of a few into "a mass retail market of goods and services" (Hirsch 173).

Photography's transformation from a pioneering technology into an industry in Italy finds contemporary documentation in the rapid spread of cameras, the emergence of photographic clubs, the growing demand for specialized magazines or informative handbooks (Cottini, *Art of Objects* 57), and the sudden rise of amateur and professional photographers (from 1,749 in 1881 to 3,502 in 1901; Rocchetti 43). Such increasing circulation and consumption of photographic images also led to the dual attempt to create a critical discourse on photography and aestheticize its language.

In this context the acclaim surrounding Stieglitz's photographic work at the first international exposition of Turin in 1902 (Costantini, "L'esposizione" 95–105) signalled a major turning point in Italian photography. Moved by the aspiration to create an Italian equivalent to Stieglitz and Steichen's journal *Camera Work*, the Turin photographers Secondo Pia, Guido Rey, Vittorio Sella, Ernesto Schiaparelli, and Edoardo di Sambuy built on the exposition's successful momentum by launching the journal *Fotografia artistica* (*Art Photography*) in December 1904. Funded by the local Società Fotografica Subalpina (Subalpine Photographic Society), guided by Annibale Cominetti, and published in Italian and French until 1917, the journal introduced new visual repertoires, lobbied for the safeguard of archival patrimony (after the 1904 burning of Turin's national library), fostered critical debates on authorship, organized photographic expositions in 1906 and 1911, and ultimately launched the Italian school of pictorialism.[1]

In addition to new photographic culture and repertoires, innovative American models of cinematographic production and consumption had an impact on contemporary Italian society. The 1903 release of *The Great Train Robbery*, directed by Edwin Porter and produced by the American studios of the Edison Manufacturing Company, was a key event in reconfiguring cinematography into a stable market and a legitimate alternative to theatre.

Prior to *The Great Train Robbery*, Thomas Alva Edison's company had primarily manufactured batteries for telegraphs and telephone systems, machinery, X-ray equipment, medical instruments, phonograph cylinder wax, and kinetoscopes in its Silver Lake, New Jersey, headquarters. Capitalizing on the international acclaim of Georges Méliès's 1902 *Le voyage dans la lune (A Trip to the Moon)*, however, Edison's company began to invest in the production of longer films in its New York studios. In *The Great Train Robbery* the pioneering director (and former projectionist for Edison) Edwin Porter developed the original technique of dramatic editing, which pieced together scenes shot at different times and places. The movie is considered the first ever to achieve continuity of action in a realistic setting (Cook).

More than for its artistic qualities, the success of the film was tied to a novel model of consumption, as selected New York theatres started to be used for movie screenings and cinema began to move from an ephemeral attraction into a stabler business. The opening of the movie theatre The Nickelodeon in Pittsburgh, on 19 June 1905 – the first permanent venue running a program exclusively based on cinema – ratified the success of a new "dime entertainment," which followed the same model of nineteenth-century "dime novels" (Sassoon 478).[2] Similar cinematographic hubs spread throughout the Unites States (Bowser 4–6), and by 1907 purpose-built theatres for motion pictures (and piano accompaniment) had also begun to appear in Great Britain, France, Germany, and Italy. The Nickelodeon format of distribution, which guaranteed consistent audiences for the growing cinematographic industry, forced producers to modify the language of films. As theatres extended their cinematographic programs from ten minutes to an hour or more, movies in fact evolved into longer multi-shot productions (Grieveson 83) and acquired an artistic dimension, shifting from previous representations of actualities or current events to more elaborate and varied themes.

The American industrial approach to cinema profoundly influenced Italy, as confirmed by the contemporary establishment of the first production companies (Ambrosio in 1905 and Cines in 1906), the extraordinary diffusion of movie theatres after 1907, and the later growth of Italian silent cinema in the early 1910s.

Three early texts of 1907 – by Gualtiero Fabbri, Giovanni Papini, and Edmondo De Amicis – document this transition and the industrial emergence of cinema in Italy. In March 1907, Gualtiero Fabbri published the short story "Al cinematografo" ("At the Cinema"), which the scholar Sergio Raffaelli describes as "the first encounter of cinema and literature" (81). The text was part of a promotional booklet published by Milan's Cinematografo Marconi (in Via Torino 61) and was the winner of a contest organized by the *Rivista fono-cinematografica e affini* (*Journal of Phono-Cinematography & Related Issues*) – the first Italian journal dedicated to cinematography, which Fabbri had founded in the same year with Pietro Tonini (Raffaelli 83).[3] The story has both archaeological and sociological value. In one way, as the first-ever Italian narrative on cinematography, it reconstructs the early experience of movie theatres, offering scholars valuable information on screenings, titles, subjects, and audiences. In another way, as a staged narration of the cinematographic "conversion" of an educated middle-class person (the author's alter ego Gastone Fedi), the story attests to the transformation of cinema from a popular attraction into an accepted trend for a bourgeois audience. Such legitimization of cinema takes shape around the protagonist, who initially is uncomfortable with the crowds surrounding the cinema and with its "lower" aspects (e.g., costs, episodes of theft, or the immorality favoured by the dark room).[4] Overcoming his concerns, Fedi attends a show and discovers the marvel of cinema, which in his words offers "more sensational emotions than theatre" (emozioni più sensazionali di quelle del Teatro; Fabbri 39) and represents the new century's industry.

A couple of months after Fabbri, on 18 May 1907, Giovanni Papini published in the newspaper *La Stampa* the article "La filosofia del cinematografo" ("The Philosophy of Cinema"), commenting upon the opening in Vicenza of Odeon, the first Italian theatre exclusively dedicated to cinema. Papini's text opens with the acknowledgment that "over a brief time, in every big Italian city, we witness the almost miraculous multiplication of cinemas" (da pochissimo tempo, in ogni grossa città d'Italia, assistiamo a una quasi miracolosa moltiplicazione di cinematografi). While registering the perplexities of his fellow intellectuals towards the phenomenon (and their fear that cinema will "little by little oust theatre […] as newspapers did with books"), Papini invites them not just to go to the movies but to consider them as "objects worth reflections" (sono oggetto degno di riflessione). Unlike Fabbri's "commercial" narrative, Papini engages in an intellectual reflection on movie theatres, presenting cinema as the expression of a new modern philosophy, where "nothing in the world, however humble, small, or ridiculous it may be […] cannot become object of thought" (non c'è nessuna cosa nel mondo, per quanto umile, piccola, e ridicola sembri, che non possa divenir materia di pensiero). In his reading, cinematography's power to reproduce complex events, lively transformations, and unlikely fantasies to a "brief phantasmagoria of twenty minutes" (una breve fantasmagoria di venti minuti) constitutes then an original source of reflection, enriching Italian culture with "new modes of thought, and perhaps even new moral emotions, suggestions, or metaphysics" (nuovi motivi di pensiero, e chissà perfino nuove emozioni morali e suggerimenti di nuove metafisiche).

In the same year, the writer Edmondo De Amicis also engaged with cinema. In his short story "Il cinematografo cerebrale" ("The Cerebral Cinematographer"), published on 1 December 1907, in *L'illustrazione italiana*, De Amicis constructs a textual equivalent of such "20-minute phantasmagoria" (Papini, "Filosofia del cinematografo"). Albeit not mentioning the cinematographer directly, the text fictionalizes "cinema" itself, visually representing the psyche and a self-projection of thought. The protagonist of the story is an undefined "Cavaliere" who needs to kill time, after his wife and children leave him home alone. While he is sitting in his armchair in front of his house's chimney (echoing the setting of Poe's "The Raven"), the story develops as an irregular stream of his mental associations and submerged remembrances. Subsequently, the fireplace turns into a screen, on which fictional and real images in the head of the Cavaliere continuously overlap. He travels to other worlds (in the past and in the present) "where his thought would not be disturbed by any image of the world where he lived" (in cui il suo pensiero non fosse turbato da alcuna immagine del mondo dov'egli viveva; De Amicis, "Il cinematografo cerebrale" 5). At the same time he processes fragments and bits of contemporary debates on physical education or psychoanalysis.[5] At one point, he even arrives at "mentally betray[ing]" (tradimento mentale; 15) his wife with the house maid, prior to abruptly reawakening "as a man caught at the crime scene" (si riscosse poi bruscamente come un uomo colto in flagrante delitto; 7).[6] In De Amicis's text, cinematography is no longer associated with an ephemeral attraction but rather coincides with a new mental space of self-examination, projection of desires, and constant transformation. As the character awakens from the phantasmagoria of his "cerebral cinematographer," he observes this experience with astonishment as "he thought about everything he had been during the brief time alone: a child, a hero, a saint, a vile, a crazy person" (pensò a tutto quello ch'egli era stato in quel breve tempo da che era solo: un bambino, un eroe, un santo, un vigliacco, un pazzo; 13).

In different ways, the three texts of 1907 record the advent of American permanent cinematography in Italy by acknowledging a new emerging market and connecting it to a new industrial mentality. The fashioning of cinema as a space of acceleration, self-questioning, and continuous metamorphosis matches the contemporary Italian elaboration of American culture as an accomplished form of industrialism, similarly centred on speed, change, and mutable identities.

The Italian Imagination of the American West

In addition to cinema, new models of theatrical performance and cultural self-representation came from Buffalo Bill's *Wild West* show (see ch. 3). William Cody was an important source of inspiration for Italian Futurism. His artistic reconfiguration of his biographical self, his managerial ability to formulate "combinations" (Sagala 8) of circus and drama, and his show, which simultaneously involved animals, clowns, and acrobats on multiple stages, offered Marinetti an archetype of his own persona, a model of cultural entrepreneurship, and a creative model for his Futurist theatre. The *serate* were in fact centred on a similar self-portrayal of the artist-entrepreneur, an analogous structure of serial performance and free improvisation, and a comparable marketing strategy based on histrionic provocation, scandal, and cultural opportunism.

The ties of Marinetti with Buffalo Bill emerge more deeply thematically, as confirmed by the references to animal energy or American eccentricities in his *Manifesto* (1909) and theory of "Variety Theatre" (1913). In the first part of the Futurist manifesto, Marinetti equates the vital energy and speed of automobiles to the wild force of "snorting beasts" (Umbro 20; "belve sbuffanti," Marinetti, *Teoria* 8). The association of mechanical elements with animals establishes a narrative of primitiveness and primordiality that certainly relates to the Nietzschean self-identification of Futurism with the beginning, or prehistory, of a new age, but also enforces Buffalo Bill's rhetoric of taming and conquest. Against the backdrop of the *Wild West* show, automobiles appear as expressions of vertigo, speed, and fear of death that are to be controlled and domesticated: "death, *domesticated*, met me at every turn, gracefully holding out a *paw*, or once in a while hunkering down" (Umbro 20; "la Morte, *addomesticata*, mi sorpassava ad ogni svolto, porgendomi la *zampa* con grazia, e a quando a quando si stendeva a terra con un rumore di *mascelle* stridenti," Marinetti, *Teoria* 8; my italics).

In the "Manifesto del teatro di varietà" ("Manifesto of Variety Theatre") the representation of animals turns instead into a deliberate theatrical strategy for raising a performance's energy, as attested by Marinetti's explicit call for the "greatest development of animal intelligence (horses, elephants, seals, dogs, trained birds)" (Umbro 129; "massimo sviluppo dell'intelligenza degli animali (cavalli, elefanti, foche, cani, uccelli ammaestrati)," Marinetti, *Teoria* 87). At the same time, the animal circus is associated with theatre by way of Marinetti's deliberate invitation to emulate "the type of the eccentric American, the impression he gives of exciting grotesquerie, of frightening dynamism; his crude jokes, his enormous brutalities" (Umbro 130; "il genere degli eccentrici americani, i loro effetti di grottesco esaltante, di dinamismo spaventevole, le loro grossolane trovate, le loro enormi brutalità," Marinetti, *Teoria* 89). Against the backdrop of Buffalo Bill's multifaceted show, Marinetti's *serate* represent a similar mix of concomitant elements: as a circus of animals, a simultaneous movement "of jugglers, ballerinas, gymnasts, colorful riding masters, spiral cyclones of dancers spinning on the points of their feet" (Umbro 127; "di giocolieri, ballerine, ginnasti, cavallerizzi multicolori, cicloni spiralici di danzatori trottolanti sulle punte dei piedi," Marinetti, *Teoria* 83), an art exhibit, a live enactment of poetry, music and the visual arts, and an improvised show.

Unlike Marinetti, who drew from William Cody a dynamic and eccentric model for his variety theatre, Emilio Salgari and Giacomo Puccini saw instead in his performances a rich repository of narrative material. Their Italian reappropriations of the American West offer a testimony of the Italian trend of emulation and reinvention of the United States.

In 1908, Salgari published *Sulle frontiere del West* (*On the Far West Frontiers*), the first book of a Western novel trilogy that would later include *La scotennatrice* (*The Scalping Lady*, 1909), and *Le selve ardenti* (*The Burning Woods*, 1910). *Sulle frontiere del West* is the story of Yalla, an Indigenous girl who is forcibly married to the US colonel Duvandel. Yalla chases him after he separated her from their daughter and scalps him for revenge. Emulating Buffalo Bill's vengeance for Custer's scalping and the *Wild West* show's narrative of loss and revenge, Salgari structures his novel around the similar framework of the encounter or clash of civilizations and the domestication of the Indigenous tribes. By setting the action at the frontier, an imaginary border of civilization and primitiveness, Salgari mimics the exploration of pioneers, mapping their advancement through long geographic and ethnographic digressions. At the same time, as the explorers move forward, Salgari sets up a climactic progression of taming acts of a white stallion, Mexicans, the "thoroughbred" Indigenous woman Yalla (seen as a wild soul to subdue and a sexual trophy to conquer), and the Sioux, who are brutally slaughtered in the final scene in revenge for their previous brutality. Salgari's pre-made format, opposing the primitiveness of Indigenous tribes (whose assaults are equated to those of wolves, coyotes, or bears) with the laboriousness of American pioneers (whose haciendas appear as opulent oases in the desert), asserts a racial and colonial subtext for his narrative. Mirroring the Italian rhetoric that followed the 1896 defeat in Adwa, Salgari's appropriation of Buffalo Bill's trope of revenge after a humiliation would provide a key reference in the Italian military ideology supporting the Italo-Turkish War of 1911 and 1912 and, later on, in the Fascist construction of the Ethiopian campaign of 1935 and 1936.

Paralleling Salgari, elements of the *Wild West* show also appear in Puccini's opera *La fanciulla del West* (*The Girl of the Golden West*), which premiered in New York City on 10 December 1910. While the opera's main structure follows the model of David Belasco's play *The Girl of the Golden West,*[7] common themes and explicit references from the *Wild West* show can also be detected in Puccini's work. *La fanciulla* includes such typical tropes as the protection of West-bound train lines (in reference to Cody's personal life), the motive of robberies (associated with Mexican bandits), public bravados (from William Cody to Rance's bet with Minnie), and stylized figures (like the Wells Fargo agent Ashby and the sheriff Rance). While absorbing and re-elaborating these stereotypical elements, the Italian opera also fashions the setting of the American West with an Italian perspective. Two instances reveal such creative interaction between Italian and American substrates: the characterization of the female protagonist Minnie and the introduction of migrants in the plot.

Minnie, who openly recalls Annie Oakley of the *Wild West* show, is reinterpreted as a modern-day *Locandiera* (*Innkeeper*), according to the archetype of Carlo Goldoni's eighteenth-century comedic play. She similarly owns a saloon on the Western frontier and is the object of desire for the sheriff Jack Rance, but falls in love with a Mexican bandit, Ramerrez, who is disguised as Dick Johnson to evade the law. As an emancipated Western woman, Puccini's Minnie educates the saloon visitors by way of her beauty. Through her faith she "civilizes" her clients, reading the Bible to them and leading the bandit to a final conversion. Minnie reflects the idea of the frontier as a site of exploration and encounter through her dual role as a love trophy (for the sheriff Rance and the criminal Ramerrez) and a reassuring maternal figure (especially for migrant workers).

The figures of migrants additionally connote the frontier as a locus of instability and nostalgia. Shifting from the forward-looking outlook of pioneers (as in Cody's show) to the backward gaze of migrants, Puccini reconfigures the West as a terrain of risk, adventure, and discovery (as alluded to in their portrayal during a game of poker), and, at the same time, a site of homesickness and melancholy. The character of Larkens, "always thinking about his mother waiting for him" (alla madre lontana che l'aspetta; Puccini 8), offers an example of this nostalgic outlook. This theme is further enforced by the representation of his companions, who mourn the distance from their families – "what could my old folks be doing over there, far away" (che faranno i vecchi miei là lontano; Puccini 10) – or curse the fever of gold or "yellow fever" (la malaria gialla; Puccini 8) that brought them to America. By tinging the frontier with nostalgia, Puccini's opera captures for his American audience not just the drama of contemporary migration from Italy to the United States but also the prolonged displacement of Italian emigrants who at the time were moving West in search of new opportunities.

A New View of Emigration: Americanism as a Form of Self-Discovery

While Italian emigration reached its peak in the early 1910s,[8] a significant manifestation of Italian Americanism also came from Italian returnees, who travelled to the United States, embraced an American mindset, and eventually decided to settle permanently back in Italy. As their salaries abroad had allowed them to acquire land or properties,[9] the return to their birth cities or villages often coincided with new financial independence. Facing local scrutiny, displacement, and even alienation from their original communities, however, returnees often underwent an uneasy reintegration process. The lack of narratives on their experience confirms their silent marginalization (see ch. 1).

A uniquely positive view of this phenomenon is Luigi Capuana's novel *Gli "Americani" di Ràbbato* (*The "Americans" of Ràbbato*), which fictionalizes the story of a group of returnees in between Ràbbato (a neighbourhood of Capuana's Sicilian hometown of Mineo) and New York City. Written in 1906 and published in 1912, the novel narrates the transatlantic story of the Lamanna family members, which emblematically depicts the "emotional and cognitive shift" (Poggioli-Kaftan 30) of their local community from an early situation of manipulation and psychological pressure at home to the elaboration of a new identity, first in New York and then in their definitive return to Sicily.

By way of the returnees' dual perspectives as both insiders and outsiders, Capuana not only overcomes the traditional narrative silence regarding the migrants' life in their new destinations but, more importantly, configures the American experience as a "third space," capable of giving rise "to something different, something new and unrecognizable, a new area of negotiation of meaning and representation" (Bhabha 211).

The New York experience of Stefano and Santi Lamanna, on the footsteps of the enriched Rabbatano Coda Pelata, and the tale of their

American life strikingly contrast with contemporary anti-migratory narratives, which primarily focused on the voyagers' tragic dooms or the "blind" narratives of those who remained.[10] Although not omitting the effects of departure on local communities or the difficulties at the destination, Capuana nonetheless places these elements within the horizon of a larger Bildungsroman, reframing emigration from a self-deceiving myth of abundance into a "formative" journey of self-discovery. For the author, the American experience coincides with self-discernment, granting characters the possibility to negotiate their identity and acquire a new mentality. Such trajectory from the initial status quo to their new financial agency, individual emancipation, and cultural reappropriation (Poggioli-Kaftan 47) finds symbolic expression in the story of the younger Lamanna brother, Carmelo, known as Menu.

At the beginning of the novel Menu is curious about the American stories circulating among the Rabbatani and ponders their truthfulness, contrasting them with his grandfather's suspicious incredulity and the information in his school textbooks. The arrival in town of the returnee Carmine Liotta, better known as Coda Pelata, offers him a direct witness of the United States and sets the plot in motion. Coda Pelata's cigar and elegant attire catalyse Menu and the reader's attention (as visually stressed in a dedicated illustration; fig. 4.1). His entrepreneurial adventure as the owner of a barbershop in New York and his new wealth (allowing him the new power to purchase lands) operate in the community as an implicit form of American "propaganda" (Capuana, *Gli "Americani"* 49). The Rabbatani ponder his invitation to go see such new world.[11] Among them, Menu's older brothers Santi and Stefano Lamanna follow this promise and decide to leave.

In this initial setting, Capuana adopts two narrative clichés of the emigration narrative: the pre-departure illusion of America as a land of abundance and opportunities, and the post-departure trope of the migrants' silence or supposed betrayals, as family members anxiously await news from them. Unlike contemporary dramatizations, however, Capuana does not resolve this initial suspension in a tragic way (for example, through the depiction of a shipwreck and the characters' disillusion or madness) but rather through unexpected relief, as he describes the arrival of the first remittances. In a dialogue of the Rabbatani with the local priest, Capuana dwells on the transformative impact of "American money," showing how "little by little the city is changed" (a poco a poco il paese si trasforma; *Gli "Americani"* 208). The priest looks with gratitude at the new altar of the church, "Paid by the 'American' Rabbatani" (A spese dei Rabbatani di America; 210), and

Figure 4.1. Illustration from Luigi Capuana's *Gli "Americani" di Ràbbato* (Milan: Remo Sandron, 1912, 43).

sees the charitable contributions of the returnees as a remedy against "the cheapness of the government" (la carità dei fedeli supplisce alla tirchieria del governo; 210). At the same time, the priest assesses the positive effects of their new conditions as landowners, which "means that they will return and they will cultivate them with more love, now that they know they own them" (significa che torneranno e le coltiveranno con più amore, ora che sanno di essere proprietari; 210).

The first actual return of the American Rabbatani coincides with a deepening awareness of this ongoing transformation, as both villagers and returnees start to notice their change in mentality. One migrant compares life at his village and in America, identifying cleanliness as the most immediately visible element of difference:

La pulizia delle case comanda la pulizia delle persone. La miseria ci rende sporchi [...] sapete come ci chiamano in America? *Sporchi italiani!* E specialmente per noi Siciliani, pei Calabresi, per gli Abruzzesi hanno proprio ragione. Là, però, i nostri contadini si trasformano. Troppo forse. (Capuana, *Gli "Americani"* 211)

[The cleanliness of houses reflects the cleanliness of people. Misery makes us filthy [...] Do you know how they call us in America? *Dirty Italians!* And they are right, especially for us Sicilians, for the Calabresi and the Abruzzesi. Once there, however, our peasants are transformed. Perhaps too much.]

The growing understanding of America's transformative power fuels the enthusiasm of Menu, who also decides to leave and follow his brothers to New York.

His arrival in America represents a double-edged moment of marvel and shock. The assessment of the grandiose American industrial civilization and urban settings, as portrayed in his textbooks, parallels the discovery of the inconsistent reports by and about his fellow Rabbatani. The hard realization of their difficult living conditions precedes the unearthing of the truth about his brother Stefano, who is involved with the Black Hand and will later be arrested for criminal activities. Notwithstanding the situation, his older brother, Santi, helps introduce Menu to Mary Keller, the daughter of a banker. Thanks to her travels to Sicily and her knowledge of Italian – "she knows Italian. She has been to Sicily" (sa l'italiano. È stata in Sicilia; Capuana, *Gli "Americani"* 297) – Mary takes Menu under her care, allowing him to escape the risks involved in being Stefano's brother and to understand the American mindset. In his new position as office boy in a bank, Menu starts his own path of education, growth, and independence. His emancipation becomes clear to the other Rabbatani in New York, as implied in the new nickname "the banker" (il banchiere; 299) assigned to him by Coda Pelata. A year and a half later, during his first return to Sicily, it also becomes evident to his fellow villagers.

Menu's return to Ràbbato with Santi marks the novel's conclusion and the apex of his itinerary of self-discovery and maturation. Menu omits to report to his dying grandfather the criminal charges that have been brought against his brother Stefano, and he refuses to fabricate a story that might perpetuate deceit. At the same time, he resolves to stay permanently in Sicily – a decision (mirroring Capuana's penchant for Hegelian dialectics over positivist thought; Romboli 95) that signifies not self-alienation from the evils of modernity but rather the embracing of a new mature identity. His empowered Sicilian-ness stems from rejection of the American and Sicilian status quo and is imbued with both Americanism and national pride. In his own words:

> Voglio essere siciliano, italiano, non americano bastardo! … Sapete che farò nonno? Prenderò la patente di maestro di scuola […] Insegnerò un po' di americanismo qui: la gran volontà, il grande amore al lavoro. Ah, se la miseria non scacciasse via i nostri paesani! Finirà anche questa! (Capuana, *Gli "Americani"* 346)

> [I want to be Sicilian, Italian, not a bastard American! … You know, Grandpa, what I will do? I will get a licence to be a school teacher […] I will teach a bit of Americanism here: the great will, the great love for work. Oh, if only misery did not force our fellow villagers to leave! But it will end!]

Menu's decision to teach "Americanism" in the local elementary school denotes the endeavour to adopt the American experience as a pedagogical tool for debunking false myths about the United States and inspiring the economic and social emancipation of his village. In this sense, the hapax legomenon *Americanism* indicates a formative journey, allowing a provincial kid to become aware of the world,[12] and a driving force of cultural and financial rebirth (reflected in the intellectual change of returnees and the impact of remittances on the nation's debts; Cinel 217).[13] In the narrative climax of the book, however, when Menu decides to be Sicilian, Americanism is reconfigured into the second term of a larger dialectics, ultimately aimed at inciting a patriotic revival, as also echoed in the title of the novel's final chapter ("Oh, the Homeland"; "Oh, la patria") and its concluding words ("homeland is always homeland"; la patria è sempre la patria; Capuana, *Gli "Americani"* 348).

Americanism as a Philosophical Model: *Leonardo* and Pragmatism

A similar idea of Americanism as a positive force for the education and renewal of Italian society took theoretical shape in connection with the Italian reception and reinvention of American pragmatism (see ch. 3).

The platform for the diffusion of Charles Sanders Peirce's and William James's philosophies in Italy would be the journal *Leonardo*, founded in 1903 by a group of young Florentine intellectuals – including Giovanni Papini (under the pseudonym of Gian Falco), Giuseppe Prezzolini (under the pseudonym of Giuliano il sofista), Adolfo De Carolis, Alfredo Bona, Ernesto Macinai, and Giuseppe Antonio Borgese – and self-proclaimed as the official organ of Italian pragmatism.[14]

Its project aimed at rejuvenating Italian contemporary culture and offering a new model of intellectual activism. As indicated in the mission statement in the first issue of 4 January 1903, the *Leonardo* intellectuals saw themselves as "a group of youngsters wishing for liberation, universality, and a superior intellectual life" (un gruppo di giovini, desiderosi di liberazione, vogliosi di universalità, anelanti ad una superiore vita intellettuale), and the journal as a creative platform to "intensify their own existence, elevate their own thought, and exalt their own art" (intensificare la propria esistenza, elevare il proprio pensiero, esaltare la propria arte; "Programma sintetico"). From 1903 until its closing in 1907, *Leonardo* represented a provocative and influential laboratory of philosophical debate, which reacted against positivism or Croce's idealism and actively promoted American pragmatism as a fertile source of cultural renewal. In spreading Peirce's and James's ideas, *Leonardo* intellectuals assumed a creative attitude, translating American pragmatism, interpreting it as an anti-Cartesian reaction to rationalism and empiricism,[15] and adding to it "a personalist existential tone and a nihilist disquiet" (Maddalena and Tuzet 8).

In his later book *Sul pragmatismo* (*On Pragmatism*, 1913) Giovanni Papini defined Italian pragmatism as a self-standing, non-academic school of thought and a posteriori singled out its two veins: "that of [...] logic pragmatism, and that of psychological or magic pragmatism" (quella [...] del pragmatismo logico e quella del pragmatismo psicologico o magico; 7).[16] The first, which was rooted in Giovanni Vailati and Mario Calderoni's work on the writings of C.S. Peirce, explored pragmatism as a philosophical and mathematical method for the acquisition of scientific knowledge. The second, which grew out of Papini's (and Prezzolini's) appreciation for the psychological work of William James, re-elaborated pragmatism as a method to "get rid of philosophy" (fare a meno della filosofia; Papini, *Sul pragmatismo* 59) and a spiritual-mystical tension. Such overlapping of pragmatism with occultism, magic, or the American New Thought (Baldacci XVI) can be detected in the debates of *Leonardo* and in long bibliographic lists of the journal's lending library, which, as advertised, included "2000 volumes of philosophy, psychology, theosophy, mysticism, history of Religions, psychic sciences, magic, occultism, *Christian Science, New Thought* and many other Italian or foreign reviews."[17]

While Papini became de facto "the intellectual and emotional heart of *Leonardo*" (Maddalena and Tuzet 3), his personality attracted the interest of the American psychologist and pragmatist William James, who praised him "in the most extravagant terms for his originality, rhetorical flair, and uncompromisingly militant pragmatic spirit" (Colella 187). The first encounter between the two took place in Rome in 1905, when James participated in the Fifth International Congress of Psychology (26–30 April 1905).[18] A few months later, in *Leonardo*'s June–August 1905 issue, Papini published the Italian version of James's essay "The Conception of Conscience," translated as "La concezione della coscienza."[19] In the following year the interaction between the two became more intense, after the publication of Papini's essay "Uomo-Dio" ("Man-God") in the February 1906 issue of *Leonardo* and his book *Il crepuscolo dei filosofi* (*Twilight of the Philosophers*, 1906).

William James explicitly commended Papini's article and book. In a letter on 7 April 1906 to the British pragmatist philosopher F.C.S. Schiller, he praised the "fecundity," "courage," "humor," and "truth" of the Italian intellectual, extravagantly describing him as "a jewel" and a "little Dago putting himself ahead of every one of us" (W. James, *Letters* 245–6).[20] On 21 June 1906 James even published a dedicated article in the scholarly *Journal of Philosophy, Psychology and Scientific Methods*, entitled "G. Papini and the Pragmatist Movement in Italy," in which he portrayed contemporary Italy as "engaged in the throes of an intellectual *rinascimento*" ("G. Papini" 337),[21] and the "Florentine band of Leonardists" (338) as "an extraordinarily well-informed and gifted, and above all an extraordinarily free and spirited and unpedantic, group of writers" (341).[22]

Notwithstanding his admiration for Papini, James personally warned him against his excessive reliance on spiritism, as implied in his unpublished letter of 27 April 1906: "I myself suspect that you are hoping too much from telepathy, mediumship, etc; but no matter, we can all gather from you the example of courage" (qtd. in Bagnoli 11). The issue of conscience and spiritism would be fiercely debated in the *Leonardo* issue of April–June 1907, featuring Papini's piece "Franche spiegazioni (a proposito di rinascenza spirituale e occultismo)" ("Frank Explanations Regarding the Spiritual Renaissance and Occultism"),[23] and would spark its eventual closure in August 1907. In that same year, the Papini–James correspondence ended, even though the American philosopher continued to influence the Italian writer's fictional and critical writings.

In 1907 Papini published the collection of short stories *Il pilota cieco* (*The Blind Pilot*, 1907), which pairs with the previous year's book *Il tragico quotidiano* (*The Tragic Quotidian*, 1906) and explores through paradoxical fictions such Jamesian themes as the role of conscience, the doubling of the self, the occult, and spiritual phenomena.[24]

The 1907 publication of James's comprehensive volume of lectures on pragmatism also elicited another Italian re-elaboration, once again by way of Papini. James's detailed analysis and pragmatic reading of Walt Whitman's poem "To You"[25] led in fact to the release in 1907 of Luigi Gamberale's *Foglie d'erba*, the first Italian (and European) translation of *Leaves of Grass*. The review of the volume and the ensuing essay on Walt Whitman authored by Papini the following year for *La nuova antologia* would make the American poet known in the Italian milieu.[26] Whitman's poetic work would be praised again in Papini's mid-life autobiography *Un uomo finito* (*A Finite Man*, 1913) and would profoundly affect Dino Campana's *Canti orfici* (*Orphic Songs*, 1914).[27]

The Emergence of Theosophy in Italian Society and Literature

As Papini's work documents, the diffusion of American pragmatism in Italy often overlapped with the spreading of new religious experiences coming from the United States. The French-imported vogue of neo-mysticism and the social prominence of the Positivist school provide two additional subtexts to read the Italian reception of American spiritism, occultism, and theosophy in the 1890s.

The French wave of spiritualism launched by the *Revue des deux mondes* found fertile ground in Italy, in conjunction with the literary works of Antonio Fogazzaro and internal ecclesial debates (see ch. 1). Brunetière's proposal to return to the Catholic Church as a moral compass against society's self-destructive impulses (as outlined in his piece on 1 January 1895, "Après une visite au Vatican" ["After a Visit to the Vatican"]) stirred a new public interest in religion as a remedy against the fears raised by industrialization, urbanization, and universal suffrage (Mangoni, *Civiltà* 24). This *esprit nouveau* found positive echoes in Italian *conciliatorismo* and harsh criticism from the Italian Positivist school, as documented in Lombroso's 1901 essay "Il pericolo nero in Francia" ("The Dark Peril in France"), which scorned the new vogue and denounced France as an enemy of free thought.

Although disregarding the new mystical trend as anti-scientific, Italian positivists took much interest in occult phenomena and dedicated significant attention to the manifestations of the "beyond," as attested by Lombroso's contemporary studies on the medium Eusapia Palladino or Capuana's photographic pursuit of hidden spirits in dead people. The origins of this practice can be traced to the contemporary discoveries of "hidden" realities, as seen in Röntgen's unveiling of X-rays in 1895, Marconi's first experiments with radio waves and wireless telegraphy in 1896, and Secondo Pia's 1898 photograph of Turin's Shroud (which first revealed a Christ-like figure in its negative impression).[28]

In this receptive milieu the diffusion of American-born religious experiences like spiritism and theosophy introduced a new dimension to Americanism, associating it with an anti-rational philosophy (in dialogue with French neo-mysticism) or to a "scientific religion" (seeking sensible patterns in paranormal phenomena and forging syncretic forms of spirituality).

American spiritualism stemmed from the experiences of three sisters from New York – Leah (1813–90), Margaretta (1833–93), and Catherine Fox (1837–92) – who claimed to be mediums able to communicate with occult beings and popularized the practice of seances as a way to contact hidden spirits or dead people. Margaretta publicly confessed that their "rappings" were a hoax, but the spiritualist trend continued to grow both in the United States and Europe, as attested by the later two-volume study *History of Spiritualism* that Arthur Conan Doyle edited in 1926.

The most important Italian representative of the spiritualist movement was the medium Eusapia Palladino (1854–1918), who held her first demonstration in Milan in 1892 and became a sensation for her alleged ability to levitate tables, communicate with the dead, and produce supernatural phenomena. Palladino travelled extensively to England, France, Germany, and the United States, where she enjoyed vast popularity, as seen in the coverage of her American trip of 1909 by the *New York Times* and *Cosmopolitan*. Despite being caught in trickery on several occasions (as relayed by Harry Houdini in his 1924 memoir *A Magician among the Spirits*, 50–65), Palladino nonetheless found the endorsement of the Italian intellectual community, as confirmed in Cesare Lombroso's description of one of her seances in his 1909 scientific essay "Ricerche sui fenomeni ipnotici e spiritici" ("Inquiries on Hypnotic and Spiritic Phenomena"). Paralleling her fame, the phenomenon of seances also became a recurring trope in contemporary Italian literature.

In Fogazzaro's *Piccolo mondo antico* (*Little Ancient World*, 1895), the *seduta spiritica* (seance) organized by Professor Gilardoni to evoke the spirit of Luisa's dead daughter, Maria, represents a secluded space of wishful imagination and a self-deceiving mental projection. The figure of Gilardoni, described as "a strange mix of free thinker and mystic" (uno strano miscuglio di libero pensatore e di mistico; 254), similarly connotes the seance as both a scientific and a mystical play (Mangoni,

Una crisi 211). From prison the disenchanted Franco debases it as an irrational space of fictional illusion,[29] but the ecstatic Luisa sees it instead as a beatifying state of divine revelation, allowing her the vision of her little Maria through her beats on a table:

> Il tavolino si rimise tosto in movimento e batté queste parole: "Son qui. Maria." "Maria, Maria, Maria mia!" sussurró Luisa con una espressione in viso di beatitudine. (Fogazzaro, *Piccolo* 258)

> [The table started to move and beat these words: "I am here. Maria" "Maria, Maria, my beloved Maria!" whispered Luisa with an expression of beatitude on her face.]

Moving away from Fogazzaro's gravity, Pirandello's novel *Il fu Mattia Pascal* (*The Late Mattia Pascal*, 1904) instead presents the seance organized by the philosopher Paleari to evoke the spirit of the dead musician Max Oliz (chs. 13–14) as a ludic space of fiction and ironic mockery of bourgeois society. By combining the element of darkness (of Adriano's blindness, of the room's setting) with the participants' deliberate suspension of disbelief (broken by the intermittence of light, the kiss to Adriana, and the protagonist's sarcasm),[30] the seance stages a lively camera obscura of fantasy, possibility, and fiction, and a "mysterious force" (forza misteriosa; Pirandello, *Il fu Mattia Pascal* 159), feeding the characters' artistic creativity and imbuing them with a state of divine possession (as seen in the Signorina Caporale who is allegedly controlled by the spirit of Max while improvising on the piano until she finally faints).

Lastly, in the later representation of Svevo's *La coscienza di Zeno* (*Zeno's Conscience*, 1922), the seance reconfigures the practice into an ambiguous fiction. The social interplay of the seance at the Malfenti house allows Zeno to defy bourgeois codes, as he jokingly evokes Guido's name through the table's movements,[31] yet also traps him into the terrible misunderstanding of his misaddressed love declaration to Augusta, instead of Ada. Zeno's play then turns from an anti-bourgeois protest into a dark space of remorse and trauma, and the seance's "dark time" (tempo all'oscuro; Svevo 174), once the site of infinite possibilities, becomes now a Freudian image of his tormented ego, as expressed by the character:

> Io avevo tuttavia bisogno di un po' di oscurità che m'isolasse e mi permettesse di raccogliermi. Avevo scoperto il mio errore e il solo equilibrio che avessi riconquistato era quello sul mio sedile. (Svevo 174)

[I needed, however, a little bit of darkness to isolate me and grant me to gather myself. I had discovered my mistake, and the sole balance I had reconquered was that on my stool.][32]

In parallel with spiritualism, theosophy also gained traction in Italy during the same years. The Theosophical Society, founded in New York in 1875 by the Russian medium Helena Blavatsky and the US lawyers Henry Olcott and William Quan Judge, promoted a new esoteric universal religion that aspired "to form a nucleus of the universal brotherhood of humanity, without distinction of race, creed, sex, caste or color; to encourage the comparative study of religion, philosophy and science; and to investigate unexplained laws of nature and the powers latent in humanity" (Abdill 177). The society, which included Thomas A. Edison among its affiliates, had developed various communities in the United States and had ties with Spiritualism, New Thought, Christian Science, and Freemasonry (*A Primer* 58–61).[33] Many speakers from the Theosophical Society had also lectured at the Parliament of Religions during the 1893 exposition of Chicago, actively promoting its syncretic neo-spiritualism to a global audience (Guénon 151).

Helena Blavatsky was closely connected to Italy, as confirmed by her personal acquaintance with Garibaldi (whom she met in 1867 prior to the battle of Mentana) and Mazzini (for whom she lobbied New York City in 1878 to erect a dedicated monument in Central Park after his death). At the turn of the century Blavatsky and Henry Olcott held conferences in Venice, Trieste, Bologna, Florence, Rome, Bari, and Naples to promote the work of the society. In conjunction with their outreach and the interest raised by their "esoteric Christianity" (Guénon 159), two Centers of Teosophical Studies opened in Milan (1891) and Rome (1897), and the first section of the Italian Theosophical Society was inaugurated in Vicenza on 1 February 1902.

The Catholic Church condemned theosophy as an expression of the "Americanist" or, as it would be later called, "modernist" heresy, but its spiritual and mystical discourse attracted numerous Italian intellectuals, including Papini, who listed theosophical texts in the *Leonardo* library and published dedicated articles in the journal. The most powerful impact of theosophy on Italian thought and religiosity, however, can be found in the work of Maria Montessori, Antonio Fogazzaro, and Luigi Pirandello.

In 1907 the newly appointed president of the Theosophical Society, Anne Besant, met the Italian pedagogist Maria Montessori at a lecture in London, after publicly praising the pedagogist's newly founded Casa dei Bambini in Rome (Children's House; Wylie 53). Montessori joined the society at that time and embraced its ties to feminism and freemasonry, as confirmed by her keynote address at the first feminist conference of Rome organized in 1908 by the Consiglio Nazionale delle Donne Italiane (National Council of Italian Women), and her first American lecture at the Masonic Temple of Washington in 1913 (see ch. 5). As a lifelong member of the Theosophical Society (and honoured guest of its Indian international headquarters of Adyar during the Second World War), Montessori would include its goals as part of her pedagogical model.

Another intellectual who developed a particular interest in theosophy was Antonio Fogazzaro. Beyond the connection to his home city of Vicenza, where the first Italian section of the Theosophical Society was based, the writer's attention to such themes as evolution, ecumenic dialogue, and new forms of religiosity made it the object of his initial interest. However, after the accusations of modernism and "theosophism" following the publication of his novel *Il santo* (*The Saint*, 1905), Fogazzaro distanced himself from theosophy, assuming a defensive and sometimes ironic attitude towards it. While abasing it in public, he maintained his interest in it in his private correspondence (Pasi 231–65).

In the work of Pirandello, theosophy was openly referenced and acknowledged (often in connection to spiritualism) as both a creative influence and an accepted cultural trend. In the short story "Dal naso al cielo" ("From Nose to Sky"), first published in *Il Marzocco* in April 1907, Pirandello presents the figure of Professor Dionisio Vernoni in relation to spiritualism, characterizing him as an expert in "occultism, mediums, telepathy, premonitions, teleportation, and materializations" (di occultismo e di medianismo, di telepatia e di premonizioni, di apporti e di materializzazioni; *Novelle* 692). In the short story "La veste lunga" ("The Long Gown"), first published in February 1913, he relates theosophy to music and meditation, as seen in the portrayal of the protagonist Didì as a solitary woman who "wanted to close in herself and wander around the world meditating theosophical science, like Frau Wenzel, her piano teacher" (voleva chiudersi tutta in se stessa e andar vagando per il mondo assorta nella scienza teosofica, come Frau Wenzel, la sua maestra di pianoforte; *Novelle* 340–1).

The most important reference to theosophy, however, appears in the novel *Il fu Mattia Pascal*. In this case, the acknowledgment that Professor Anselmo Paleari was "part of the theosophical school" (era ascritto alla scuola teosofica) and was familiar with spiritism (si era dato anche agli esperimenti spiritici; Pirandello, *Il fu Mattia Pascal* 108) represents not just a mere detail but rather an invitation to know more about the trend, as confirmed by the explicit mention of his theosophical library on the shelves. The bibliographic list of "titles of this kind" (titoli di questo genere; 108), copied in the text without their authors,[34] suggests the existence of a familiar or curious readership that was willing to recognize this new cultural input and expand further on it. In these cited works, which mirror the study lists of *Leonardo*, Pirandello then manifests his inquisitiveness towards theosophy (and American thought), which finds expression as intellectual curiosity and simultaneously as creative re-elaboration in the new setting of his Italian fiction.

5 The Rise and Fall of Transatlantic Americanism (1909–1919)

By the turn of the twentieth century, Americanism had acquired parallel connotations as an image of prosperity (for Italian immigrants entering the US workforce) and an ideology of industrial, cultural, and military expansion (for Americans aspiring to broaden their influence in Europe). In the years preceding, during, and following the Great War, Americanism also began to take shape as a bilateral phenomenon, as seen in the development of interactive and collaborative projects in the fields of education, female entrepreneurship, immigration services, and health care.

This chapter examines the formation and evolution of "transatlantic" Americanism as an international network of bidirectional exchanges, through the investigation of such exemplary experiences as the New York School of Italian Industries, Montessori's first school in America, the institution of legal protection for immigrants, and sanitary aid for Italian soldiers during the First World War.

The establishment of the Scuola d'Industrie italiane (School of Italian Industries) in 1905 and the opening of the first Montessori school in Tarrytown, New York State, in 1911 illuminate the emergence of a transatlantic bond in relation to education, entrepreneurship, and female emancipation. The work of bicultural attorneys Gino Speranza and Fiorello La Guardia – who created bilingual forms of legal protection and cultural mediation and fostered mutual assistance during the First World War – reflects a legal, journalistic, and diplomatic web of transatlantic interactions. Lastly, the emergency network established by the Young Men's Christian Association (YMCA) and the American Red Cross (ARC) before and after the US military intervention in Europe showcases the growing collaboration between the Italian and American governments in rescue operations, as well as the evolution of Americanism from an international program of exchange (of aids and resources) to war propaganda, presenting Americans as trustworthy allies, Wilson as an enlightened leader, and the United States as global peacemakers.

These experiences highlight the facets of transatlantic Americanism as a diverse platform of entrepreneurial, intellectual, and sanitary exchange in connection with the political vision of Woodrow Wilson. Notwithstanding its initial success, the president's Americanism underwent an unexpected reconfiguration during and following the 1919 Paris Peace Conference at Versailles, moving from an ideal of global collaboration to an oppositional identity marker. As Wilson's Italian popularity dropped after Yugoslavia's annexation of Istria and Dalmatia, Americanism would turn into anti-American revanchism, feeding patriotic pride and the growth of Fascist nationalism. Conversely, as Congress refused to ratify the Treaty of Versailles and rejected entrance into the League of Nations, Americanism in the United States also shifted from a globalist to an isolationist ideology. With the election of Republican president Warren Harding in 1920, Americanism identified with anti-migratory nativism and provided the ideological backup to Harding's and Coolidge's immigration quotas of 1921 and 1924 that brought emigration to an abrupt standstill. The reconversion of Americanism from transatlantism to nativism finds expression in the post-war trajectory of Gino Speranza, who moved from his early commitment to immigration to a blunt call to "abolish" emigration in defence of America's "original spirit" (*Race or Nation?* 254).

A Transatlantic Network of Education and Female Entrepreneurship

In 1909 the American philanthropist and textile entrepreneur Alice Hallgarten invited the Italian pedagogist Maria Montessori to spend the summer in her Umbrian residence near Città di Castello (Pazzini, *Coltivare l'immaginario* 37).

Born in New York and raised in Frankfurt, Hallgarten moved to Rome in the late 1890s to work as volunteer in the San Lorenzo neighborhood, and met Montessori. During her time in Rome, Hallgarten also met the economist and politician Leopoldo Franchetti (whom she married in 1901; Bisi Albini)[1] and became involved with Industrie femminili italiane (Italian Female Industries), an association founded by a group of upper-class women in 1903 to promote education and emancipation of women through the revival of decorative arts.[2]

The American baroness was interested in new educational methods aimed at encouraging creative skills and promoting new forms of independence for women. In 1901 she opened an elementary school for local peasant women in her summer residence of Villa Montesca in Umbria, and in 1907 she and her husband funded Montessori's first Casa dei Bambini (Children's House) in the San Lorenzo neighbourhood of Rome (Alatri 121). Hallgarten was also committed to entrepreneurship. Following the mission of Italian Female Industries, she started the embroidery and lacemaking business Tela Umbra (Umbrian Weaving) in 1908 in Città di Castello (Pazzini, *Coltivare l'immaginario* 38).

Her model (and then commercial partner) was Romeyne Robert, an American expatriate in nearby Perugia who was married to Count Ruggero Ranieri di Sorbello. In 1903 Robert had similarly started an elementary school for local women in her summer residence of Villa del Pischiello and opened the embroidery shop Arti Decorative Italiane (Italian Decorative Arts) in Perugia (Ranieri, "Romeyne Robert"). Italian Female Industries' president, the textile designer Carolina Amari, had partnered with Robert to rediscover, redesign, and commercialize the "Umbrian stitch" (later called *punto Sorbello*), training local women in this ancient embroidery technique. Robert and Hallgarten also created a cooperative for the European export of their artefacts and textile craft (Pazzini, *Maria Montessori* 183).

As Hallgarten's guest during the summer of 1909 (Maccheroni 49–50), Montessori came to appreciate the American women's philanthropic and entrepreneurial vision of education as a force for female emancipation. She trained teachers and tested new materials with students at the Montesca school and visited Romeyne Robert's Pischiello school (inspiring the American lady to experiment with the method on her own children; Valoroso and Ranieri 14). During this time in Umbria, Montessori drafted her manual *Il metodo della pedagogia scientifica applicato all'educazione infantile nelle Case dei Bambini* (*The Montessori Method: Scientific Pedagogy as Applied to Child Education in the Children's Houses*). The text, published in Città di Castello in 1909 at Franchetti's expense (Busenghin 85), formalized her experiments and became the cornerstone of her pedagogy.

During these years two parallel projects developed in the United States around the same juxtaposition of education, emancipation, and entrepreneurship: the New York Scuola di industrie italiane, and the first Montessori school (in the city of tycoon John D. Rockefeller). Moving away from the educational model of secular and religious institutions, which were mainly concerned with heritage preservation, Carolina Amari and Maria Montessori gave form to a new intercultural schooling, proactively focused on social assimilation and mutual integration of values. Their schools represent early laboratories of transatlantic exchange and, simultaneously, of a new bilateral Americanism as a broader horizon of cultural reinvention and mutual synthesis.

Amari saw the School of Italian Industries as a cultural extension of Industrie femminili italiane and an ideal extension of Romeyne Robert's business. Her project to export the Umbrian educational and entrepreneurial models of Alice Hallgarten and Romeyne Robert and her commitment to female emancipation (as Roman president of Italian Female Industries) found support in Italy, from Queen Margherita, and, in the United States, from Florence Colgate, a prominent American woman whom Amari had met during a business trip to New York (Pazzini, *Maria Montessori* 26–7). Like the Pischiello school, the New York School of Italian Industries aspired to train lower-class women (in this case, migrants) and provide them with an expressive outlet, a decent working environment, and a starting salary through their work, granting them settlement and worthy living conditions in America. Like Arti Decorative Italiane, which Amari and Robert had developed in Perugia, the school also produced and sold artisanal pieces for the American market (which are now conserved at the Cooper Hewitt Museum and the Boston Museum of Fine Arts; Ranieri, "Artistic Philanthropy"). This project of social betterment and creative integration of cultures received public praise in a 1907 piece for the American magazine *The Craftsman*, in which the author states that "here [at the school] the Italian instinct for creating the beautiful finds full play, and full pay," and "no child laborers, no overtime, no evening work are found" (E. Irwin 406).

The first Montessori school in the United States likewise sparked new forms of international cooperation. After the publication of *The Method* in 1909, a young teacher from Chicago, Anne George, travelled to Rome to receive extensive training from the pedagogist. In the following year she curated the first English translation of *The Method*. During the same period Montessori trained two other American ladies in Rome: the journalist Josephine Tozier, who would write a series of pieces on her for *McClure's Magazine*, and the educator Roberta Fletcher, who would co-found with Anne George the first Montessori school in Tarrytown.

Solicited by S.S. McClure, who had met Montessori in England in 1910, Tozier published two articles on her pedagogy in the magazine, propelling a wider diffusion of her method to its female audience. In the first piece, published in May 1911 with the title "An Educational Wonder-Worker: The Methods of Maria Montessori," Tozier presented Montessori's pedagogical theory and the newly opened Tarrytown school. In the second piece, published in December 1911 under the title "The Revolutionary Educational Work of Maria Montessori as Carried Out in Her Own Schools," she gave a detailed report of her didactic practices in Rome. While mirroring the journal's call for a renewed involvement of women in society, Montessori's emancipatory principles (summed up by her conviction that "children teach themselves") coincided with a growing entrepreneurial trend in American education, as schooling began to shift from the teacher-centred classical curriculum to a more creative and individualized dimension. Against this backdrop, thanks to the initiative of S.S. McClure and Roberta Fletcher, Montessori's work began to acquire a new entrepreneurial dimension in North America.

S.S. McClure was a regular guest of the Wednesday evening meetings that inventor Alexander Graham Bell and his wife, Mabel, organized at their mansion in Washington, DC. Aware of their dissatisfaction with the traditional curriculum, she had invited them to visit Montessori's school in response to their search for alternative methods. After Mabel Bell and her daughter Daisy's stay in Tarrytown in February 1912, the Bells invited the school's co-founder Roberta Fletcher to teach a class at their Washington house on 1331 Connecticut Avenue. Soon afterwards, in the summer of 1912, they convinced her to open a "Children's Laboratory" in the loft of an unused warehouse close to their summer mansion in Baddeck, Nova Scotia, thus establishing the first Montessori school in Canada (Association Montessori Internationale – Canada).[3]

A year later, after inviting Fletcher back to their Washington house, the Bells funded the opening of a school in the city at 1840 Kalorama Road on 15 October 1913 and invited Montessori to the United States for the project's public launch. Two months later, with the help of McClure, George, and Fletcher, Montessori was hosted in the Bells' mansion during her first trip to America (Kramer 158–76; see ch. 4). The reception organized in her honour on 6 December 1913, which was reported the following day in the *New York Times*, confirms not just her increasing popularity in North America but also the evolution of her method from an Italian schooling practice to a transnational educational philosophy.

Americanism as Transatlantism in the Early Work of Gino Speranza

A key figure in the growth of the School of Italian Industries was the American-born Italian attorney Gino Speranza, husband of Florence Colgate and, in the words of Thomas A. Guglielmo, "perhaps the most prominent Italian-American public intellectual of the early twentieth century" (169). In his work as volunteer, immigration attorney, and journalist, Speranza exemplified a new idea of Americanism, which moved from a mirror of the age's progressivism – focusing on the integration of migrants and education as a remedy to American social warfare, poverty, and racism – to a new transatlantic dimension, as institutional collaboration and cultural dialogue among nations.

The son of Carlo Leonardo Speranza, a professor of Italian literature at the universities of Yale and Columbia, Gino Speranza was educated between his parents' native city of Verona and New York City. After completing his training in international law at New York University (bachelor of laws, 1894) (Salerno 133),[4] he started his career working as an attorney for Italian immigrants and as legal adviser to the Consulate General of Italy in New York City. He then became a member of the Emigration Commission (established by the Italian government for the legal defence of Italians abroad), secretary of the Society for the Protection of Italian Immigrants (founded in 1901 by New York settlement-house worker Sarah Wool Moore), director of the Investigating Bureau for Italian Immigrants (an agency designed to pursue cases of industrial safety negligence or fraud), and, in 1906, an adviser to the U.S. State Department on the labour riots of Italian American workers in West Virginia's mining districts (Gino Speranza Papers).[5]

While creating a network of assistance to Italian immigrants and establishing a labour bureau to counteract the exploitative padrone system, Speranza more actively engaged with the Scuola d'Industrie italiane after marrying Florence Colgate in 1909. He supported his wife's mission to train Italian immigrants in embroidery and lacemaking, provided advice on transportation and housing, and encouraged women to retain their cultural identity and embrace their new life in America. In 1912 he definitively abandoned his legal practice to focus on writing, moving from early legal reports (exposing Americans to the problems and advantages of Italian immigration) to broader work on cultural mediation in his articles and short stories for *Atlantic* and *Atlantic Monthly* ("explaining the nature of immigrant institutions such as the mutual-aid societies, Italian language newspapers, immigrants' banks, and religious festivals, but also dealing with crime, the Black Hand and Mafia"; Pozzetta 61). Moved by the progressive idea of Americanism as a process of social betterment and assimilation of diversity (through service, education, and work), his writings not only aimed at fostering intercultural understanding but also aspired to offer Americans a "systematic interpretation of Italy to America and America to Italy" (Livingstone xiii).

As Italy entered the European war on 24 May 1915, Speranza decided to travel to the country with his wife, Florence Colgate. He served in Italy between August 1915 and April 1919, first as a correspondent for the *New York Evening Post* and then as an attaché of the Political Intelligence Division at the US embassy in Rome beginning in 1917. His sixty articles represent a unique historical documentation, capturing the "feel" of the Italian war from both an inside and an outside perspective.[6] At the same time, Speranza's journal (which was published posthumously in 1941 as *Diary of Gino Speranza: Italy, 1915–1919*) reflects not just the "sentimental paradox" (Livingstone xv) of his two identities, as he swung between his Italian heritage and his self-identification as American (or rather as a Wilsonian; Livingstone xv), but also the refashioning of his Americanism into a conscious transatlantism, intended as an original recreation of cultures across the ocean.[7]

In his role as reporter, military envoy, and diplomatic adviser to US ambassador Thomas Nelson Page, Speranza developed his work of assistance to immigrants and cultural mediation within a transatlantic framework. He would continue to support the cause of immigrants: for example, by extolling Italian Americans travelling with him – "yesterday [they] were solving the problems of industrial America; today they are going to fight the battle of freedom in Europe; tomorrow, perhaps, they will police the peace of the world" (*Diary* 3; 12 August 1915) – and by reproaching Italian authorities for treating naturalized Americans as deserters, as they refused "to allow the wives of some native Italians to join their husbands in America" (*Diary* 180; 18 February 1916). He would also continue his mission as cultural translator, identifying the war as an ideal circumstance for understanding Italy – "now is a most acceptable time for an outsider to see Italy, for this is the great hour when he may see her face, her lovely, unforgettable face, free of conventional smiles, unadorned, and indifferent to the opinions of strangers" (*Diary* 12; 26 August 1915)[8] – and witnessing the American relief effort. On board his liner he recorded the exact cargo of American aids (antityphoid serum and shoes; 18 August 1915)[9] and solicited shipments of wool to support Italian fighting in the Alps (26 August 1915).[10] In his later role as a member of the Committee for War Relief, he regularly visited the hospitals set in place by US officials in Italy, stressing the value of American help in bringing sanitary relief, lifting morale at Christmas time, and improving the soldiers' diet.[11]

In addition to providing a retrospective record of his personal mission, Speranza's diary offers a valuable testimony on the diplomatic relations and collaborative exchange between Italy and the United States, prior to and after the US military intervention in 1917.

During the first years of the conflict Speranza extensively travelled the country – from his home base in Florence to Rome (where he visited the Vatican and the Italian senate) and the war rearguard (in Vicenza, Treviso, Padua, and Gorizia) – collecting intelligence on such topics as the effects of war on Italian cities, high-altitude combat in the Alps, the Italian war front in Albania and the Balkans,[12] the Vatican stand on the conflict,[13] and Austrian military strategy. His mission to Venice in October 1915 exemplifies his work, as his courtesy visit to the American consul Harvey Carroll turns into a profitable time to gather strategic information on the economic and sanitary necessities of the Italian army.[14]

After Italy's military defeat and withdrawal from Caporetto (October–December 1917), Speranza became more involved with the American war effort, serving in Rome as adviser to the US ambassador Thomas Nelson Page.[15] As diplomatic attaché, he came in contact with the professionals of Wilson's propaganda, including the high commissioner for public information Charles Merriam (later the founder of behaviourism and adviser to US presidents Taft and Hoover), and the New York State representative Salvatore Cotillo (later named first Italian American justice of the New York supreme court).[16] Speranza collaborated with them in the work of the American Committee on Public Information (CPI), which aimed at swaying Italian public opinion from the anti-war arguments of the Socialist Party and persuading Italians to continue the fight with the Allies. In his service Speranza actively promoted Wilson's vision of Americanism as a platform for peaceful dialogue among nations, as outlined in the Fourteen Points presented by the president to the US Congress on 8 January 1918 (and later ratified in the formation of an international League of Nations).[17] In this role as cultural diplomat Speranza also interacted with US representative Fiorello La Guardia (later mayor of New York City) in the early months of 1918, when La Guardia was convalescing in Rome after an aeroplane crash on a test flight (Brodsky 103).

The ARC and YMCA in Italy between Public Diplomacy and Propaganda

Speranza's mission to Italy offers valuable insights on the American strategy during the war, as well as on Wilson's propaganda machine, which had already been operative since 1915.

Before the United States entered the conflict, on 6 April 1917, American soft power had taken shape around the diplomatic, cultural, and sanitary network of the YMCA and the ARC. After the Italian retreat from Caporetto on 28 October 1917, the work of emergency relief professionals paired with that of soldiers (dispatched on the Italian front line in early 1918) and of the "propaganda regiment" (Rossini 102), set in Rome by the US embassy with the tasks of gathering political intelligence, countering anti-American prejudice spread by German misinformation, and advancing Wilson's view of America as a global force for peace.[18]

In the initial phase of the war the United States made its presence felt in Italy through first-aid provisions, dispatch of medical personnel, and the establishment of hospitals or centres of assistance. Humanitarian service was approved by the American war council (honorarily chaired by President Wilson), financially supported by public fund-raising campaigns or private donations, and organized on site by the US ambassador to Rome, Thomas Nelson Page.[19]

The mission of ARC professionals was that of providing medical assistance to hospitals and immediate relief to the starving, homeless, and orphans affected by the war. While displaying the US commitment to Italy's war effort (without jeopardizing neutrality),[20] ARC members favoured a transnational exchange of ideas and fostered social reform projects (waging anti-tuberculosis crusades, founding nursing schools, and promoting child welfare).

In parallel with their sanitary and diplomatic work, YMCA professionals established a network of "comfort stations" (Ellwood 66), setting up hostels throughout the national territory – in Nurri (Sardinia), Stilo (Calabria), Cassino, Volterra, Avezzano, Padula, and Santa Maria Capua Vetere. Charged with the task of assisting Italians materially and psychologically, they distributed morale commodities (like chocolate and cigarettes),[21] organized entertainment, offered English lessons, and provided education to soldiers' children. In 1916 the organization proposed to the Italian army that the YMCA bring its services near the front line in support of the existing network of Case del Soldato (Soldier's Houses) founded by the Italian priest Giovanni Minozzi, but the offer was declined (Cecchin 11).

After the United States' declaration of war against Germany and the dispatch of the expeditionary force to France, the American strategy of sanitary aid, moral support, and diplomatic collaboration did not change in Italy (Rossini 53). Although not engaging in direct combat against Austria, the US government intensified the activities of the ARC and YMCA, coordinating them more openly in conjunction with Italian authorities.

In early summer of 1917 the head of the ARC Permanent Commission, Colonel Robert Perkins, visited the peninsula to enhance and reorganize war-time relief. In collaboration with the American consul in Venice, Harvey Carroll, he enacted a more explicit form of American presence, based on the concepts of efficiency, fraternity, and militarized virility. In dialogue with Italian authorities and in collaboration with US agencies, he also swayed American public opinion to increase the number of ambulances in the peninsula (J. Irwin 418–21). In June 1917, American Ambulances for the Allies (AAA) had founded the Italian Ambulance Fund in New York City, and the Midwest branch of the American Field Service had launched "American Ambulances for Italy" in a public demonstration on 19 June in Chicago of 100,000 people (including a young Ernest Hemingway, the Italian minister of treasury Francesco Saverio Nitti, and the Italian senator Guglielmo Marconi). "Ambulanze Americane per l'Italia" opened its dedicated office inside the US consulate of Milan on 13 August 1917, and a few days later – as Speranza records on 15 August 1917 – the first US ambulances were spotted on the Italian front (Cecchin 10).

In the late summer of 1917 the New York financier and philanthropist George F. Baker travelled to Italy to assess the country's social and military conditions and provide the war council of the ARC with accurate information on new potential aid packages. At the end of his inspection he declined the ARC's request for increased funds and instead delivered a $200,000 war-council grant to supplement the system of charity set in place by the US ambassador in Rome, Thomas Nelson Page (J. Irwin 413). Soon after Baker's return to America, however, his projections were suddenly overturned, as news arrived that the Austrian army had broken the Italian front line in Caporetto.

In the two months between the unexpected collapse of the front line (on 28 October 1917) and the "halting battles" of Monte Grappa (11–26 November, and 11–21 December 1917; Cutolo), blocking the Italian withdrawal and the Austro-Hungarian penetration along the line of the Piave River, the Italian war front acquired a new strategic importance in the broader context of the conflict. On 5 November 1917 the Allies met in Rapallo for their first Supreme War Council and approved the dispatch of British and French troops to the Italian front; on 9 November Italy's Supreme General Cadorna was forced to resign ("Cadorna Removed"); and on 7 December the United States declared war against Austria. In the months spent preparing military action in the peninsula (at the time, the only US contingent in Italy was La Guardia's aviation camp in Foggia), American relief services implemented emergency aid near the Piave line, first with independent initiatives and then with a more organized structure.

In the immediate aftermath of the Caporetto debacle, the US consul in Venice, Harvey Carroll, organized an impromptu relief effort with the help of ARC professionals, distributing two tons worth of chocolate, cigarettes, and scarves to withdrawing Italian troops. In November 1917 the Ambulance Committee of American Poets, chaired by Robert Underwood Johnson, dispatched fifty Ford ambulance trucks to the front line (McGrath Morris 44–5), and in early December the ARC redirected two loads of sheets, canned food, and first-aid kits from Paris to Italy's front (Cecchin 17). It was at this time that American writers John Dos Passos and John Howard Lawson moved from the Verdun battlefield to the Italian war front.

Only in the early months of 1918 did Americans develop a more structured presence behind the Piave front line. In coordination with Italy's military leadership, which officially recognized the YMCA as an Italian association in January 1918,[22] US soldiers (many of them writers) served between the YMCA of Ca' Erizzo in Bassano del Grappa and the ARC hospital of Schio, providing moral support to Italian troops, distributing aid to refugees in the area, and setting up field hospitals. John Dos Passos and Jack Lawson served as ambulance drivers. Sydney Fairbanks worked as a reporter (publishing *Come sta*, the first American journal in Italy on 10 March 1918; Cecchin 43) and as an interpreter for Robert Underwood Johnson (chair of American Poets' Ambulances in Italy, president of the New York Committee of the Italian War Relief Fund of America, and US ambassador in Rome from April 1920 to July 1921). In June 1918 Ernest Hemingway also reached the Italian war front, driving ambulance trucks behind the front line and dispensing chocolate and cigarettes to soldiers.[23] A month later, on 8 July, he was wounded by Austrian mortar fire in Schio and soon thereafter was honoured with the Silver Medal of Valour by the Italian government. His convalescence in Milan (until November 1918) and his love story with the nurse Agnes von Kurowsky inspired his later novel *A Farewell to Arms*.

Between the end of 1917 and the early months of 1918, the ARC gradually moved from emergency operations to a more organized relief structure, establishing its Permanent Commission in Rome on 20 December 1917 (Cecchin 21) and systematically enhancing its public narrative throughout the peninsula. Two public demonstrations – organized in collaboration with Italian authorities in Milan and Rome – launched the ARC's renewed effort to rout German anti-American propaganda and promote American democracy as a force of international peace.

On 13 December 1917 the ARC organized in Milan "a grand spectacle to introduce its men and its message to Italy," parading a hundred US volunteers and forty Ford ambulances. Its speakers included the mayor of Milan, members of the Italian army's health division, representatives from the French and British military, and the president of the Italian Red Cross (J. Irwin 407). Attending with the Ambulance Corps, John Dos Passos lambasted the event in his diary, laconically noting that "we

are here for propaganda it seems – more than for ambulance work [...]
we must show Italy that America is behind them" (115).[24]

A month later, on 15 January 1918, the ARC celebrated the establishment of its Permanent Commission in Rome through a grandiose
gathering in Piazza del Campidoglio that included as guests King
Victor Emmanuel III, the Italian minister of treasury Francesco Nitti,
the mayor of Rome, and various Italian senators and ministers. After
the introductory speeches by ARC commissioner Robert Perkins and
US ambassador Thomas Nelson Page, the Italian scientist and senator
Guglielmo Marconi gave the keynote address, praising ARC leaders
and endorsing the common fight of Italy and the United States for "the
triumph of those democratic principles which are the life and hope of
all progressive communities" (qtd. in J. Irwin 423).

Through these public demonstrations the ARC not only made explicit
its ties to Italian institutions but also obtained the approval of Italy's
prime minister, Vittorio Orlando, to enact large-scale cash distributions
in support of soldiers' families. By April 1918, ARC officials had distributed a total of 6,850,000 lire (about US$1 million) to a reported 318,000
families of Italian soldiers all over the national territory (J. Irwin 423).
Cash handouts, which did not require an expense report on the recipi-
ents' end, represented powerful statements of America's friendship
as well as formidable marketing events of American democracy,[25] as
evidenced by their careful preparation, execution, and media diffusion. In collaboration with the propaganda committee in Rome, ARC
professionals set up preliminary visits to distributing sites, organized
parades of US soldiers in military uniform, scheduled interviews in
local newspapers, and distributed writing materials for husbands and
fathers at the front, whether they be postcards featuring the portrait of
Woodrow Wilson or posters, pamphlets, and publications of various
kinds (J. Irwin 424). Many gatherings included inspirational speeches
(often by Fiorello La Guardia) as well as American-style celebrations,
as seen in the patriotic festivities organized on 4 July 1918, in Milan,
Rome, Naples, Palermo, Turin, and Bologna, which marked the peak of
Wilsonianism in Italy (Rossini 133).

The most daring form of collaboration between the ARC and the Italian state, or rather the most powerful expression of Americanism as a
transatlantic force of international cooperation, was the so-called Pisa
Village. The project, proposed by US consul Harvey Carroll in Venice
and approved by US ambassador Page in March 1918, aspired to build a
medical colony in the outskirts of Pisa for the assistance and relocation
of 15,000 displaced Venetians. This urban site, provided by the Italian
government and initially named after the ambassador's wife, Florence

Page, was conceived as a new space of assistance where refugees and wounded soldiers "could reestablish their lives and their communities, support themselves through employment rather than charity, and raise their families in a stable and orderly climate" (J. Irwin 425). At the same time, the Pisa Village (comprising eighty concrete homes, offices, shops, a community kitchen, a church, schools, a hospital, and even a replica of Venice's Piazza San Marco) also aspired to showcase a modern-day American city in Italy, exposing Italians to more advanced housing systems and sanitary behaviours. Despite ample coverage by the American press and the declared intention to complete work by the end of the summer, the colony was never finished, because of poor planning, unreliable labour, and the sudden end of the war. The buildings that were completed between May and November 1918 were turned over to the Italian government and reassigned by the Italian Ministry of War, but refugees never moved into the city and the project that aspired to memorialize America's help to Italy became an omen of Wilson's political collapse.[26]

The War-Time Americanism of Fiorello La Guardia

Like Gino Speranza, Fiorello La Guardia was a key figure of American propaganda in Italy, not only for his ability to mediate and translate worlds but also for his political charisma.

La Guardia and Speranza shared bilingual upbringings and parallel professional paths, from their early service to Italian immigrants to their direct involvement in the Italian war.

La Guardia was the son of a composer and accompanist. His father, Achille, born in Foggia in 1849, had first travelled to the United States in 1878 for a tour of the opera singer Adelina Patti. After serving as the director of an Austrian veterans' band, he resettled in Trieste, where he married Irene Cohen Luzzatto (from one of the city's most prominent Jewish families) and had two children: Gemma (1881) and Fiorello (1882).[27] Hired as bandmaster of the US Eleventh Infantry Regiment in 1885, he moved back to America, and, following his assignments, the La Guardia family moved with him to Fort Sully (Dakota Territory, 1885), Watertown (New York, 1887), Arizona (Fort Huachuca, 1890; Fort Whipple, 1892), and Tampa (Florida, 1898) (Foraker). An episode of food poisoning forced him to leave service in the wake of the Spanish-American War and return to Trieste, where he managed a hotel until his death in 1904. Fiorello refused to join the family business in Trieste and, thanks to the help of Raymond Willey, a US consular agent in the nearby city of Fiume, moved to Budapest, where he took a post as clerk-secretary of the American consul in Hungary (Mangiafico). In 1903, at the end of Willey's term, he returned to Fiume as consul and first introduced medical inspections of emigrants in the city port prior to their embarkment (Brodsky 18). After being denied transfer to the US consulate in Belgrade due to his lack of academic credentials, La Guardia moved back to New York in 1906, where he completed his law degree at New York University in 1910 and worked at Ellis Island as a certified interpreter in Italian, Yiddish, German, Hungarian, and Croatian. Building on these experiences, he opened a law firm with his associate Raimondo Canudo at 50 Broad Street in New York City. His legal services for Italian and Jewish immigrants soon earned him the reputation as "the people's attorney" (Brodsky 44). Thanks to his popularity, he ran for Congress in 1916 and was elected as the first Italian American congressman, taking office on 4 March 1917.

As La Guardia and Speranza crossed paths in Rome in 1918, they shared not just a parallel background or a common commitment to the social, cultural, and political assimilation of immigrants into American society but also a strong vision of Americanism as an ideology to assert a new US international influence and Americans as global citizens (Rossini 3), as outlined by Wilson prior to and after America's entrance into the war. In the early years of the conflict, Wilson promoted Americanism as a non-committal assistance role, which limited US involvement in Europe to the dispatch of sanitary and economic aids (as documented by Gino Speranza). As public pressure escalated following the release of the Zimmermann Telegram (January 1917)[28] and Congress approved military intervention in Europe (April 1917), Wilson's Americanism acquired a more pronounced political connotation as military intervention (also voted by Congressman La Guardia) and "ideological warfare" (in the dual work of propaganda to support troops and promote America's democratic ideals; Rossini 54).

In this context, La Guardia decided to take action, applying for a leave of absence from Congress, joining the US Army Air Service in the summer of 1917, and setting up the first American military camp in Italy on 16 October 1917 in his father's hometown of Foggia. During his time in Italy he wore many hats: as second in command of the Eight Aviation Instruction Center at Camp Foggia, combat flyer, US Army's representative on the Joint Army and Navy Aircraft Committee, propagandist for the American Expeditionary Forces, smuggler for the Italians, and US congressman (Brodsky 93). Until his departure in October 1918, he was a key figure of American combat, propaganda, and diplomacy in Italy, anticipating the need for American boots on the ground in Italy (prior to military deployment on the northeastern front in early 1918) and transferring his skills as legal and cultural mediator to the Italian context.

His involvement with American and Italian aviation earned him the aura of political leader and flying ace. On the one hand, La Guardia built his fame as a loyal leader at the US base of Camp Foggia, by catering meals for his troops and teaching the game of baseball to Italian troops (Brodsky 95). On the other hand, as he trained his pilots, survived an aeroplane crash, and engaged in aerial combat on the Italian-Austrian front (as major in command of the Foggiana unit of Caproni Ca 44 bombers), he acquired the status of a hero. His aviation feats and his abilities as motivator, leader, and multilingual speaker equated him to the Italian poet and war legend Gabriele D'Annunzio, who similarly inspired Italy to join the conflict with his speech at Quarto (Genoa) on 5 May 1915, survived an aeroplane crash (remaining blind for a few months), and recklessly led risky aeroplane missions over enemy territory.[29] La Guardia too became an influential intellectual, leveraging his feats to reassure Italians against German propaganda and building trust towards Americans by way of his reputation as "a shrewd and ambitious politician with a strong sense of social justice, a fighter against corruption, a defender of the poor and the underdog" (Muson).

Summoned by Ambassador Page (through Gino Speranza) as the "only man capable of delivering the proper propaganda" (Brodsky 101), La Guardia spearheaded the team of US-trained propagandists. While addressing the "indifference" of Italians towards the United States and their confused understanding of the American role in Europe (Rossini 17–19), he promoted Wilson's transatlantic ideal of military and civil cooperation. In his rallies throughout the peninsula's major cities, La Guardia urged Italians to double their efforts to win the war, scolding their bad habits (Muson) and boosting their morale with powerful motivational speeches. In aggrandizing the impact of US military contingents, he also grew the network of health services and distributions (of sanitary aids, chocolate, cigarettes, and money) that the YMCA and the ARC had set in place in Italy since the early years of the war.

While enacting a new form of public diplomacy with his "near-hagiographic" profile (Brodsky 106), La Guardia also established ties with the Italian political leadership, reaching out to Italian minister of treasury Francesco Nitti, the army's Supreme General Armando Diaz, and King Victor Emmanuel III (whom he confidently addressed as "Manny" at a luncheon in Padua in August 1918; Rossini 108). In his political role he worked to cultivate an Italian change in attitude towards Americans, inviting the military leadership to coordinate engagements and draft orders in Italian and English, and he organized public welcome ceremonies to announce American support (as documented in the parades accompanying the three battalions of William Wallace in many Italian cities after their first arrival on 27 July 1918).[30]

Following his return to the United States in the fall of 1918, La Guardia was re-elected to Congress, but, a few months later, he resigned from his post in disagreement with Wilson's denial of Italy's Adriatic claims at the Paris Peace Conference of Versailles. Although disappointment with Wilson and Italy's anti-Wilson reactions led his colleague Gino Speranza to radically shift his attitude, La Guardia's war service paved the way not just for his political career as mayor of New York (from his first unsuccessful bid in 1921 to his later appointments from 1934 to 1945) but also for his creative re-elaboration of Americanism from a transatlantic platform of shared responsibility into a pragmatist program of reformism, assimilation, and merit.[31]

The Failure of Wilsonianism and the End of Transatlantic Americanism

When war suddenly ended with the armistices of 4 November (for Italy) and 11 November 1918 (for the Allies), US officials were caught "relatively unprepared" for demobilization (Barry). Logistical difficulties in ship transportation and medical efforts to prevent the spreading of the influenza pandemic delayed the discharge of US soldiers, which would be fully completed by the end of the Paris Peace Conference in June 1919.

In the spring of 1919, as US officials increased recreation activities for soldiers in reaction to their mounting protests and petitions, General Pershing approved the construction of a stadium in the outskirts of Paris to host the Inter-Allied Games – an Olympic outlet for disengaged soldiers (1,500 from eighteen nations), celebrating the fraternity of Allied forces gathered in Paris for the peace conference, and setting a final discharge of American troops. After the games the stadium was turned over to France as a memorial of the American Expeditionary Forces (Chavinier-Réla).[32]

During the same months, Americans who were still stationed in Italy (YMCA, ARC, and Committee on Public Information members) also continued in their work of assistance, relief, and propaganda. YMCA professionals organized activities to keep up their own and the civilians' morale. In this context, the new game of basketball, which US instructors had taught Italians on the Piave line since 1918, became an expression of American closeness and ingenuity. The sport gained popularity in June 1919 in connection to the Inter-Allied Games of Paris, when the teams of Italy, France, and the United States played their first international competition. Following the two teams' losses to the US (respectively, 93–6 versus France, and 55–17 versus Italy), Italy's 15–11 victory over France acquired a new connotation, as the match fuelled a wave of national pride and revamped the frustrations over war negotiations.[33]

Over the same period, ARC officials worked to provide remedies against the spreading of the Spanish influenza and shifted from the failed project of the Pisa Village to broader post-war reconstruction plans. While maintaining its focus on children left orphaned by war, the ARC implemented sanitary and civic reforms in Italy, working to spread literacy and improve hygienic standards for refugees (seen as potential new emigrants). In collaboration with the Italian Committee on Public Information, ARC workers acted as social reformers and ambassadors of America's global leadership – showing the mutual benefits of international cooperation yet also promoting the exceptional nature of US democracy, promoting reforms as mutual exchange, and also imposing the Fourteen Points agenda outlined by Wilson in his 8 January 1918 speech to the Congress.

In conjunction with the YMCA and ARC network, the Italian section of the CPI propagated Wilson's agenda of peace among nations under the guidance of the United States and actively promoted the image of the American president as a "modern saint" (Rossini 134). Capitalizing on years of health cooperation, military support, and systematic propaganda over the Italian national territory,[34] Wilson acquired an extraordinary consensus in Italy, as confirmed during his first visit to Italy (2–6 January 1919), when adoring crowds welcomed him in Rome, Milan, Turin, and Genoa, acclaiming him as "the Messiah of the new world that was about to spring from the rubble of warfare" (Rossini 180).

Despite this strong foothold in the "real" country, Italian political leadership increasingly saw the American president with antagonism and distrust: first, for his war-time lack of interest in Italian affairs, given his choice to postpone post-war goal talks until the end of combat (the so-called "doctrine of postponement"; Rossini 141); and then, during the peace talks of Versailles, for his staged ignorance over the 1915 secret pacts of London (promising Istria and Dalmatia to Italy; Salvemini, *Dal patto di Londra*). The breaking point with the Italian administration came on 23 April 1919, when, in open defiance of Italy's Adriatic claims (and Ambassador Page's recommendation), Wilson pushed to assign Istria and Dalmatia to the newly formed Yugoslavia and confidently called Italians to disregard their leaders' opposition, from the pages of the French newspaper *Temps*. Outraged by the decision, Italian prime minister Orlando left the negotiation table at Versailles on

24 April. His minister of foreign Affairs Sydney Sonnino joined him a few days later. Upon their return to Rome, the Italian press began a campaign of popular indignation against Wilson, rapidly turning him from a beloved saviour into the hated individual responsible for the nation's so-called mutilated victory. The wave of irredentism and national revanche following these events (echoed a few months later in Italy's basketball victory at the Inter-Allied Games) found immediate expression in Italian newspapers in the quick diffusion of vehement anti-Wilson rage. On 26 April, a month after founding his Combat Fasces, Benito Mussolini described Wilson's decision in the pages of *Il popolo d'Italia* as "the most memorable monument of the most hypocritical bad faith" (qtd. in Yarrow 163). On 3 May, in the op-ed for *L'unità* "La camicia di Nesso" ("The Shirt of Nessus"; Salvemini 270–4), the philosopher Gaetano Salvemini examined Italy's rejection of American politics and explained why Italy had rebelled against the US "difference in treatment" (differenza di trattamento). The most notable reaction to Wilson's annexation of Istria and Dalmatia to Yugoslavia came on 12 September, however, when Gabriele D'Annunzio took action to occupy the city of Fiume and proclaimed the independent Reggenza Italiana del Carnaro (Italian Regency in Carnaro) in opposition to the Versailles resolutions.

The anti-American backlash following the Paris Peace Conference brought political instability to Italy (as confirmed by the collapse of Orlando's cabinet on 23 June 1919) and fuelled the emergence of nationalist forces, eventually leading to the rise of the Fascist party in 1922. During Wilson's semester in Paris in the first half of 1919, the American political system also faced multiple pressures: rushed demobilization, the spreading of influenza, the outbreak of race riots, and the scare of a potential Bolshevik revolution (Berg 609–10). Upon Wilson's return, Congress curtailed his vision of US global leadership, denying ratification of the Treaty of Versailles[35] and rejecting American entrance into the League of Nations that he had promoted (Cooper 319–57). Weakened by political crisis and failing health, Wilson rapidly lost consensus, and Warren Harding was elected president in 1920 amidst increasing fears of a new wave of war refugees. The new Republican administration would pass two laws forcefully limiting immigration: the Per Centum Act, signed by Harding in 1921 (reducing the number of immigrants to 3 per cent of a given country already living in the United States, according to the 1910 census); and the Immigration Act of 1924, signed by his successor Coolidge, which prevented immigration from Asia, established border patrol, and reduced the annual quota of any nation from 3 to 2 per cent (according to the 1890 census).

Such reconfiguration of Americanism from an ideal of assimilation and global cooperation to an isolationist and nativist ideology delimiting the nation's "original" identity finds intellectual correspondence in the post-war trajectory of Gino Speranza. Returning to America at the initial outbreak of anti-Wilsonian rage in April 1919 and feeling frustrated with Italians and the US president, Speranza reconsidered his pre-war commitment to pluralism and soft integration and instead embraced the middle-class philosophy of American nativism (Salerno 134).[36] In his new view, Americanism coincided not with the need to preserve or strengthen ethnic ties but instead with the necessity to reconstruct society around the core values of the American native stock. While tolerant of cultural diversity, Speranza buoyed Americanism as a new identity politics (aimed at weeding out radicalism or opposition to the nation's ideals), campaigned for immigration quotas, and theorized the forced Americanization of immigrants in his 1925 book *Race or Nation? A Conflict of Divided Loyalties.*

Speranza's intellectual conversion ratifies not just the conclusion of Italian emigration (as stated in the Immigration Act of 1924) but also the end of Americanism as a transatlantic ideal of cultural and political cooperation. Speranza's parable from his early immigration service to the shocking conviction that the immigrant "must be not only barred but abolished" (*Race or Nation?* 255–6) ultimately mirrors the trajectory leading Americanism from an international vision of global interconnectedness to a nationalist ideal of social homogeneity and political order.

Epilogue

The crisis of Wilsonianism veered Americanism from external to internal, reshaping it from an international ideology of expansion or brotherhood into a national debate on citizenship and immigration.

The intellectual path of Gino Speranza exemplifies this shift (see ch. 5). His 1925 treatise *Race or Nation?* outlines a clear-cut synthesis of 1920s Americanism, moving from multiculturalism to anti-immigrant isolationism. In relation to citizenship, he narrows down American identity to "historic American stock" (15) and "new stock minorities" (30) – pending their acceptance of the "fundamentally Anglo-Saxon and Protestant character of American civilization" (16). In relation to immigration, he rejects the "permitted invasion of huge blocks of foreign stocks, of alien minorities that found it hard to fit into any European state, of entire single districts and provinces from the Continent pouring in unabsorbable masses into a nation" (71) and proposes as remedy a program of "complete American conformity" (266), featuring the elimination of foreign-language teaching, the suppression of non-English press, and the establishment of a "federal racial census or national ethnological survey" (261–2). The call for forced Americanization matches his bid to abolish immigration tout court, as outlined in the following passage:

> What then can there be but "Abolition" – the absolute prevention of any further accretions to this vast mass? […] We must abolish "the immigrant" from our minds and from our lives; from our polity and from our policies. The country is to-day a nation, full-fledged and complete; its period of colonization and expansion is a thing of the past […] we have no longer a frontier, nor have we any more free lands. We do not need settlers, we do not need population from outside sources; we do not need it because we do not want to become a crowded state like the countries of Europe and

> Asia, and we wish to transmit our "freedom of space" to our own people
> in the future. (Speranza, *Race or Nation?* 254–5).

Speranza bluntly spells out the specific and contingent association of
Americanism with the political platform in support of immigration
quotas and isolationism. His work more broadly attests to the reconfiguration of the term in relation to exclusiveness, as expressed in the
contemporary stand-alone associations of the United States with capitalism, industrialism, and modernism.

In parallel with the direct exaltation of US exceptionalism (vis-à-vis
Communist Russia), Americanism would also acquire an indirect
connotation in the 1920s as the negative polarity of American Italianism and European modernism. This epilogue explores these countering ideologies, starting from the anti-American sentiment of Italian
migrant communities and the "Americanization syndrome" (Carlson)
of French and German intellectuals. While considering the resurgence
of an American myth in the 1930s, this conclusion also briefly investigates forms of anti-Americanism from the 1940s to the present and the
continuity between the Americanist debate and contemporary criticism
of the United States.

Italianism in the United States

Post-war disapproval of Wilson spearheaded a powerful antagonistic
narrative in Italy in the early 1920s. As nationalists and Fascists reconfigured anti-American resentment into revanchist pride and framed the
relationship with the United States in terms of a clash of civilizations,
Wilsonianism (which was then a synonym for *Americanism*) became the
de facto ideological opposite of Italianism.

For migrant communities in North America, Italianism was similarly
turned into an identity marker or a cultural self-defence against forced
Americanization. Capitalizing on American fascination for Mussolini's
political charism, Fascist authorities invested in the "Italian colony in
America" (Viscusi xxi), supporting the Italian American press, organizing national feasts, and establishing American *fasci*. Thanks to a wide
network of educational outlets (e.g., Dante Alighieri societies and par-
ish schools), Italian language and culture "became a major arena for
propaganda" (Carnevale 151), fostering allegiance to Fascist Italy and
eliciting ethnic pride. A prohibition-era example of this dynamic is the
transformation of wine into a national symbol, representing not only a
key component of the Italian diet and the Catholic liturgy but also a cultural token revealing the hypocrisy of restrictions and, as theorized by
gangster Al Capone, a moral defence against puritanism (Viscusi xx).

At the time of Sacco and Vanzetti's court case, which divided American public opinion and raised global protests in 1927, Mussolini veered from his early focus on the organization of American *fasci* to soft cultural diplomacy in the attempt to "project a positive image of the nation and promote the idea that Fascism had turned Italy into a modern country" (Bedarida). In 1927 the Italian government established the Casa Italiana in New York under the directorship of Giuseppe Prezzolini and from the early 1930s dispatched lecturers to teach Italian courses in American universities (exemplified by Uguccione Ranieri di Sorbello's work at Middlebury College and Yale University between 1930 and 1936; Valoroso 39–42). At the same time, Italian contemporary art also tried to promote a modern image of the nation in America, as wished for by Futurist painter Fortunato Depero during his time in New York between 1928 and 1930. Although his experience was largely unsuccessful, due to the uneven reception of Futurism[1] and to the Wall Street financial crash,[2] Depero nonetheless promoted his choice of New York over Paris and his American work for *Vogue*, *Vanity Fair*, and *Atlantica* as triumphal achievements, in the endeavour to pressure Fascist authorities into accepting Futurism as a state art (Berghaus 484) and gain himself a leadership role in the contemporary European debates on America.

Moving beyond the defensive logic of Italianism (by immigrant communities) and anti-Italianism (by American society at large), Italian academic culture in the United States also forged an interesting space of dialogue with American society and intellectual resistance to the pervasive Fascist presence between the 1920s and 1930s.

In the pioneering experience of Italian American educator Leonard Covello,[3] language teaching fashioned a new pedagogical space in US public schools, offering second-generation Italians an alternative to the ideologization of Fascist Italianism and promoting bilingualism as a remedy to homologating Americanization.[4] Similarly, in the experience of anti-Fascist exiles like Arturo Toscanini, Giuseppe Borgese, and Gaetano Salvemini, Italian language and culture became a free vehicle to elaborate critiques of the Fascist regime, as well as an early vision of the country's later transformation into a democracy.

European Modernism and the Fear of Americanization

Disillusionment over Wilson and puzzlement over the US refusal to join the League of Nations (which the president had proposed) triggered a phase of an "uncomprehending transatlantic dialogue" (Roger 259).

Despite isolationism, the United States continued to exert significant influence over Europe in the post-war years, as confirmed by the success of Hollywood cinematography and the capillary diffusion of American products, trends, and ways of thinking. In the 1920s, *Americanism* was in fact an "umbrella term" that related to "anything that was 'modern' and could even remotely be linked to materialism, efficiency, size, mechanization, standardization, automation, technocracy, uniformity, pragmatism, reform consciousness, naive optimism, spontaneity, generosity, openness, advertising, democracy, or influence exercised upon the masses" (Gassert 220).

During the same years, a new wave of anti-Americanism spread throughout Europe, first as a discourse downplaying US war intervention (presenting Americans as latecomers) and then as a more elaborate critique of the American industrial model. The epicentre of the intellectual project to defend Europe against the machine civilization was Paris, which in those years became not just the European alternative to New York but also the fertile milieu of a new modernist movement, self-labelled as a new humanism (Roger 400).

The philosophical debate on Americanism, which manifested itself as a form of elitist resistance, revolved around the indictment of machinism, the quest for individuality against the "spectre of mass culture" (Sassoon 947), and the affirmation of national rootedness against the abstractism (and perceived totalitarianism) of Americanism.[5] While French intellectuals generally decried US imports as "low" culture, polluting national values (Sassoon 938–9), German thinkers like Adolf Halfeld (in his essay "Amerika und Amerikanismus" ["America and Americanism"], 1927) or Fritz Lang (in his dystopian movie *Metropolis*, 1927) adopted the American prototype as a negative term of comparison to investigate or denounce the effects of the mechanization of life (as later attested by Walter Benjamin's *Work of Art in the Age of Technological Reproducibility*, 1936).[6] The Italian philosopher Antonio Gramsci elaborated in those years a study on Fordism, alternating praise of Sinclair Lewis's novel *Babbitt* (which he saw as proof that "the USA was building a society critical of itself"; Sassoon 941) and criticism of prohibition (which he saw as a form of state control over productivity).

In political terms, reaction to the "American challenge" (Sassoon 935) manifested in a heightened form of state protectionism and the elaboration of national alternatives. While large parts of society embraced the American way of life, as promoted by Hollywood cinematography, European leaders increasingly sought to endorse oppositional cultural models, defining national identities, promoting domestic markets, or – as in the case of Italian Fascism – advancing autarchy as an ideology of self-reliance.[7] In the Italian case, Fascism contained Hollywood's monopoly and influence upon the Italian masses through dubbing (as a form of cultural censorship), state support of the industry (with the establishment of the Venice Film Festival in 1932 and the studios of Cinecittà in 1937), and a direct embargo of US films starting in 1938.

As Donald Sassoon conclusively frames it, with regard to the 1920s and 1930s, "the various attempts to resist Americanism, whether from politically hostile forces (communism, fascism) or from the exponents of elite culture, at best contained the phenomenon," and the influence of the United States in Europe during these years ultimately comes down to an inextricable divide of opinions, as "for every statement by a European lamenting the inexorable tide of American trash, the infectious germs of brash modernity, the coarse and low taste of American people, one can find a countervailing one praising America's politics, its culture, its technology, its lifestyle" (939).

From Americanism to Anti-Americanism

In the 1930s the word *Americanism* designated in Italy a market, a trend, and a latent political and cultural unease, which found expression both inside and outside Fascism.

As for Mussolini's swaying attitudes towards America, which "changed over time in light of shifting political circumstances" (Mariani 53), Americanism represented "a phenomenon both terrifying and fascinating" (Gentile 12), which broadly applied to a mix of disillusionment and excitement regarding modern life. While Emilio Cecchi voiced his disenchantment towards the United States in his famous book *America amara* (*Bitter America*, 1939), large sectors of the Fascist literary establishment nonetheless saw the American model as an example to imitate. Ermanno Amicucci chose the Columbia School of Journalism as inspiration for Italy's first school of journalism in Rome in 1929. Similarly, Giulio Einaudi, Carlo Frassinelli, and Arnoldo Mondadori expanded their market by publishing translations of American authors (including Herman Melville, Edgar Allan Poe, Nathaniel Hawthorne, Edith Wharton, Edgar Lee Masters, Sinclair Lewis, and John Dos Passos) (Sassoon 908).

During the same years, an "Americanist strain in Italian letters" (Viscusi xxvii) also matured in connection with the anti-Fascist writers Cesare Pavese and Elio Vittorini, who saw America as an alternative space of freedom (vis-à-vis the dictatorship) and a mythical land of pure imagination, as expressed in the former's idealized vision of the "middle West" and the latter's anthology of US authors, *Americana* (1941).[8] Such interest would later inform Pavese's post-war "Saggio sull'Americanismo" ("Essay on Americanism," 1951), Beppe Fenoglio's novel *Una questione privata* (*A Private Affair*, 1963), and Calvino's short story "Autobiografia di uno spettatore" ("Autobiography of a Spectator," 1974), respectively portraying America as a space beyond grids, an "over the rainbow" land of self-determination, and a youthful cinematographic remembrance, nurturing creative imagination.[9]

The outbreak of the Second World War marked a definitive break between the tacit Americanism of Italian publishers, writers, and moviegoers and Mussolini's official rebuff of the US "demoplutocracy." As Italy joined the war, Americanism came to mean enemy propaganda, as well as the force behind the "betrayal" of many *italoamericani*, who refused to fight for Italy after the US government's decision to register unnaturalized Italian citizens as enemy aliens, thus ending the "Fascist dream" of an Italian colony in America (Viscusi xvi–xvii).

From the armistice of 1943 to the immediate aftermath of the war, Americanism mainly related to a call for national liberation, but anti-Fascist forces maintained an ambivalent attitude towards it. Italian socialists (as then the radical left) alternated between disdain for American capitalism and intellectual fascination with American literature. Italian Catholics vacillated between the rejection of America's consumerism or Protestant ethics, and the Christian Democracy party's push to join the North Atlantic Treaty Organization. While these bipolarisms "can in no way be meaningfully interpreted according to the category of anti- (or pro-)Americanism" (Mariani 54), they nonetheless highlight a transitory phase of incubation and reconfiguration of the term.

After 1945 the word *Americanism* gradually disappeared from European dictionaries,[10] and traditional forms of "culturally oriented criticism" of the United States, "premised on European superiority and American cultural inferiority" (O'Connor 12), took on a new tone of open resentment towards American politics and ideals. Over the following decades the negative *anti-Americanism* emerged as a leading term in Italy and Europe, alternately identifying the reaction against the Vietnam War (in the broader scenario of the cold war), the protest against Americanization in Europe (after the fall of the Berlin wall), and a clash of civilizations (after the terrorist attacks of 2001).

Conclusion

The study of Americanism in Italy provides a new perspective on the phenomenon, as the country's unique flow of departing and returning migrants turned the concept from an export ideology into a lively platform of cultural, social, and economic exchange. This multifarious network of relationships not only confirms that Italy was the most favourable terrain for American penetration in Europe – thus offering evidence that the Americanization of Italy started long before its full-fledged manifestation in the post–Second World War era – but also offers a valuable term of comparison for assessing the American influence-building process in other contexts and periods.[11]

In the Italian milieu, American hegemony advanced in relation to financial empowerment (from returnees and investors), commercial capitalism (from navigation to import), mass communication (serial narratives and propaganda), sanitary aid (prior to the soft military intervention of the First World War), and political leadership (from Roosevelt to Wilson). The antagonistic and symbiotic ties between Italy and the United States illuminate the hidden traits of America's soft power and the foundations of its "Market Empire," which Victoria De Grazia sums up in five principles: the assumption of the other nations' limited sovereignty over their public space; the connection of social and scientific knowledge to economic exports; the primacy of best practices over formal legislation; the association of democracy with equality of consumption; and the choice of peaceful means over military power (6–9).

America's early "consumer revolution" (De Grazia 9) in Italy documents the first European manifestation of the American belief that economic development is key to democratic stability and peace in the world (De Grazia 14), as well as the remote origins of the post-1945 cultural dialectics, opposing the European rhetoric of resistance against alien hegemony or "cultural invasion" to the American counter-narrative of free market and consumer choice.[12]

The encounter or clash of Italian and American cultures finally reveals the nature of Americanism (and anti-Americanism) as a "war of words," or as a wide-ranging "discourse," whose well-rooted narratives and argumentations became self-conscious in the late nineteenth century (Roger ix–xviii).[13] This reconstruction of the complex and varied meanings of Americanism in Italy aspires not just to offer new elements for a historical re-evaluation of the term or to establish a point of comparison for current scholarly debates (mostly on anti-Americanism),[14] but also, and most importantly, to reconfigure anti-Americanism from "a battle cry or a smug assumption" (Kazin and McCartin 1) into a legitimate critique of America's ultimate adherence to its self-proclaimed ideals.

Notes

Preface

1 In his *Americanism: The Fourth Great Western Religion*, David Gelernter explains the concept as a "sacred narrative" (52), exploring its transformation from the biblical self-representation of a chosen people in a new promised land into a project "to perfect the world, to spread liberty, equality, and democracy to all mankind" (147).

2 Enlightened projection about America followed the sixteenth- and seventeenth-century vision of the New World as "an earthly space for the mythical paradise in the West" (Friedman 8), as expressed in its connection to El Dorado, Eden, and Atlantis and as documented in the New World setting of Thomas More's *Utopia* (1516) and Francis Bacon's *New Atlantis* (1627).

3 Guido Bonsaver's most recent volume, *America in Italian Culture* (2023), offers a systematic overview of the cultural, political, and industrial ties between Italy and the United States from 1861 to 1943. Against this backdrop, my study on "Americanism" specifically focuses on the domestic debate and global discourse on "America" at the turn of the twentieth century.

Introduction

1 A significant instance of Franklin's fame in Italy is represented by the Calabrian city of Filadelfia, which was rebuilt on the model of the US founding father's hometown of Philadelphia after the village of Castelmonardo was destroyed by an earthquake in 1783. For more information on the Calabrian tribute to American independence, see Marianna Barone's volume *Massoneria, istituzioni ed elite politiche*.

2 The trade agreement was signed by Benjamin Franklin on 6 February 1778, a year after his first arrival in Paris and the inclusion of the entry "Americans" in the supplement of Diderot and D'Alembert's *Encyclopédie* (Roger 24).

3 In his thirty-six-volume *Histoire Naturelle, générale et particulière, avec la description du Cabinet du Roi* (*Natural History, General and Particular, with a Description of the King's Cabinet*), published between 1749 and 1804, the scientist Comte de Buffon argued that, having emerged from a late flood, the American continent was "a lesser world, atrophied and shrunken, a world where living things vegetated, men withered away, and species got smaller" (Roger 8).

4 Roosevelt wrote the essay while serving as president of the New York Police Board of Commissioners. As indicated in the memoirs of Jacob Riis, his 1894 encounter with the photographer and social reformer first stirred Roosevelt's interest in the issue of emigration and Americanization (Riis 3).

5 In defining the three sides of broad Americanism, Roosevelt indicated that (1) "we wish to be broadly American and national, as opposed to being local or sectional"; (2) "the patriotism of the village or the belfry is bad, but the lack of all patriotism is even worse"; and (3) with reference to newcomers, "we must Americanize them in every way, in speech, in political ideas and principles" (Roosevelt, "What 'Americanism' Means").

6 Roosevelt also included Native Americans in his myth of Americanism. By reframing "the racial stereotype of their uncivilized ferocity into a praise of Indian 'rugged individuality,'" he called them to earn their part in the nation. To counter their imagery as "noble savages," he depicted them as "noble warriors" characterizing "Indian 'ferocity' as a response to weak-willed whites" (Dorsey 71).

7 "There is no such thing as a hyphenated American who is a good American. The only man who is a good American is the man who is an American and nothing else" (Roosevelt, "Americanism"). By affirming this, Roosevelt aimed at rekindling the spirit and soul of the American experiment, not at legitimizing a renewed nativism, as he argues in the following passage: "Political movements directed against men because of their religious belief and intended to prevent men of that creed from holding office, have never accomplished anything but harm. This was true in the days of the 'Know-Nothing' and Native-American [nativist] parties in the middle of the last century; and it is just as true to-day. Such a movement directly contravenes the spirit of the Constitution itself" (Roosevelt, "Americanism").

8 In response to Wilson's decision, Roosevelt wrote his own account of the situation and an indictment of the president in the 1917 book *The Foes of Our Own Household*.

9 The 1888–9 world baseball tour was organized by Albert Goodwill
Spalding, owner of the Chicago White Stockings, creator of a sporting
goods brand, and influential professional in the sport. The tour became
"a transnational enterprise that marketed the national pastime abroad"
(Zeiler 179) but also spread America's imperialist and racist ideologies.

10 "By the end of 1913 US films were already invading the European markets.
First came the wave of Keystone comedies, and by the summer and
autumn of 1915 the films of Charlie Chaplin […] By the end of the war the
American cinematic invasion of Europe had become an established fact:
for every 5,000 meters of French films presented weekly in France there
were 25,000 meters of imported films, mainly American" (Sassoon 816).

11 In Wilson's words: "let your thoughts and your imagination run abroad
throughout the whole world, […] wherever you go, go out and sell goods
that will make the world more comfortable and more happy, and convert
them to the principles of America" (qtd. in De Grazia 2).

12 "If Baudelaire created the word *Americanize*, a verb with an illustrious
future, it was not through a slip of the pen or some accidental impulse.
The neologism logically and inevitably arose from a series of his writings
that gave it life and force" (Roger 62). The word appeared for the first time
in an article on the 1855 World's Fair that Baudelaire published in *Le Pays*
and was lastly used in his *Fusées* (*Rockets*, in "L'art romantique," published
posthumously in 1887).

13 "This long-lasting diglossia partly explains […] the almost complete lack
of popular literature in Italy. Italian had been, after Latin, the dominant
European language in the sixteenth and seventeenth centuries. Then it
lost ground to French. For six hundred years Italian literature 'floated' –
as the Italian literary critic Alberto Asor Rosa wrote – 'in an immense
ocean of non-Italian speakers.' The majority of those who spoke only the
local dialect were illiterate. So any writer who wished to be widely read
had to use the language of the elite minority. Inevitably, this made the
construction of a text-based wider popular culture somewhat difficult. In
nineteenth-century Italy, popular narrative was unable to match that of
either France or Britain: the narrow linguistic base of Italian prevented it"
(Sassoon 31).

14 This portrayal was grounded in contemporary writings on the South,
from Pasquale Villari's *Lettere meridionali* (*Letters from the South*, 1875)
to Leopoldo Franchetti's *Condizioni politiche e amministrative della Sicilia*
(*Political and Administrative Conditions in Sicily*, 1876). In these sources, and
in Giovanni Verga's short stories and novels, the South often appears as an
anomaly, or "a perverse realm of social disorder and moral degradation in
which human existence cannot be conceived of according to the standard
measure of European civilizations" (Moe 63).

15 "The emigrant was doubly wrong: objectively, he lowered the pressure
   in Europe, and subjectively, he gave credence to the idea that elsewhere,
   somewhere in the world, there was a more breathable atmosphere.
   He believed in the lie of fresh air. European socialism, on principle,
   condemned the individual escape hatch of emigration because it delayed
   the revolution. More mutedly but more passionately, it detested the air
   duct known as America" (Roger 233).
16 "Quello che ho trovato soprattutto nella vita degli italiani nell'America
   meridionale è lo stesso difetto che io trovo nell'azione dei Governi italiani,
   cioè, la mancanza di un programma pratico di vita transoceanica" (Ferri
   1236; What I have found, above all, in the life of Italians in South America
   is the same defect that I find in the action of Italian governments, that is,
   the lack of a practical program of transoceanic life).
17 "Sino alla metà del secolo decimonono le guerre si facevano o per il
   principio di nazionalità o per la conquista dei confini naturali. Ora la lotta
   internazionale si dibatte per la conquista del mercato" (Ferri 1238; Until
   the mid-nineteenth century, wars were waged either for the principle of
   nationality or for the conquest of natural borders. Now the international
   struggle is for the conquest of the market).
18 "E sarebbe invano che il nostro paese, in tante sue parti, continuasse lo
   slancio notevole e promettente di sviluppo economico, se poi l'aumento
   di produzione non trovasse, oltre gli aumentati consumi all'interno,
   gli sbocchi assicurati nel grande mercato internazionale. Ma l'Italia è
   una grande esportatrice di uomini più che di merci" (Ferri 1239; And it
   would be in vain for our country, in many of its parts, to continue the
   remarkable and promising impetus of economic development, if the
   increase in production did not then find, in addition to increased domestic
   consumption, secure outlets on the great international market. But Italy is
   a bigger exporter of men than of goods).

1. The Emigration Debate and the Spreading of Anti-Americanism in Italy

 1 "By 1861 war expenses and war reparations to the Austro-Hungarian
   Empire amounted to 1,482 million lire. The debt of the new nation was
   2,446 million lire. In the next four years the national debt increased by
   an additional 2,187 million, while total state revenues from 1861 to 1865
   totaled 2,842 million" (Cinel 37).
 2 "The price of wheat declined from 39 lire per quintal in 1874 to 34
   in 1880, to 23 in 1887, to 20 in 1894. The price of corn dropped from
   23 lire in 1873 to 13 in 1894. Competition from Europe affected other
   Italian commodities. Wine dropped from 85 lire per hectoliter in 1880

to 59 in 1890; olive oil from 159 lire per hectoliter in 1884 to 115 in 1891"
(Cinel 40).

3 "The abolition of slavery created an immense demand for work on tropical
plantations, which was filled by free or semi-free migrations that had
already developed in parallel with the slave trade" (Colucci and Gallo 21).

4 "Reversed seasons could guarantee work all year long, and a successful
trip could produce a profit of 350–450 lire, which equalled a farm
labourer's salary at home. In this way, earnings could be doubled,
avoiding a fall into poverty" (Clementi 199).

5 Rubattino, which was a partner of the Genoese steel company Ansaldo,
bought an outpost in Eritrea in 1869 to open its line to the Red Sea. The
port of Massawa, acquired by the Italian state in 1882, was the initial
point of Italy's colonial penetration in Eritrea. Florio, which was based in
Palermo, controlled the Atlantic route.

6 Among them were political exiles, businessmen, artists, beggars, children and
"practitioners of such wandering trades as exhibiting bears, making plaster
figurines, building walls and streets, and cleaning chimneys" (Gabaccia 26).

7 "From 1881 to 1887, yearly exports to France had totaled 444 million lire
and imports 307. In 1888 imports from France declined to 164 million lire
and exports to 165 […] wine exports to France declined from 2.6 million
hectoliters in 1887 to 1.8 million the following year" (Cinel 42).

8 "In 1888 a commercial war with France had begun which had annulled
customs agreements that were in place, triggering retaliative measures
from Italy; following these conflicts Italy lost over 40 per cent of exports
to France for a number of years. The Italian economy risked drastically
impoverishing itself and, what is more, risked suffering a serious increase
in unemployment, which was already high due to the agricultural crisis,
and as a consequence, social conflict grew" (Soresina 724).

9 As a consequence of Argentina's new policy, in 1891 returnees significantly
outnumbered arriving migrants (58,000 versus 16,000). The emigration rate
returned to its previous flow only in 1896 (Devoto 37).

10 "Remittances registered unprecedented yearly increases, especially from
1895 to 1913. The yearly average for the 1891–5 period was 254 million lire.
In the following five years the yearly average climbed to 347 million. In the
1901–5 period, the yearly average was 691 million, and 846 [million] in the
1906–10 period" (Cinel 143).

11 "For the draft, young Italians living abroad had either to return to Italy
for the service or to report to the Italian consul in their jurisdiction. Failure
to do so resulted in a warrant of arrest effective as soon as the delinquent
person set foot on Italian soil. Ignorance of the requirements of the law
and distrust for consular officers prevented many young Italians from

reporting. Their return became impossible, even after many years. Draft evaders were afraid of arrest upon arriving in Italy" (Cinel 151).

12 "It was a question of culture, but also a political and economic question; in Italy the assimilation of emigrants in the United States was viewed with suspicion, linked to the fear of a loss of influence over these communities by the homeland, and also a dwindling of the finances being sent back in that valuable U.S. currency" (Soresina 729).

13 "This misrepresentation of immigrants from Italy drew in part upon the transnational spread of the findings of such Italian positivists as anthropologists Giuseppe Sergi and Luigi Pigorini, criminologists Cesare Lombroso and Enrico Ferri, and sociologist Alfredo Niceforo. Their writings found a prompt echo on the other shore of the Atlantic in xenophobic essays by, among others, Edward Alsworth Ross and Madison Grant. Reflecting national stereotypes in their homeland, these Italian scholars contrasted northern Italians, who allegedly belonged to an Alpine race, with southern Italians, who were supposedly inferior to the former because they were part of a Mediterranean race that presumably shared a significant number of distinctive features with the African race. Since the great bulk of Italian newcomers to the United States had been born in southern Italy, it was almost unavoidable that the characteristics of the people from this specific region were ascribed to all individuals from the nation" (Luconi 127).

14 "Church historians shy away from collective enterprises and are not interested in emigration, not even in relation to the pastoral care of migrants, whereas scholars in migration studies overlook Church history and disdain Vatican sources" (Sanfilippo, "Chiesa, ordini religiosi" 129).

15 This renewed phase of clash between the Italian state and the Catholic Church would find symbolic expression in 1889 in the controversy following the erection of Giordano Bruno's statue in the Roman Campo de' Fiori.

16 "L'emigrazione è un fatto naturale, provvidenziale. È una valvola di sicurezza data da Dio a questa travagliata società […] Impedendola si viola un sacro diritto umano; abbandonandola a sé la si rende inefficace" (Scalabrini, *L'emigrazione italiana* 203–4; Emigration is a natural, providential fact. It is a safety valve given by God to this troubled society […] By preventing it, we violate a sacred human right; by leaving it to its own devices, we make it ineffective).

17 "É così che in meno di un anno, sotto il nome glorioso di Cristoforo Colombo, sorse nella mia diletta Piacenza, primo in Italia, l'Istituto di patronato italiano per gli emigrati italiani. È così che nello scorso luglio dodici missionari, otto sacerdoti e quattro laici, salparono dal porto di Genova e dell'Havre per New York e l'interno del Brasile […] Colà i nuovi

missionari hanno pure carattere di ufficiali di Stato Civile, vantaggio anche questo non lieve per i nostri poveri connazionali, ignari della lingua del paese" (Scalabrini, *Il disegno di legge* 252). (Less than a year ago, under the glorious name of Christopher Columbus, in my beloved Piacenza, there first arose in Italy an institute for the Italian patronage of Italian emigrants. Last July, twelve missionaries (eight priests and four laypeople) left from the ports of Genoa and Le Havre for New York and Brazil […] Once there, the new missionaries even have the character of civil officials – a significant advantage for our poor fellow Italians, who don't speak the local language.)

18 In the "Note Vaticane" rubric in *Corriere della sera* on 4–5 March 1889, the secular journalist Fra Pacomio reports on the visit of Bishop Scalabrini to Rome and commends his work: "è in Roma da qualche giorno monsignore Scalabrini […] l'ottimo vescovo di Piacenza ha veduto il Papa e alcuni cardinali, e ha avuto da tutti lodi e incoraggiamenti per la sua santa opera a pro dell'emigrazione. Il Papa l'ha accolto con particolare affetto, promettendogli di sussidiare più largamente l'istituto Cristoforo Colombo, al quale ha dato, com'è noto, un sussidio di ventimila lire. Anche Propaganda aumenterà l'assegno. L'opera di monsignore Scalabrini è così alta, e ispirata a tanta carità, che dovrebbe trovare favore grandissimo nel laicato ricco e colto di ogni parte d'Italia." (A few days ago, Monsignor Scalabrini arrived in Rome […] The excellent bishop of Piacenza saw the Pope and some cardinals and received praise and encouragement from all for his holy work in favour of emigration. The Pope welcomed him with affection, promising to more generously subsidize the Istituto Cristoforo Colombo, to which, as is known, he has already given 20,000 lire. Propaganda will also increase its contribution. Monsignor Scalabrini's work is so high, and inspired by so much charity that it should find great favour among the wealthy and educated people of every part of Italy.)

19 This view is epitomized in an article published in *Corriere della sera* on 22–23 December 1888 entitled "Le nuove migrazioni dei popoli" ("The New Migrations of Peoples"): "l'emigrazione degl'italiani nell'America meridionale non è dovuta a sterilità del suolo italiano, ma a cause economiche, quali tasse eccessive, scarsezza di capitali, ordinamenti rurali difettosi, specialmente nella bassa Italia, tutte cose a cui si potrà rimediare col tempo." (The emigration of Italians to South America is not caused by the unproductiveness of Italian soil, but rather by economic reasons, such as high taxes, scarcity of capital, and flawed rural organization (especially in Southern Italy), all issues that can be remedied over time.)

20 "The very first voyage of the emigrants is full of perils and hardships, for they fall for the most part into the hands of avaricious *traders*, whose slaves they in a manner are, and thrown together by droves in the narrow

spaces of the ships, with but slight clothing, they are gradually driven into depraved *habits*. When they reach the lands for which they are destined, […] they fall into the hands of the dishonest, and into the snares of those more powerful men to whom they *enslave* themselves" (*Quam aerumnosa*, sec. 1; my italics).

21 "È da qualche tempo che si fa circolare, forse a studio, la voce che l'arcivescovo di Baltimora, cardinale Gibbons, possa essere il futuro Pontefice. La cosa in sé è assurda, ma che la voce vi sia non v'ha dubbio […] un papa americano, forse eletto prima che egli intervenga al Conclave, sarebbe il maggior trionfo dell'ignoto. La verità è che, nelle presenti condizioni politiche di Europa, e con un papa quasi ottantenne, non si possono fare previsioni, ma soltanto ipotesi" (Fra Pacomio, *Corriere della sera*, 15–16 December 1888). (A rumour has been spreading lately, perhaps on purpose, that the Archbishop of Baltimore, Cardinal Gibbons, could become the next pope. The idea in itself is absurd, but there is no doubt of the existence of this rumour […] an American pope, possibly elected prior to his arrival at the Conclave, would be the biggest triumph of the unknown. The truth is that, in the current political conditions of Europe, and with the current pope almost in his eighties, one cannot make any predictions, only hypotheses.)

22 "Upon the explicit request of Emilio Treves, Ferraguti travelled on a ship of migrants from Genoa to Buenos Aires in 1889 to find inspiration for his work. The artist had brought not only canvases and brushes on the trip but also a camera, in order to describe the situations that he would witness in the most accurate way possible" (Giannini and Baratta).

23 Among contemporary novels on emigration, no book except for *Sull'oceano* endured beyond its initial publication. Other contemporary titles include Antonio Marazzi, *Emigrati* (1880–1); Francesco Paolo Matticoli, *Maria: Scene americane* (1881); Giovanni Guidotti, *Ebe: Romanzo politico* (1895); Francesco Saverio Rondina, *L'emigrante italiano* (1891–2); Giorgio S, *I due fratelli ovvero il ritorno dell'emigrato* (1897); Achille Salzano, *Verso l'Ignoto, il romanzo dell'emigrante* (1903); Carolina Invernizio, *I drammi degli emigrati* (1910); and Guglielmo Ferrero, *Fra i due mondi* (1913). For a more complete list and overview of Italian literature on emigration see Emilio Franzina's volume *Dall'arcadia in America*.

24 "Cogli occhi spenti, con le guance cave, / pallidi, in atto addolorato e grave" (lines 1–2; with dead eyes, hollow cheeks, / pale, sorrowful and serious in their actions).

25 The theme of "inganno" reappears in a contemporary poem by Mario Rapisardi, "Emigranti" ("Emigrants," 1883), denouncing the politicians' made-up myth of American wealth as a way to relieve the national state of the burden to feed them.

26 "E la triste processione cominciò. Triste, non solo in sé medesima, ma perché quella numerazione della folla come d'un armento, del quale non importava a nessuno di conoscere i nomi, faceva pensare che tutta quella gente fosse contata per essere venduta, e che non ci passassero davanti cittadini d'uno Stato d'Europa, ma vittime d'una razzia di ladri di carne umana fatta sopra una spiaggia dell'Africa o dell'Asia" (*Sull'oceano* 248). (And the sad procession commenced. Sad, not only in itself, but because, counting that throng like a herd of animals without care for any name, gave the idea that the poor creatures were told off for sale: that we saw not citizens of a European state, but victims of a raid of kidnappers upon the shores of Africa or Asia"; *On Blue Waters*, 371–2.)

27 "Operai, contadini, donne con bambini alla mammella, ragazzetti che avevano ancora attaccata al petto la piastrina di latta dell'asilo infantile passavano, portando quasi tutti una seggiola pieghevole sotto il braccio, sacche e valigie d'ogni forma alla mano o sul capo, bracciate di materasse e di coperte, e il biglietto col numero della cuccetta stretto fra le labbra [...] Di tratto in tratto passavano tra quella miseria signori vestiti di spolverine eleganti, preti, signore con grandi cappelli piumati, che tenevano in mano o un cagnolino, o una cappelliera, o un fascio di romanzi francesi illustrati, dell'antica edizione Lévy" (*Sull'oceano* 5).

28 "Quando misi piede a terra, mi voltai a guardare ancora una volta il Galileo, e il cuore mi batté nel dirgli addio, come se fosse un lembo natante del mio paese che m'avesse portato fin là. Esso non era più che un tratto nero sull'orizzonte del fiume smisurato, ma si vedeva ancora la bandiera, che sventolava sotto il primo raggio del sole d'America, come un ultimo saluto dell'Italia che raccomandasse alla nuova madre i suoi figliuoli raminghi" (*Sull'oceano* 257). (As I put foot on shore, I turned to look at the *Galileo,* and my heart swelled at bidding her adieu, as if she were a little strip of my own country which had sailed across the sea and brought me to that spot. She was but a black dash upon the horizon of that mighty river, yet I could see her flag as it flowed and floated in the early rays of the American sun. It was as if Italy, with a last salute, commended her wandering children to their new adopted mother"; *On Blue Waters* 386–7.)

29 The original reads: "rivarcare quei mari"; "tornare ai villaggi umili e cari" (De Amicis, "Emigranti," lines 91–2).

30 The representation of departure is also related to the projection of the future in the new land (as seen in the caress of a mother to her daughter while waiting on a tier in the 1891 sculpture *Emigranti* by Domenico Ghidoni).

31 A similar representation appears in the unfinished last painting by Giuseppe Pellizza da Volpedo *Famiglia di emigranti* (*Emigrant Family*), depicting the tribulation of seasonal workers from the mountains to the

paddy fields near Vercelli through a similar contrast between the imposing forces of nature and the weak resources of migrants.

32 In Pirandello's short stories dedicated to the theme – "Il vitalizio" ("Retirement Funds," 1901), "Scialle nero" ("Black Scarf," 1904), "Il fumo" ("Smoke," 1904), "L'altro figlio" ("The Other Son," 1905), "Filo d'aria" ("Gust of Air," 1914), "Nell'albergo è morto un tale" ("Someone Died in the Hotel," 1917) – emigration appears as "a great silent shadow emptying houses and street, desertifying landscapes, leaving indelible signs of disease, disgrace, and ruin" (Martelli 441).

33 "– Che cosa faranno in casa sua a quest'ora? Guardai l'orologio e risposi: – A quest'ora la mia casa è al buio, e tutti dormono. Egli si mise a ridere, fregandosi le mani: – Anche vosciâ sciâ gh'è cheito! – disse – (Anche lei c'è cascato.) – A quest'ora in casa sua ci batte il sole, e i suoi ragazzi domandano il caffè e latte" (*Sull'oceano* 244). ("'What do you think your friends at home are about just now?' I looked at my watch and answered: 'At this hour my house is all dark and everyone is asleep.' He began to laugh and rubbed his hands more than ever: 'Ah! My dear sir, have I caught you too! At this hour it is broad day at home and your children are wanting their coffee and their milk'"; *On Blue Waters* 368.)

34 The most important reports of the age are: Carlo Gardini, *Gli Stati Uniti, Ricordi* (1887); Adolfo Rossi, *Un italiano in America* (1891) and *Nel paese dei dollari* (1893); Giuseppe Giacosa, "Gli Italiani a New York ed a Chicago" (1892); Alfonso Lomonaco, *Da Palermo a New Orleans* (1897); and Ugo Ojetti, *L'America vittoriosa* (1899).

35 "Nel 1880, in città [New York] esistono appena 15 associazioni mutualistiche, salite a 25 nel 1885, a 48 nel 1889, a 78 nel 1892, a 145 nel 1896, a oltre 200 nel 1902, a più di 2000 nel 1910 e a un numero stimato vicino a 3000 nel 1915" (Bugiardini 561).

36 The most important Italian newspapers in the United States were *La voce del popolo* (San Francisco, 1859), *Il progresso italo-americano* (New York, 1880), *L'Italia* (Chicago, 1886), and *L'eco d'Italia* (New York, 1894).

37 The United States would pass the Anarchist Act in 1903, after McKinley's killing, stating the inapplicability to foreigners of the first amendment of the American constitution, and the Literacy Act in 1917, denying admission to migrants who were not able to prove their literacy.

38 "The resort to lynching in the struggle to uproot the supposed presence of the Mafia from New Orleans was also exploited to intimidate Italian Americans in order to break their monopoly over the importation of tropical fruits, to snatch the control of the city's French Market from their hands, to curb their inroads into the lucrative fishing and oyster trade, to force them out of longshoremen activities on the harbor's docks, and to hamper their rise in local politics. Italian Americans' economic success

and early stages of involvement in civic affairs had caused envy and fear among numerous native residents. By the time Hennessy was assassinated, the Sicilian immigrants allegedly operated more than three thousand fruit and other food retail outlets in New Orleans" (Luconi 131–2).

39 "U.S. state officials rhetorically and legally constructed Italian lynching victims as American citizens. If Italian lynching victims were U.S. citizens, state officials could avoid making indemnity payments to the Italian government for the wrongful death of Italian subjects. Meanwhile Italian officials, as part of their own state-making endeavor, used these lynching crises and indemnity debates to claim Sicilians as Italians and enfold them within the Italian state" (Barbata Jackson 18).

40 The parallel designation of Archbishop Francesco Satolli as apostolic delegate in Washington, DC, in 1892 also functionally strengthened the Catholic Church's diplomatic relations with the American government, in support of its work for Italian migrants of missionary congregations. At an ecclesial level, the move, justified by the pretext of sending a pope's envoy to the exposition of Chicago, was a way to mediate the tensions with local bishops.

41 In a similar way the diplomatic crisis following the massacre by the hand of French villagers of 150 Italian immigrant workers in Aigues-Mortes in 1893 would give vent to a larger commercial war with France, or as Argentina's 1911 decision to block Italian arrivals after an outbreak of cholera would result in the attempt to create an independent Italian colony in Buenos Aires.

2. From Columbianism to Americanism

1 For information on the Genoa exposition see Mario Bottaro's volume *Genova 1892 e le celebrazioni colombiane.*

2 A month after the regatta, during his visit to the exposition, the French writer Emile Zola confirmed that, under the aegis of Columbus and Italy's leadership, the event represented "un gran passo verso l'era della pacificazione universale" (a great step forward towards universal pacification; *Corriere della sera*, "La visita di Zola a Genova" 29–30 September 1892).

3 "Colombo era costretto a mendicare l'aiuto dei Re di Spagna, per poter portare lontano, al di là dell'Oceano, il pensiero della civiltà cristiana ed il genio investigatore italiano" (*Corriere della sera*, "Domani," 7–8 September 1892; Columbus was forced to beg for the help of the Crown of Spain, to be empowered to take far, across the Ocean, the thought of Christian civilization and the Italian investigatory genius).

4 "De dov'era? Lo vedi com'è er monno? / Quann'era vivo, ch'era un disgraziato, / Se pô di' che gnisuno ci ha badato, / E mò che nun c'è più,

tutti lo vonno" (Pascarella, sonnet 45, lines 1–4; Where was he from? You see how the world is? / When he was alive, he was disgraced / You can say no one even cared about him / and now that he is no more, everyone wants him).

5 The original reads: "la più grande e meravigliosa di quante mai se ne videro nell'ordine delle cose umane" (*Quarto*, sec. 1).

6 The project to canonize Columbus was first launched by Antoine Roselly de Lorgues in 1856 (through the publication of his *Christophe Colomb* [*Christopher Columbus*]) and then made official in 1866 with the opening of his cause of beatification under Pius IX.

7 The Parliament of Religions "was the longest, most ambitious, most visited, most admired of the many congresses; and it evoked the most extensive comments in books, newspapers, and magazines" (Badger 263). The congress, which was founded upon the rule of "no proselytizing, no discrimination, no controversy" (264), acquired further visibility because of the presence of the archbishop of Chicago, Patrick Feehan, and Cardinal Gibbons.

8 "Cody and his managers were inspired to bring their show to the gates of the Columbian Exposition for many of the same reasons that had brought it to Rome, Paris, and London. The series of performances in Roman amphitheaters, on the grounds of the Windsor Castle, and at the foot of Mount Vesuvius had given Cody and his publicists ample occasion to reflect on the course of Western history" (Kasson 98). In the celebration of Columbus, for instance, Cody not only introduced in his "colorful, polyglot, high-energy performance" of the *Wild West* show the episode titled "Pilot of the Ocean, 15th Century – the First Pioneer," but also presented himself in a parallel scene as the "Guide of the Prairie, 19th Century – the Last Pioneer" (Kasson 98).

9 In *La gazzetta letteraria* of 31 March 1900, Enzo Sacchetti confirmed the attribution of Semplice to the Tuscan deputy Edoardo Arbìb, who was "a valiant army officer who founded and directed *La libertà*, and who, until recently, under the pseudonym of Semplice for *Corriere della sera*, along with General Clemente Corte, dealt with military and political topics, with a clarity, a good sense, and a fluid style that charmed people" (un valoroso officiale dell'esercito, che fondò e diresse la *Libertà*, e che, fino a poco tempo fa, sotto il pseudonimo di *Semplice* nel *Corriere della sera*, trattò volontieri, assieme al generale Clemente Corte, argomenti politici e militari, con una chiarezza, un buon senso ed uno stile fluido che innamorava; 6).

10 Arbìb was also a senator (from 1904 to his death in 1906) and the author of four novels and the essay "Cinquant'anni di storia parlamentare del regno

d'Italia" (1898; "Fifty Years of Parliamentary History of the Kingdom of Italy").

11 "Chi può farlo […] se ne venga in America, venga all'Esposizione di Chicago […] ci sarà molto, molto da imparare, e val la pena d'affrontare la fatica e la spesa del viaggio, per tornarsene a casa colla mente più aperta e il cuore più saldo per le battaglie della vita" (Semplice, *Corriere della sera*, 2–3 May 1893; Whoever can afford it […] come to America, come to the Chicago Exposition […] There will be lots to learn, and it is worth the effort and expense of the trip to return home with a more open mind and a more resolute heart for the battles of life).

12 In his *Corriere della sera* piece from Hartford, on 2–3 August 1893, Semplice outlines the gigantic proportions that industrial modernity acquired in America, where for example everybody already uses bicycles – "qui tutti li adoperano e le gare sono frequentissime" (here everyone uses them and there are very frequent races) – or typewriters – "Qui si fanno anche innumerevoli macchine da scrivere, che tutti oramai adoperano" (here they produce innumerable typewriters, and everyone already uses them).

13 "Mi pareva di vedere in quella facilità, e non certo per me solo, d'avvicinare il Capo dello Stato, come un emblema di tutto l'organismo politico di questo paese inimitabile. Quest'uomo, […] sa benissimo che il suo ufficio è soltanto temporaneo, e che fra quattro anni, se non lo rieleggono – cosa difficile – sarà un cittadino come tutti gli altri" ("L'esposizione di Chicago," *Corriere della sera*, 18–19 May 1893). (It seemed to me, and not only to me, that the facility by which I came close to the Head of State was an emblem of all the political organism of this inimitable country. This man […] knows too well that his office is only temporary, and that in four years, if they don't re-elect him – a difficult thing – he will be a citizen like all the others.)

14 "Noi altri italiani manchiamo delle attitudini necessarie a riuscire a determinati scopi con mezzi determinati e precisi. Spendiamo, per alcuni rispetti, tanto quanto spendono altri paesi, ma dovecché essi traggono un frutto dal denaro che impiegano, […] noi dal nostro non ne caviamo quasi nessuno. Sappiamo pur troppo spendere, ma non sappiamo guadagnare" ("Sull'esposizione di Chicago," *Corriere della sera*, 23–24 April 1893). (We Italians lack the necessary attitudes to reach determinate goals with precise and determinate means. We spend, for many respects, as much as the other countries, but if they draw profit from their investments […] we don't obtain much back. We know how to spend, but we don't know how to earn.)

15 "La Mostra di Chicago poteva essere un'eccellente occasione per migliorare le nostre relazioni commerciali, le sole importanti, cogli Stati Uniti e per assicurare al nostro paese una riputazione più degna. Ma

la lasciammo sfuggire, senza trarne il partito che potevamo cavarne. […] Da noi non c'è stato un cane che […] abbia tentato di persuadere i nostri industriali di maggior grido di far sì che l'Italia potesse farsi onore a Chicago in faccia ad una riunione mondiale" ("L'Italia agli Stati Uniti," *Corriere della sera*, 18–19 August 1893). (The Chicago Exposition could have been an excellent occasion to improve our commercial relations – the only important ones – with the United States and to assure our country of a more dignified reputation. But we let it go by without much advantage. […] No one in Italy managed to convince the top industrialists to bring honour to Italy at such an international gathering.)

16 "A bordo, qui, gli emigranti sono 500; in grandissima parte lombardi, della provincia di Como, venti di Vicenza e Verona, e qualche toscano. Per lo più, vanno perché li hanno chiamati quelli che andarono prima di loro e che hanno già una buona posizione […] Partono veramente a famiglie, con le donne anziane e le giovani, coi bambini grandicelli e coi lattanti. Hanno pagate per il viaggio ciascuno 160 lire, e non se ne lagnano. Ognuno ha la sua cuccetta, caffè la mattina, due pasti al giorno, con carne" (*Corriere della sera*, 2–3 April 1893). (Here onboard there are 500 emigrants; mostly Lombard, from the province of Como, about twenty from Vicenza and Verona, and a few Tuscans. For the most part, they leave because those who left before them and already have a good position have invited them […] They leave in family groups, with elderly and young women, with children and infants. Each of them paid 160 lire for the trip, and they don't complain about it. Each one has a bunk, coffee in the morning, and two meals a day, with meat.)

17 "Questi emigranti si divertono un mondo qui sul bastimento. Alle 5 ½ della mattina c'è ballo sul ponte al suono d'un organetto a mano: nelle ore pomeridiane, giuocano per gruppi, alla tombola o fanno comunella insieme fra 10 o 12; mazzi di carte non ne ho visti in giro, ma qualche partita alla morra la fanno. La sera, dal tramonto alle prime ore di notte, cantano in coro le canzoni del villaggio, ch'è un gusto a sentirli, sì bene sono modulate e intonate le voci degli uomini e delle donne" (*Corriere della sera*, 2–3 April 1893). (These emigrants have a lot of fun on the liner. At 5:30 in the morning there is dancing on the deck as a barrel organ plays; in the afternoons, they play bingo or gather in groups of 10 or 12 people; I saw decks of cards, and they play morra as well. At night, starting at sunset, they sing the songs of their villages, and the voices of the men and women are so well in tune that it is a pleasure to hear them.)

18 The original reads: "tutti i piagnistei contro l'emigrazione che si sogliono fare in Italia, specialmente se trattasi di quella che va agli Stati Uniti" (*Corriere della sera*, 23–24, April 1893).

19 The original reads: "Dal momento che a noi non basta l'animo d'assicurare a tante creature umane un'esistenza pacifica e ben nutrita, volerli trattenere in paese sarebbe dar prova di feroce egoismo rispetto a loro e di poco affetto alla patria comune" (*Corriere della sera*, 23–24 April 1893).

20 In his report from Philadelphia, Semplice tells the success story of Italian bricklayers: "Alcuni che sono qui da anni hanno una posizione agiata, e non mancano neppure coloro che sono diventati due e tre volte milionari. […] Non dico che la loro vita sia tutta color di rosa; ma quando penso a quella che conducono i nostri contadini del Mezzogiorno, del Mantovano e di alcuni distretti del Veneto, benedico l'America che li libera in parte dal rimorso di lasciare tante creature umane in balia della più squallida miseria e delle più atroci sofferenze" ("Filadelfia," *Corriere della sera*, 25–26 July 1893). (Some of them who have been here for years have a good position, and there are also those who have become millionaires […] I am not saying that their lives are all fun, but when I think of the life that our peasants live in Southern Italy, near Mantua, or in some districts of Veneto, I bless America, which frees them in part from the regret of leaving so many human creatures at the mercy of the most squalid misery and the most atrocious sufferings.)

21 In his piece for *Corriere della sera* on 2–3 May 1893, Semplice downplays the difficulties of entering the United States – "a New York non ci sono così tante difficoltà come dicono" (There are not as many difficulties in New York as they say) – in relation to customs: "val la pena che si sappia in Italia che, almeno da quanto ho veduto io, per me e per altri, i doganieri non sono punto seccanti. Tutte le storie che si raccontano, di difficoltà incontrate per un vestito nuovo, o per mezza dozzina di paia di guanti, o per le gioie delle signore, non hanno fondamento." (It should be known in Italy that, at least from what I have seen, the customs agents were not at all annoying to me or others. All the stories that people tell, of difficulties related to a new dress, a half dozen pairs of gloves, or ladies' jewels, are unfounded). And in relation to prices: "la vita in America non è più cara di quello che viaggiando possa essere altrove […] una volta qui, si spende come dovunque" (life in America is not more expensive than anywhere else you might travel […] once here, one spends like anywhere else).

22 "Tutto quello che ne fu scritto più volte in Europa, l'Italia compresa, è addirittura una esagerazione. Non è niente affatto vero, per esempio, che qui gli abitanti vadano per le strade correndo come indemoniati, premuti dalla smania di sbrigare le loro faccende a vapore. Camminano tale e quale come noi, ad un passo ordinario e non eccessivamente sollecito" (*Corriere della sera*, 6–7 May 1893). (Everything that was written about America in Europe, Italy included, is an exaggeration. It is not at all true, for example, that here citizens run wildly about the streets, driven by the frenzy to

get their jobs done. They walk just like we do, at an ordinary and not excessively hurried pace.)

23 Fra Pacomio reports Monsignor Scalabrini's visit to Rome in his "Note Vaticane" of 4–5 March 1889 (*Corriere della sera*): "il Papa l'ha accolto con particolare affetto, promettendogli di sussidiare più largamente l'istituto Cristoforo Colombo, al quale ha dato, com'è noto, un sussidio di ventimila lire" (The Pope welcomed him with particular affection, promising to more generously subsidize the Istituto Cristoforo Colombo, to which, as is known, he has already contributed 20,000 lire). Fra Pacomio praises Scalabrini's work as a model for the secular world – "l'opera di monsignore Scalabrini è così alta, e ispirata a tanta carità, che dovrebbe trovare favore grandissimo nel laicato ricco e colto di ogni parte d'Italia" (Monsignor Scalabrini's work is so high, and inspired by so much charity, that it should find great favour among the wealthy and educated people of every part of Italy) – and encourages the reader to follow his noble goals: "disciplinare col vincolo religioso la povera emigrazione nostra; assisterla durante il viaggio; allogarla nei punti dov'è diretta, e mercè provvidi comitati di assistenza in Italia e in America, illuminarla e sorreggerla, ecco un grande scopo cristiano, degno dell'uomo che l'ha ideato: ecco un grande bisogno sociale, al quale si vuol provvedere." (Disciplining our poor emigrants through the bonds of religion; assisting them during the trip; lodging them wherever they are headed, supporting and illuminating them through committees in Italy and America: here is a great Christian goal, worthy of the man who conceived of it; here is a great social need, to which we could contribute.)

24 Fra Pacomio also weighed the financial repercussions of Satolli's appointment and the potential withdrawal of American dioceses from their contribution to the papal fund: "L'America è ricca, ed è la più larga contribuente dell'obolo. [...] Dal 1870 ad oggi la sola diocesi di New York ha dato all'obolo due milioni e mezzo di lire. Nel Giubileo sacerdotale di Leone ne offrì 220,000 [...] Qual differenza tra le diocesi italiane e quella di New York! A Torino si sono appena raccolte 11,000 lire; a Napoli circa 20,000; a Messina 8000; a Venezia 2000, a Sassari 600!" (*Corriere della sera*, 8–9 February 1893). (America is rich and is the largest contributor to the pope's charity [...] From 1870 to today, the diocese of New York alone has given it two and a half million lire. During Leo's priestly jubilee it offered 220,000 [...] What a difference between the Italian dioceses and that of New York! In Turin only 11,000 lire were collected; in Naples about 20,000; in Messina 8,000; in Venice 2,000, in Sassari 600!)

25 "For when America was, as yet, but a newborn babe, uttering in its cradle its first feeble cries, the Church took it to her bosom and motherly embrace. Columbus, as We have elsewhere expressly shown, sought,

as the primary fruit of his voyages and labours, to open a pathway for the Christian faith into new lands and new seas. Keeping this thought constantly in view, his first solicitude, wherever he disembarked, was to plant upon the shore the sacred emblem of the cross" (*Longiqua oceani*, sec. 2).

26 Along the lines of Gibbons's presentation at the Parliament of Religions of Chicago, *Longiqua oceani* includes mention of the need to care for Native and African Americans: "We cannot pass over in silence those whose long-continued unhappy lot implores and demands succour from men of apostolic zeal; We refer to the Indians and the negroes who are to be found within the confines of America, the greatest portion of whom have not yet dispelled the darkness of superstition. How wide a field for cultivation! How great a multitude of human beings to be made partakers of the blessing derived through Jesus Christ!" (sec. 18).

27 Leo XIII calls Catholics "to be not followers but leaders" in the advancement of knowledge and invites them, under papal authority, to "cultivate every refinement of learning and zealously train their minds to the discovery of truth and the investigation, so far as it is possible, of the entire domain of nature" (*Longiqua oceani*, sec. 6).

28 On the occasion of the Chicago fair, Ireland related the discovery of Columbus to American progress: "the exposition of Chicago will show forth the results of the discovery of Columbus [...] What Columbus gave to the world was not only the America of the year 1492 [...] what he gave was America of the year 1892 [...] What Columbus gave was, in a large measure, the marvelous progress of modern times" (137–8).

29 "America treats us well; her flag is our protection. Patriotism is a Catholic value" (Ireland 91).

30 "Una guerra fra questi due paesi presenterà numerosissime novità ed anomalie. Quale sarebbe, innanzi tutto, il teatro di questa guerra? [...] Più delle corazzate saranno in giuoco i corsari. Questa prospettiva esercita sin da questo momento un'azione profondamente perturbatrice sul commercio mondiale. Gli enormi scambi tra l'Europa e l'America, in quanto erano fatti con navi di bandiera spagnuola o nord-americana, hanno già cominciato ad arrestarsi [...] La guerra non è ancora scoppiata e già i primi effetti si fanno sentire. Essi diventeranno ben altrimenti importanti per le sorti del grande mercato internazionale quando le apprensioni siano diventate realtà. Questa ripercussione del conflitto armato sulle vicende dei traffici è forse la più grave conseguenza che possa venire all'Europa dalla guerra" ("Alla vigilia della guerra," *Corriere della sera*, 28–29 March 1898). (A war between these two countries will present numerous novelties and anomalies. Above all, where would such a war be fought? [...] Corsairs will be in play more than battleships. This situation

has already had a perturbing impact on global trade. The enormous
exchanges between Europe and America, since they were made with
Spanish or North American ships, have already begun to halt […] The war
has not yet broken out, and the first effects are already being felt. They
will become far more impactful on the broader international market when
apprehensions will become reality. This repercussion on trade is perhaps
the most serious consequence that Europe can receive from the war.)

31 Despite their sympathy for Spain, Europeans nations did not show "any
inclination to act against the United States without assurance of support
from all the others" (Trask 46).

32 "La Spagna ha una flotta superiore a quella americana, la Spagna ha un
esercito e l'America non ne ha che l'embrione. Ma l'enorme potenzialità
finanziaria degli Stati Uniti e l'ardente patriottismo di quella grande
popolazione di 70 milioni bastano certamente a pareggiare la partita"
(*Corriere della sera*, 28–29 March 1898). (Spain has a fleet that is superior to
the American one; Spain has an army and America has only the embryo
of one. But the enormous financial potential of the United States and the
ardent patriotism of that vast population of 70 million are certainly enough
to tie the game.)

33 In the piece of 9–10 April 1898, "L'attualità all'estero: Spagna e Stati Uniti"
("News from Abroad: Spain and the United States"), *Corriere della sera*
reports the words of an American diplomat about the papal mediation:
"disse che l'intervento del Papa aveva fatto pessima impressione. Non è
il caso di ricordare la superiorità numerica dei protestanti sui cattolici […]
ma bisogna tener presente che agli Stati Uniti è radicato potentemente
il senso della separazione assoluta della Chiesa dallo Stato […] Ora è
evidente che l'intervento del Papa, per quanto ispirato a sensi d'umanità,
è parso ai più un'inframmettenza dovuta alle condizioni politiche
della Spagna e diretta ad affermare un'autorità superiore a quella dello
Stato." (The diplomat said that the Pope's intervention had made a
bad impression. There is no need to recall the numerical superiority of
Protestants over Catholics […] but we must bear in mind that the sense
of the absolute separation of Church and State is powerfully rooted in
the United States […] Now it is evident that the intervention of the Pope,
though inspired by senses of humanity, seemed to many to be an intrusion,
due to the political conditions in Spain and aimed at affirming an authority
superior to that of the State.)

34 "La prima conseguenza della guerra è … l'aumento del prezzo del pane!
Fra tutti gli infiniti e parolai commenti, che i giornali d'ogni parte del
mondo fanno alla dissennata contesa fra i due popoli divisi da tanta
estensione dell'Oceano, quello che meno emerge è il più inavvertito, ma
il più pratico, il più grave, il più doloroso: bisogna andarlo a cercare nei

prezzi correnti del mercato, nelle "mercuriali"!" ("La prima conseguenza della guerra," *Corriere della sera*, 6–7 May 1898). (The first consequence of the war is … the increase in the price of bread! Of all the endless and verbose comments that newspapers from all over the world make about the senseless dispute between the two peoples divided by the ocean, the one that emerges the least is the most inadvertent, but the most practical, the most serious, the most painful: it must be sought in the current market prices!)

35 Against this backdrop, the American press immediately indicted Italian anarchists as suspects in the killing of President McKinley in Buffalo the year afterwards. *Corriere della sera* expressed relief at the news that the killer of McKinley was not an Italian anarchist as initially conjectured: "McKinley è colpito […] Per fortuna questa volta, l'assassino non è italiano, ma d'italiani sempre è costituito il maggior contingente anarchico" ("Nota sul delitto anarchico," *Corriere della sera*, 8–9 September 1901; McKinley is hit […] Fortunately, the assassin is not Italian this time, but the largest anarchist contingent is still made up of Italians).

36 Considering a new colonial administration, the American government "developed a new respect for Catholic opinion that had never before existed" (Reuter xi), minimizing the anti-Catholic prejudice and seeking help for the organization of new, formerly Catholic colonies.

37 "Son troppo recenti in Italia le lotte per la libertà, perché non vi si comprenda tutta la ignominia di quello che per decine d'anni è avvenuto in Cuba […] Noi non desideriamo ché la pace […] è dovere di ogni cristiano pensare e sentire così. […] Ma desiderar la pace non è far la pace, e non siamo noi due e tre volte vincitori che dobbiamo chiederla" (*Corriere della sera*, 29–30 July 1898). (The struggles for freedom in Italy are too recent for us not to understand all the ignominy of what went on in Cuba for decades […] All we want is peace […] it is the duty of every Christian to think and feel this way […] But to desire peace is not to make peace, and it is up to us, two- and three-time victors, to ask for it.)

38 "Le ostilità son dunque durate oltre tre mesi e mezzo, o più precisamente 114 giorni […] La sterminata ampiezza dei due teatri strategici senza rapporto tra loro e abbraccianti due continenti, due oceani, quasi due mondi, le enormi distanze cosi marittime che terrestri, le difficoltà delle comunicazioni anche telegrafiche, la dispersione delle forze navali e militari, tutto faceva prevedere un conflitto lunghissimo ed asperrimo, il quale non sarebbe finito che per reciproca stanchezza, senza parlare delle possibili complicanze diplomatiche, a cui la sospensione del traffico in tanta parte di mondo poteva offrire argomento e pretesto. Ma, d'altra parte, la sproporzione delle forze nautiche e più ancora delle economiche non permetteva alcun dubbio sull'esito e sulla durata della impari lotta"

(Ojetti, *Corriere della sera*, 18–19 August 1898). (Hostilities therefore lasted more than three and a half months, or more precisely, 114 days […] The immense dimensions of the two strategic theatres, which are not connected to each other and include two continents, two oceans, almost two worlds, the enormous distances, both on sea and on land, the difficulties of communication, including by telegraph, the dispersion of naval and military forces, all predicted a very long and bitter conflict, which would only end due to mutual fatigue, not to mention the possible diplomatic complications, to which the suspension of traffic in so much of the world could offer an argument and a pretext. But, on the other hand, the disproportion of the nautical forces, and even more of the economic forces, left no doubts regarding the outcome and the duration of the unequal struggle.)

39 "Ormai siamo tutti d'accordo: l'America è una scuola d'energia, l'Italia è il museo d'Europa" (Ojetti, "Giudizi e pregiudizi sull'America," *Corriere della sera*, 28 June 1904; By now we are all in agreement: America is a school of energy, Italy is the museum of Europe).

40 "Pel novantanove per cento dei cittadini dell'Unione, tutta l'Europa è pronta a seguire le sorti della Spagna nel '98. L'old world, il vecchio mondo, si regge sulle grucce della storia finché lo zio Sam non voglia dargli una spallata" (Ojetti, "La grande America e il piccolo mondo," *Corriere della sera*, 3 October 1904). (For 99 per cent of the citizens of the Union, all of Europe is ready to follow the same fate as Spain in 1898. The Old World stands on the crutches of history until Uncle Sam wants to give it a shove.)

41 "The church in the United States prior to 1898 was not a monolithic organization, nor was it about to become one. But by 1904 it was more conscious of itself as a national organization than it had ever been before" (Reuter xi).

42 "Che diverrebbe il papato, se trasportasse la Sede da Roma a Baltimora? Materia da combinazioni industriali e finanziarie di ogni specie. Vedremmo il Papa alto patrono di Società industriali, presidente di miniere e di ferrovie, promotore di imprese folli destinate a clamorosa rovina. *Rèclame* su tutta la linea! L'idealità svanirebbe, e il papato morrebbe, perduta l'intima sorgente della vita sua; ovvero, in omaggio alla legge di adattabilità, assumerebbe forma nuova, e che forma!" (*Corriere della sera*, 28–29 July 1892). (What would become of the papacy if the Holy See were transported from Rome to Baltimore? This is a matter of all kinds of industrial and financial machinations! We would see the Pope as the patron of industrial companies, the president of mines and railways, the promoter of mad undertakings destined for clamorous ruin. Advertising across the board! Ideality would vanish, and the papacy would die, the

intimate source of its life lost; or, in homage to the law of adaptability, it would assume a new form, and what a form!)

43 Similarly to Hecker, who worked in the ecumenical dialogue between Catholics and Protestants, Klein (who was also the translator of Ireland's speeches) saw Ireland as a new modern priest, trying to harmonize church and the modern age.

44 The book would have a profound impact on the liberal Catholicism of Tommaso Gallarati Scotti, who later founded in 1907 the journal *Il rinnovamento*, which advocated for a renewal of the Catholic Church and was condemned as modernist by the Holy See.

45 "Leggevamo nei giorni scorsi i discorsi di un prelato Americano, monsignor Ireland, arcivescovo di Saint Paul negli Stati Uniti, che una colta signora, la contessa Sabina di Parravicino di Revel, ha tradotti e pubblicati allo scopo che il clero italiano potesse trarne partito per il bene morale e sociale" (*Corriere della sera*, 22–23 May 1898; In recent days we were reading the speeches of an American prelate, Monsignor Ireland, archbishop of Saint Paul in the United States, which an educated lady, the Countess Sabina di Parravicino di Revel, translated and published, so that the Italian clergy could take advantage of them for the moral and social good).

46 "Due diversi indirizzi per cui l'azione cattolica si è messa: da una parte la libera, ansiosa sete di bene, il rinato bisogno dell'apostolato morale, che si afferma colla rampogna non intinta nel veleno dell'odio o dell'interesse; dall'altra la preoccupazione politica e la formula chiosastica che inaridisce la spiritualità religiosa" (*Corriere della sera*, 22–23 May 1898; Two different directions for Catholic action to take: on the one hand, the free, anxious thirst for the good, the renewed need for the moral apostolate, which is affirmed with reproaches not dipped in the poison of hatred or self-interest; on the other, the political concern and the formulaic glossaries that wither religious spirituality).

47 On 1 March 1889 the Florentine journal *Rassegna nazionale* published the anonymous article "Roma e l'Italia e la realtà delle cose. Pensieri di un prelato italiano" ("Rome and Italy, and the Reality of Things: Reflections of an Italian Prelate"), which argued that the non-participation of Catholics in the Italian political life (*non expedit*) was materially and spiritually damaging the Church. After Leo XIII accused the writer of arrogance and insubordination, Bonomelli admitted on 21 April 1889 to being the author of the essay and affirmed his obedience to the pope in his own cathedral of Cremona.

48 "Between 1890 and the first decades of the twentieth century, the press played a central role in confirming and spreading a predominantly negative image of Italian immigration, in consolidating an idea of Italians

as belonging to an inferior race, and in legitimizing concerns about
the concrete possibility of making them assimilable to American social
behaviours and values" (Garroni 105).

49 "While flatly denying the presence of heretical or schismatic elements in
the context of Catholicism in the United States, American liberal Catholics
[...] in fact returned to positions of deference to ecclesiastical authority,
settling on an attitude of prudence and reserve, which was clearly
detectable in the temporal and Roman 'conversion' of the most important
and significant exponent of the American trend, Msgr John Ireland"
(Confessore 8).

50 *Corriere della sera* reads the letter through an Italian lens, by comparing
Americanism to Rosminianism (the philosophy of Rosmini) and indicating
with a certain degree of irony that "come nel rosminianismo si trova più
male che in Rosmini, così nell'americanismo come istituzione o religione,
trovasi più da riprovare che negli atti del padre Hecker" ("L'Italia e il
Papa nei contatti internazionali," *Corriere della sera*, 22–23 February 1899;
as in Rosminianism there is more evil than in Rosmini, in the same way, in
Americanism as an institution or religion there is more to reproach than in
the acts of Father Hecker).

51 "Il Papa non consentì però a mettere all'indice il libro non trovandosi
gli estremi rigorosi e l'opportunità del provvedimento, anche perché la
traduzione non rispecchiava molto fedelmente il testo americano e i precisi
intenti della propaganda di Hecker. Bensì Leone XIII si indusse a scrivere
la lettera che confuta e combatte l'americanismo in ciò che non si ritiene
conforme alla dottrina della Santa Sede e specialmente all'autorità del
Papa" (*Corriere della sera*, 22–23 February 1899). (However, the Pope did
not agree to index the book, as he did not find reasons and appropriateness
for the decision, also because the translation did not reflect very faithfully
the American text and the precise intentions of Hecker's propaganda.
Rather, Leo XIII was induced to write the letter refuting and rejecting in
Americanism what is not considered to be in conformity with the doctrine
of the Holy See, and especially with the authority of the Pope.)

52 "It gives Us pleasure at the same time to express our commendation of
the Institute of the Paulist Fathers. They have wisely adopted the plan
of addressing our dissenting brethren openly, both to explain Catholic
teachings and to refute objections brought against them. If each of the
bishops would promote in his diocese the practice of these Fathers and the
frequent attendance at sermons, it will be most gratifying and acceptable
to Us, for we trust that it will result in no little profit toward the salvation
of souls" (Leo XIII, Apostolic dispatch to Satolli, 18 September 1895).

53 With the death of Leo XIII in 1903, and the election of Pius X (after
the Austrian emperor had rejected Rampolla, who was elected by the

conclave), the Church became more open politically, with the inclusion of Catholics in Italian politics after the Gentiloni Pacts of 1913, yet more intransigent doctrinally, after the condemnation of modernism and the establishment of the anti-modernist oath.

3. Americanizing Italy

1 Edison's electrical plant opened in Milan's Via Santa Radegonda in 1883, a few months after the establishment of the world's first plant in New York's Pearl Street and a few months before the building of the first German plant in Berlin's Friedrich Strasse in 1884.

2 Starting in the 1890s, the need for electricity stimulated the exploration of other sources, as seen in the later construction of the hydroelectric plants of Paderno sull'Adda (1898) and Vizzola sul Ticino (1901). As Toninelli points out, "between 1898 and 1911, the overall contribution of electricity, both of thermal and water origin, to the total power installed in industrial plants grew impressively, rising from 17.5 to 47.7 per cent" (369).

3 Morgan's impact extended to the First World War, when his firm purchased "$3 billion worth of supplies […] representing nearly half of all the American supplies sold to the European Allies" ("History of JP Morgan Chase").

4 Theodore Roosevelt was "welcomed to Europe as a world hero" and "the most famous American of his era." His unprecedented 1910 reception, as he toured European capitals and visited heads of state, signals an attitude shift towards the United States and "a more mature and balanced recognition of the meaning of America's progress" (Ellwood 56–7).

5 "Il Taylor esprime con cinismo brutale il fine della società americana: sviluppare nel lavoratore al massimo grado gli atteggiamenti macchinali ed automatici, spezzare il vecchio nesso psico-fisico del lavoro professionale qualificato che domandava una certa partecipazione attiva dell'intelligenza, della fantasia, dell'iniziativa del lavoratore e ridurre le operazioni produttive al solo aspetto fisico macchinale" (Gramsci, *Americanismo e fordismo* 42–3). (Taylor expresses the purpose of American society with brutal cynicism: to develop the worker's mechanical and automatic attitudes to the maximum degree, to break the old psycho-physical link of skilled professional work, which demanded a certain active participation of the intelligence, of the imagination, and of the initiative of the worker, and to reduce productive operations solely to the physical aspect.)

6 "The relationship between the European industrial world and that of the U.S. was defined, above all, in terms of difference: a difference that was not always clearly perceived, and which too often had to resort to a

generic adjective ('American' method, 'American' machines, 'American' type, 'American' salary) to indicate something that escaped the usual parameters of reference. The trips and missions to the United States served precisely to overcome indeterminacies and misunderstandings. The most immediate perception of the observers was the widespread passion for mechanics, accompanied by an ingenuity that led to the effective replacement of human labour with machines and automatic devices" (Bigazzi 911).

7 "La cosa che mi fece più impressione fu il grande uso delle macchine agricole [...] L'America fu la nuova patria dell'industria agricola" (Mosso 7; The thing that impressed me the most was how much they used agricultural machinery [...] America was the new land of the agricultural industry). In addition to mechanization, Mosso identifies the difference between Italian and American agriculture in the fact that American farmers often own their lands.

8 "Uno dei fatti più utili a conoscersi nella storia moderna è la separazione della Chiesa dallo Stato. Tale progresso lo dobbiamo agli Stati Uniti dell'America" (Mosso 118; One of the most useful facts to know in modern history is the separation of Church and State. We owe this progress to the United States of America).

9 "Per l'americano tipico il lavoro è lo scopo della vita individuale e sociale, è la stessa felicità, per noi invece è un mezzo verso il riposo" (Ojetti *L'America e l'avvenire*, 18; For the typical American, work is the goal of individual and social life, it is happiness itself; for us, instead, work is a means towards rest).

10 Ojetti uses as an example Monsignor Ireland's diplomatic glitch on the occasion of the US ultimatum to Spain before the war of 1898: "guardate la storia anzi la cronaca della guerra con la Spagna. Tra il 15 febbraio 1898 quando esplose il Maine, e il 5 aprile, quando il console generale Lee fu richiamato dall'Habana, corre più di un mese e mezzo di domande e di risposte dai vari Stati alla Presidenza e viceversa. Tra l'ultimatum mandato alla Spagna il 19 aprile e la chiamata dei primi centoventicinquemila volontari corre una settimana. La sera avanti all'invio dell'ultimatum, Monsignor John Ireland esciva a tardissima ora dalla Casa Bianca portando con sé la promessa sincera che la guerra non sarebbe stata dichiarata: la mattina dopo, l'ultimatum era telegrafato a Mr. Woodford in Madrid, solo perché i telegrammi ricevuti nella notte dal West e dal Middlewest avevan costretto il presidente Mac Kinley a mutar parere" (Ojetti, *L'America e l'avvenire*, 10–11). (Look at the history, or rather, the narrative of the war with Spain. Between 15 February 1898, when the USS *Maine* exploded, and 5 April, when Consul General Lee was recalled from Havana, there was more than a month and a half of questions and answers

from the various States to the Presidency and vice versa. A week elapsed between the ultimatum sent to Spain on 19 April and the call for the first 125,000 volunteers. The evening before the ultimatum was sent, Monsignor John Ireland left the White House at a very late hour, bringing with him the sincere promise that war would not be declared: the next morning, the ultimatum was telegraphed to Mr Woodford in Madrid, only because the telegrams received overnight from the West and the Midwest had forced President McKinley to change his mind.)

11 "Noi abbiamo il torto di giudicar l'opinione pubblica americana coi criteri con cui giudichiamo l'opinione pubblica degli Stati Europei" (Ojetti, *L'America e l'avvenire*, 9; We wrongly judge American public opinion with the criteria with which we judge the public opinion of the European countries).

12 The Saint Louis World's Fair, which coincided with the Olympics, was not well attended because of the tensions surrounding the contemporary war between Russia and Japan. On 12 and 13 August 1904 the organizers of the Olympic Games held the so-called Anthropology Days, which featured a live "exhibit" and mock competition of natives and Indigenous Peoples (from Southeast Asia, the Pacific Islands, East Asia, Africa, the Middle East, South America, and North America).

13 The original quotes read: "gli Americani non hanno il senso dell'eterno che noi Mediterranei abbiamo" (Ojetti, *L'America e l'avvenire*, 25); "la febbre dell'imperialismo americano sbollirà lentamente davanti alla realtà" (36).

14 *Mauretania*'s twin ship was the liner *Lusitania*, launched in 1906 and sunk in 1915 by the Germans. *Mauretania* was preceded in fame by the RMS *Majestic*, a luxurious ocean crosser built in 1890 by the White Star Line and followed by the *Titanic*, which tragically sunk in 1912.

15 The Baedeker guide for Italy was divided into three parts: *Northern Italy and Corsica* (part 1), *Central Italy and Rome* (part 2), and *Southern Italy, Sicily, and the Excursions to the Lipari Islands, Tunis, Sardinia, Malta, and Athens* (part 3). The guide was published as a three-volume set in fourteen editions (in 1867, 1869, 1872, 1873, 1875, and 1876 in Coblenz; 1880, 1883, 1886, 1890, 1893, 1896, 1900, and 1903 in Leipzig), indicating a consistent flow of travellers to the peninsula. Starting in 1904, the guide was published in three independent volumes: *Italy, From the Alps to Naples* (Leipzig, 1904; reprint in 1909); *Southern Italy and Sicily, with Excursions to Malta, Sardinia, Tunis and Corfu* (Leipzig, 1908); and *Central Italy and Rome* (Leipzig, 1909).

16 Futurism "completely shuttered the old enchantment Italy had cast over susceptible young American artists [...] Some of the early adherents to Futurism abandoned Marinetti precisely because they felt he was trying to Americanize Italy. Under such circumstances there was little to be gained

to be forsaking New York for Rome. Another aspect of Futurism that made Italy less and less interesting for foreign artists was its outspoken xenophobia. Marinetti's aggressive exaltation of Italian supremacy in all fields of human endeavor […] made the atmosphere increasingly inhospitable" (Licht 132).

17 "American tastes and sensibilities tended to be anti-sculptural for religious and political reasons. The Puritan strain, ever-strong in America, regarded any graven image with suspicion but held sculpture to be the very essence of all that was suspect in art. Politically, it was difficult to reconcile monumental sculpture with the democratic ideal of equality" (Licht 134).

18 Berenson's five masterpieces are: *Venetian Painters of the Renaissance* (1894); *Lorenzo Lotto* (1895); *The Florentine Painters of the Renaissance* (1896); *Central Italian Painters of the Renaissance* (1897); and *The Drawings of the Florentine Painters* (1903).

19 The original reads: "un largo campo di osservazioni e di opportuni raffronti […] un ramo della fotografia, coltivato da pochi anni soltanto ed ispirato logicamente dall'Arte Moderna" (*Esposizione internazionale* 9).

20 "In Bologna, the Wild West played for eight days, made a huge profit, and left the Bolognese with stirring impressions of the American West and vivid memories of congested streets and oversold arenas. In Bologna and elsewhere, Wild West concessionaires introduced audiences to popcorn, giving them a lasting taste of American mass culture" (Rydell and Kroes 110).

21 In his 1906 tour Buffalo Bill performed in the following Italian cities (in alphabetic order): Alessandria (21 April); Ancona (10 April); Arezzo (31 March); Asti (27 April); Bergamo (7 May); Bologna (8 April); Brescia (8 May); Como (29 April); Cremona (18 April); Ferrara (13 April); Firenze (1–3 April); Forlì (9 April); Genoa (14–16 March); Livorno (18–20 March); Mantua (17 April); Milan (30 April–5 May); Modena (6–7 April); Novara (28 April); Padua (14 April); Parma (5 April); Pavia (20 April); Perugia (30 March); Piacenza (19 April); Pisa (4 April); Ravenna (12 April); Rimini (11 April); Rome (22–28 March); Spezia (17 March); Terni (29 March); Treviso (10 May); Trieste (12 May); Turin (22–26 April); Udine (11 May); Verona (15–16 April); and Vicenza (9 May) (Buffalo Bill Museum).

22 The five acts of the show (retitled *The Drama of Civilization*) were: "The Primeval Forest," "The Prairie," "The Cattle Ranch," "The Mining Camp," and "The Battle of Little Big Horn."

23 In the United States Cody introduced the bandit's queen Annie Oakley to mirror the debate on feminine emancipation; Sitting Bull in 1885, as a way to enact the reconciliation with Native American tribes; and Christopher Columbus, in the 1893 performance at the Columbian exposition of Chicago, as a way to present the origins of the American pioneering spirit.

In Europe Cody reconfigured the show as a universal story of all nations, introducing a reconciliation scene between the United States and England in the 1887 show of London, "The Marseillaise" in the 1889 show at the universal exposition of Paris (Griffin xx), or, in the early 1900s, mentions of the Boxer Rebellion in China or the Anglo-Boer War in South Africa.

24 At the time, Italian intellectuals lively debated different approaches to human flight. In the piece "Alla conquista dell'aria: Dirigibile o aeroplano?" ("The Conquest of the Air: Dirigible or Airplane?," *Corriere della sera*, 16 June 1908), Italian deputy Odorico pondered the lighter-than-air and heavier-than-air options. Two days later, in the short story "Quando gli uomini voleranno" ("When Men Will Fly," *Corriere della sera*, 18 June 1908), Ojetti gave form to the fascination with flying experiments. For more documentation on this early phase of flight in Italy see Caprara's volume *L'avventura della scienza* (2009).

25 The original reads: "la semplicità e la modestia di quest'uomo che ha realizzato il più antico e audace sogno dell'umanità […] Sono i missionari dell'aviazione. Hanno scoperto una verità meravigliosa e vogliono convertire l'umanità a questa loro religione alla quale hanno dato tutta l'anima, tutta la vita, tutta la fortuna" (Barzini).

26 The first attempted engine-operated flights in Italy date back to 1905 (Mancuso 23). In 1908 the French pilot Leon Delagrange also experimented on short flights in Milan, Rome, and Turin with his airplane *Voisin*.

27 In 1907, Bell had invited the motorcyclist Curtiss, known as one of the greatest American experts in motor construction, to join the Aerial Experiment Association (AEA) aimed at developing engines for flight.

28 The first airship was built in 1899, the first Italian aeronautic society (Società Aeronautica Italiana) was founded in 1904, and the first-ever pavilion dedicated to aviation was set in Milan at the exposition of 1906.

29 See Bohn for more information on the Futurist poetics of flight.

4. Italian Americanism

1 See Costantini's *La fotografia artistica* for a detailed account of the journal's development and content.

2 "This literature was the true antecedent of the popular cinema and mass television. Most of this made-in-the-USA fiction was not exported, but the foundation stones of a formidable cultural industry were being laid" (Sassoon 482).

3 The foundation of the *Journal of Phono-Cinematography & Related Issues* would be followed in the fall of 1907 by Fabbri and Tonini's establishment of the Italian cinematographic association Unione dei Cinematografisti e Affini (Union of Cinematographers and Related Associates).

4 In a dialogue with himself, the protagonist rules out all the available
   options for his free time: "Ove andare? […] A teatro? […] Solite cose"
   (Fabbri 11; Where to go? […] To the theatre? […] Usual things). "Al club
   allora?" "Dunque a casa X?" "Al caffé?" "Dall'Ersilia?" "A letto dunque?"
   (11–14; To the club then? So, to X house? To the coffee shop? To Ersilia's?
   To bed, then?). As he sees the "living stream" (fiumana vivente; 14) of
   people moving towards the cinema, he ponders the possibility of entering –
   "Ah! Un cinematografo!… E se entrassi?… ma a che prò?" (15, Ah! A
   movie theatre!… And if I went in?… But for what) – but continues to view
   the cinema with suspicion as "roba da ragazzi, niente altro […] Roba da
   ragazzi e da vecchi rimbambiti […] roba da popolino ancora!" (12; kid
   stuff, nothing more […] Kids and old fools […] stuff for the populace!).
5 De Amicis echoes the psychoanalytical theories that Freud established in
   his published works during the same years: *Studies on Hysteria* (1895), *The
   Interpretation of Dreams* (1900), *Psychopathology of Everyday Life* (1901), *Three
   Essays on Sexuality* (1905), *Jokes and Their Relation to the Unconscious* (1905),
   The Case of Dora (1905), and *Jensen's Gradiva* (1907).
6 De Amicis points out the protagonist's sense of guilt for such "orgy of
   the spirit, luckily the only one, which made him a little ashamed" (orgia
   dello spirito, fortunatamente unica, di cui un poco si vergognava; "Il
   cinematografo cerebrale" 15).
7 For more information about the relationship between Belasco's *Girl of the
   Golden West* and Puccini's opera, see Randall and Davis's volume *Puccini
   and the Girl*.
8 "In 1913, the year in which statistics record the peak of the transoceanic
   flow, there [were] 209,835 departures from Naples, 138,166 from Genoa,
   62,745 from Palermo, and 6,367 from Messina" (Molinari 247).
9 "Returnees were determined not to fall prey to moneylenders. But the
   great and ultimate goal was the purchase of land […] in the mind of
   returnees, it spelled financial security and social status" (Cinel 150).
10 Two contemporary examples of this kind of narration, focused on
   those who remain, are offered by the Sicilian short stories "La Mérica"
   ("America") by Maria Messina and "L'altro figlio" ("The Other Son") by
   Luigi Pirandello.
11 "Che vuoi che ci sia? Occorre di essere stati là per saperlo; e costoro che
   fanno i libri non hanno visto l'America neppure in sogno. Io, se potessi
   portarmi dietro tutto Ràbbato, uomini, donne, ragazzi… Bisogna vedere
   coi propri occhi per persuadersi che là è davvero un altro mondo"
   (Capuana, *Gli "Americani"* 55). (What do you want there to be? You have to
   have been there to know it; and those who make the books have not seen
   America even in dreams. Me, if I could take all Ràbbato with me, men,

women, children… You have to see it with your own eyes to be persuaded that it really is another world there.)

12 "In un anno e mezzo di vita nel fervido affaccendamento di New York quel ragazzo sembrava diventato uomo maturo" (Capuana, *Gli "Americani"* 346; In a year and a half of life in the fervent bustle of New York, that boy seemed to have grown into a mature man).

13 "Remittances registered unprecedented yearly increases, especially from 1895 to 1913. The yearly average for the 1891–5 period was 254 million lire. In the following five years the yearly average climbed to 347 million. In the 1901–5 period, the yearly average was 691 million, and 846 in the 1906–10 period" (Cinel 143).

14 On the occasion of the journal's centenary of foundation, the Florentine publisher Vallecchi released a five-volume reprint of the entire collection, entitled *La nascita della modernità* and edited by Giorgio Luti.

15 Despite the accusation that the *Leonardo* intellectuals had a simplistic understanding of American pragmatist thought, Maddalena and Tuzet identify in them "one point that unites the apparently distant philosophies of Peirce and James: Anti-Cartesianism, the rejection of rationalism as much as empiricism, seen as an impoverishment of the richness of experience" (8).

16 "Presso di noi il pragmatismo si divise quasi nettamente in due sezioni: quella che si potrebbe dire del pragmatismo logico e quella del pragmatismo psicologico o magico. Alla prima appartenevano Vailati e Calderoni ai quali moltissimo deve – per quanto i loro scritti siano letti da pochi e da pochissimi intesi – la teoria della scienza e la logica considerata come studio del significato delle proposizioni e delle teorie. La seconda era composta da me e da Prezzolini e noialtri, spiriti più avventurosi, più paradossali e più mistici, svolgemmo soprattutto quelle teorie che ci facevano sperare un'efficacia diretta sul nostro spirito e sulle cose" (Papini, *Sul pragmatismo* 7). (Here, pragmatism was divided almost neatly into two sections: that which could be called logical pragmatism and that of psychological or magical pragmatism. To the first belonged Vailati and Calderoni, to whom it owes a great deal – although their writings are read by few and understood by very few – the theory of science and logic considered as a study of the meaning of propositions and theories. The second was made up of myself and Prezzolini, and we, the more adventurous, more paradoxical, and more mystical spirits, developed above all those theories that gave us hope of a direct effect on our spirit and on things.)

17 Over the same years, another key source of book lists in German, English, and French came from the bibliographies that were regularly published

on *La Rassegna settimanale*, a journal inspired by *The Saturday Review* (see Beria).

18 The proceedings of the conference, edited by the Italian physician, psychologist, and psychiatrist Sante De Sanctis, were published in 1905 under the title *Atti del v Congresso internazionale di psicologia tenuto in Roma dal 26 al 30 aprile 1905*.

19 Papini would also later translate William James's lecture "The Energies of Men" ("Le energie degli uomini") for *Leonardo*'s February 1907 issue.

20 "What I really want to write about is Papini, the concluding chapter of his 'Crepuscolo dei Filosofi,' and the February number of the 'Leonardo.' […] Papini is a jewel! To think of that little Dago putting himself ahead of every one of us (even of you, with his *Uomo-Dio*) at a single stride. And what a writer! and what fecundity! and what courage (careless of nicknames, for it is so easy to call him now the Cyrano de Bergerac of Philosophy)! and what humor and what truth!" (W. James, 7 April 1906, *Letters* 245–6).

21 James opens the essay with the following statement: "American students have so long had the habit of turning to Germany for their philosophic inspiration, that they are only beginning to recognize the splendid psychological and philosophical activity with which France today is animated; and as for poor little Italy, few of them think it necessary even to learn to read her language. Meanwhile Italy is engaged in the throes of an intellectual *rinascimento* quite as vigorous as her political one" (W. James, "G. Papini" 337).

22 "In this Florentine band of Leonardists, we find, instead of heaviness, length and obscurity, lightness, clearness and brevity, with no lack of profundity or learning (quite the reverse, indeed), and a frolicsomeness and impertinence that wear the charm of youth and freedom. Signor Papini in particular has a real genius for cutting and untechnical phraseology. He can write descriptive literature, polychromatic with adjectives, like a decadent, and clear up a subject by drawing cold distinctions, like a scholastic" (W. James, "G. Papini" 338).

23 In the same issue, two other articles dealt with occultism, spiritism, and American New Thought: Arturo Reghini's essay "Il punto di vista dell'occultismo" ("The Point of View of Occultism") and Roberto Grego Assagioli's essay "Il nuovo pensiero Americano: Il 'New Thought'" ("The New American Thought: On 'New Thought'").

24 Despite its alleged "poor translation" (mala traducción; Borges, prologue 6), the Spanish version of the collections, *Lo trágico cotidiano y el piloto ciego* (1908) would provide the Argentinian writer Jorge Luis Borges with the later inspiration for his short story "Veinticinco de agosto 1983" ("25 August 1983"). Jorge Luis Borges's comment on the bad translations of Papini in the preface to the Spanish edition of *Espejo que huye* sheds light

on the contemporary fame of Papini and the global diffusion of his literary works.

25 "James values Whitman for this ability to overstep logical categories and create mergers where there were once separations. By such unifying aesthetic action – which is revealed in his poetry, prose, notebooks, and orations – Whitman can 'change the usual standards of human value' through a generosity of feeling that facilitates communication between not only people but elements of American culture as well" (Allison 19).

26 McCain indicates that the first Italian reviewer of Walt Whitman was Enrico Nencioni, who wrote in December 1879 a "formal presentation" on the American poet on the first page of the Roman paper *Il Fanfulla della Domenica*, "the first to appear in an Italian paper of any note" (McCain 5). The real fame of Whitman, however, was triggered by Papini's 1908 piece. See Camboni for more information about Papini and Whitman.

27 In the article "The Longest Day: Dino Campana and Walt Whitman; Across Italy and South America" (2005), Bernardini examines Campana as "the Italian poet most influenced by Walt Whitman" and the *Canti orfici* as "Campana's creative response to Whitman's idea of America as the source of an extra-European newness, freedom, and regeneration" (4).

28 X-rays particularly captured the attention of contemporary Italian writers, who often overlapped scientific and supernatural discourses on the phenomenon's implications. In his 1896 essay "Mondo occulto" ("Occult World") Capuana presented X-rays as a microscope of the "so-called beyond" (cosí detto *di là*; 194). In the article "Rinunzia" ("Renunciation") published in *La critica* on 8 February 1896, Pirandello saw the discovery in Leopardian terms, arguing that scientific knowledge imposed an act of "renunciation" to the mystery of life. Years later, in his 1907 poem "Alle soglie" ("At the Thresholds"), Guido Gozzano observed X-rays as "cold rays" (gelidi raggi; line 16) penetrating the warmth of his chest or a "fluid" (un fluido; line 17) that "painlessly draws bones and sick organs upon a background of ashes" (senza dolore disegna su sfondo di brace / e l'ossa e gli organi grami; lines 18–19). For more information on Italian literary representations of X-rays at the turn of the twentieth century, see Sorbello 547–61.

29 As soon as Franco knows about Luisa's contact with Maria, he writes from prison about people in the seance: "so positivamente che erano *illuse* ma non ho mai dubitato, quando mi riferivano conversazioni avute con gli spiriti, della loro buona fede. Pare che l'immaginazione, eccitata, possa far udire e vedere come reale ció che non é. Ma io voglio credere che nel

tuo caso non v'*inganni* l'immaginazione, che il vostro tavolino si muova e si esprima davvero come dici" (Fogazzaro, *Piccolo* 256; my italics). (I know positively that they were *deluded*, but, when they told me about conversations that they had with the spirits, I never doubted their good faith. It seems that the imagination, when excited, can cause things to be heard and seen that are not real. But I want to believe that, in your case, your imagination does not *deceive* you, that your coffee table really moves and expresses itself as you say.)

30 During the seance the table rises in the air, but Adriano observes the fact with disbelief: "Se, come sosteneva il Paleari, la forza misteriosa che aveva agito in quel momento, alla luce, sotto gli occhi miei, proveniva da uno spirito invisibile, evidentemente, questo spirito non era quello di Max: bastava guardar Papiano e la signorina Caporale per convincersene. Quel Max, lo avevano inventato loro. Chi dunque aveva agito? Chi aveva avventato sul tavolino quel pugno formidabile?" (Pirandello, *Il fu Mattia Pascal* 171; If, as Paleari maintained, the mysterious force that had acted at that moment, in the light, before my eyes, came from an invisible spirit, then evidently this spirit was not that of Max: it was enough to look at Papiano and Miss Caporale to be convinced of it. They had invented Max. So, who had acted? Who had thrown that formidable punch at the coffee table?)

31 The joke is condemned by Ada – "mi dispiace per voi che abbiate potuto credervi autorizzato ad uno scherzo simile" (I am sorry for you, that you could have believed yourself authorized to play a joke like this) – but self-justified by Zeno's histrionic laughter: "Volevo ridere! Credevo che nessuno di noi avrebbe presa sul serio quella storia del tavolino"; Svevo 177–8). (I wanted to laugh! I didn't think that any of us would have taken that story about the table seriously.)

32 The trope of the seance would also find later expression in the post-war phase of modernism, as seen in the re-emergence and centrality of the scene in Fellini's *La dolce vita* (1959).

33 Two leading members of the Theosophical Society were part of Freemasonry: Henry Olcott, founder of its international theosophical headquarters in Adyar, near the Indian city of Madras, and Anne Besant (successor of Helena Blavatsky since 1907), founder of the French lodge Le droit Humain (the only one admitting women).

34 "Quei libri recavano titoli di questo genere: *La Mort et l'au delà – L'homme et ses corps – Les sept principes de l'homme – Karma – La clef de la Théosophie – ABC de la Théosophie – La doctrine secrète – Le Plan Astral –* ecc., ecc." (Pirandello, *Il fu Mattia Pascal* 108). (Those books bore titles such as: *La Mort et l'au delà – L'homme et ses corps – Les sept principes de l'homme – Karma – La clef de la Théosophie – ABC de la Théosophie – La doctrine secrète – Le Plan Astral –* etc., etc.)

5. The Rise and Fall of Transatlantic Americanism

1 Franchetti was the co-author (with Sydney Sonnino) of an unofficial report
on Sicily, *La Sicilia nel 1876* (*Sicily in 1876*), which would become one of the
foundational texts of the so-called Southern question.

2 Italian Female Industries was initially created by Italy's Queen Margherita
in 1892 with the goal of recovering the lacemaking tradition of Burano
(Pazzini, *Maria Montessori* 22). Since 1903 Italian Female Industries had
become a more mature and extended project that developed from Rome to
the rest of Italy. For more information see Porpora.

3 More information on the relationship between the Bells and Maria
Montessori can be found in Charlotte Gray's *Reluctant Genius.*

4 More information on Speranza's life can be found in Pozzetta and
Livingstone.

5 Speranza also served on numerous committees between 1900 and 1912.
Among others, he was a member of the Law Commission of the New York
Prison Association, director of the training school for probation officers of
the Order of St Christopher, and chair of the Commission on Crime and
Immigration of the American Institute of Criminal Law. Gino Speranza's
correspondence for the Society for the Protection of Italian Immigrants
and the Scuola d'Industrie italiane and his legal papers are found in the
archives and manuscript section of the New York Public Library.

6 Speranza's correspondence and war-time papers are now archived at the
Hoover Library at Stanford University. Other testimonies of the Italian
war from an Italian American perspective include the Wilsonian report
by Salvatore Cotillo, the first Italian-born to serve as a New York State
representative (*Italy during the World War*, 1921), as well as the war sections
of Constantine Panunzio's biography (*The Soul of an Immigrant*, 1921) and
Fiorello La Guardia's posthumous *The Making of an Insurgent* (1948).

7 "Speranza believed that he had […] made his own contribution to ensure
that Italy and the United States did not look at each other with hatred or
incomprehension but instead that the war had for the first time removed
the barriers, and that […] there was truly a bridge 'over the waters' upon
which the two people could 'walk and meet'" (Staiti 31).

8 The quote ends: "There are no *forestieri* to whom she has to minister, no
tourists for whom she has to assume a welcoming smile. She can devote
herself entirely to her sons, in all her naturalness, in all her ardour, in all
her strength. It is a privilege to see her thus, to have the opportunity of
grasping the subtle, intimate spirit of united Italy and of ascertaining to
what extent the genius of her race still lives in her people, in all her people,
and in what form, new perhaps, but deeply and definitely related to the
great past, it will manifest itself" (*Diary* 12; 26 August 1915).

9 "The *Taormina* is carrying anti-typhoid serum for the Italian soldiers, the freight of which is $40.00, and one hundred thousand pairs of American shoes for the Italian army, packed in cases of fifty pairs, each of which costs $5.00 for carriage from New York to Genoa, an enormous rate of transportation it seems to me" (*Diary* 6; 18 August 1915).

10 "Italy is asking for only one thing, a small enough thing measured by the tremendous task she is facing so gallantly. '*Lana! Lana!*' is the universal cry – wool for her Alpini, wool for those fearless troops who must guard, through the long winter rigours, the peaks and passes already captured, wool for these specially picked men from the mountain provinces, who cannot be indefinitely supplied and whose places no other troops, however enduring and brave, can take" (*Diary* 13; 26 August 1915).

11 On 5 September 1915, Speranza visited the US hospital in Villa Modigliani at San Gervasio and noted that "within five weeks this villa had been converted by an American committee into a modern hospital of fifty beds with springs and comfortable mattresses" (*Diary* 18). In his later visit to the US hospital of Gorizia he noted that "men eat very well in the hospital, chicken and eggs in addition to meat, pasta and risotto" (*Diary* 373; 14 September 1916).

12 Starting from his early assessment on 24 November 1915 ("What is Italy going to do in the Balkans?"; Speranza, *Diary* 108), the American journalist and lawyer would later comment on Italian activity in Albania (8 January 1916), the Italian occupation of Valona (25 January 1916), and the arrival of Italian soldiers in Salonica (24 December 1916).

13 Speranza followed the Roman question with interest, observing that with Pius X "dreams of territorial and temporal power came to an end" and with Benedict XV "the idea of temporal dreams had fallen back on an earlier position of the Popes, that of quasi-spiritual adviser to kings and nations" (*Diary* 14–15; 30 August 1915).

14 Speranza met with Harvey Carroll on 18 October 1915; with Monsignor Apollonio, Arciprete at Saint Mark's Basilica (who indicated in dialect that "American dollars will be well accepted" [I dolari dall'America i' vegnaria ben accolti; *Diary* 76; 24 October 1915]); with US commander Jackson (for whom he collected "useful data for the United States about the new appliances and instruments of war that the Italians are using"; *Diary* 87; 26 October 1915); and with the Italian journalist Ugo Ojetti (who gave him a detailed report on the Austrian damage to local monuments; *Diary*, 28 October 1915).

15 Thomas Nelson Page served as the US ambassador to Italy from 1913 to 1919 and wrote a memoir of his Italian work called *Italy and the World War* (1920).

16 Charles Merriam served in Italy between April and September 1918. Salvatore Cotillo was sent to Italy by Wilson in May 1918 and spent a year in the peninsula as representative of the Committee on Public Information. His propaganda work in support of the Italian war effort would be recognized by Italian king Victor Emmanuel III, who honoured him with the decoration of Grand Officer of the Italian Crown ("Justice Cotillo").

17 The fourteenth point of Wilson's speech prefigures the League of Nations, indicating that "a general association of nations must be formed under specific covenants for the purpose of affording mutual guarantees of political independence and territorial integrity to great and small states alike" (Wilson, "Woodrow Wilson's Fourteen Points").

18 "What Wilson developed was an original conviction that to the republic's material power should be added an explicit moral mission in the world. 'Manifest Destiny' would be redefined again, offering the benefits of America's historical beliefs and experience in such a way that they might become a means for the salvation of all of suffering humanity" (Ellwood 61).

19 During the war the ARC received a total contribution (in money and materials) of $40 million and recruited 8,100,000 volunteer workers. Its chapters grew from 107 in 1914 to 3,864 in 1918, and its paid staff grew from 25 in 1914 to 12,300 in 1918 ("World War One and the American Red Cross"). The ARC war council allocated to Italy more than $20 million in funds and material goods, and by the summer of 1918 "949 surgeons, nurses, ambulance drivers, and other American personnel, as well as thousands of Italian workers" were employed in the country (J. Irwin 408). For more information on the ARC's impact in Europe during the First World War see Henry Davison's *The American Red Cross in the Great War* (1919), Foster Rhea Dulles's *The American Red Cross* (1950), and Patrick Gilbo's *The American Red Cross* (1981).

20 In September 1914, in agreement with the Geneva conventions and the principles of impartiality of the Red Cross Movement, the United States dispatched the SS *Red Cross* (known as "the Mercy Ship"), which carried 170 surgeons and medical supplies to Europe for relief of both sides. During the following months, passenger ships were also used as cargo ships (as Speranza notes in his journal on 8 August 1915; *Diary* 6), increasingly carrying aids in favour of the Allied forces.

21 As tobacco provisions from Turkey, Bulgaria, Macedonia, and Russia ceased with the outbreak of war, US cigarettes became a morale commodity and a marketing tool of America's capitalistic modernity. From 1917 to 1918, the YMCA "shipped more than 12 million dollars' worth of tobacco products to European battlefields" (Burns 158).

22 Italy's new Supreme General Armando Diaz allowed the YMCA to operate
    on the front at the end of 1917, and John Nollen officially established it as
    an Italian association in Bologna in January 1918 (Rossini 94).
23 Hemingway applied for service in May 1918, three months after the *Kansas
    City Star* had published a call for volunteer ambulance drivers for the
    Norton-Harjes Ambulance Corps in France (where John Dos Passos had
    been serving since November 1917). On 19 May Hemingway marched in
    a parade of nurses led by President Wilson on Fifth Avenue in New York
    City and soon afterwards left for France. From Paris he was dispatched to
    Milan, arriving on 6 June 1918. Two days later he reached Schio, where he
    first met Dos Passos (McGrath Morris 38–9).
24 "In the courtyard of an aging Milan palace, festooned with crossed Italian
    and American flags, the new and old ambulances were parked in a
    horseshoe pattern facing a podium where military officials in full regalia
    welcomed the men and their machines. Dos Passos stood at attention
    for review. Unlike his service with the Norton-Harjes Ambulance Corps
    in France, the drivers here were to be soldiers in a propaganda war. The
    ambulances weren't merely intended to save lives of Italian soldiers but
    to signal to the nation that American troops were on their way" (McGrath
    Morris 45).
25 "In Italy, in 1918, the United States deployed its programs of relief and
    propaganda on a vast scale. The spectacular success of those programs
    was in part a result of the wealth of resources deployed and the efficacy
    with which they were administered, but it was also due to the growing
    ideological thirst of the Italian masses, both civilians and fighting men,
    and to the myth of America as a paradise for the common man, a myth
    that had developed in those parts of Italy that produced major flows of
    emigrants" (Rossini 3).
26 More information on the Pisa Village can be found in "The American City
    at Pisa," *Red Cross Bulletin*, 20 July 1918, and *The Gospel of Germs* by Nancy
    Tomes.
27 Gemma La Guardia Gluck's volume *Fiorello's Sister* also offers interesting
    insights on her brother's biography.
28 The Zimmermann Telegram revealed Germany's secret offer to return
    all territories lost in the war of 1846–8 to Mexico in exchange for support
    against the United States (Tuchman 63–74).
29 D'Annunzio flew over Trieste on 7 August 1915 with co-pilot Giuseppe
    Miraglia. In a second raid over Trieste, on 16 January 1916 (with co-pilot
    Luigi Bologna), D'Annunzio hit his cheekbone over the machine gun at
    landing and lost sight. Over a period of blindness and convalescence he
    wrote *Notturno* (*Nocturnal*, 1916), dedicating it to his fellow pilot Giuseppe
    Miraglia (who had died in combat in December 1915). After his return to

aviation in May 1917, D'Annunzio delivered the eulogy commemorating the death of Italian flying ace Francesco Baracca on 26 June 1918 and flew over Vienna on 9 August 1918, stirring the Italian resistance by dropping anti-Austrian leaflets on the city.

30 Colonel William Wallace's regiment arrived in Italy on 27 July 1918 and was welcomed in Turin, Milan, and Verona. On 1 August a solemn demonstration announcing the arrival of American troops was organized in Villafranca, in the presence of the Italian king Victor Emmanuel III, the Italian prime minister Vittorio Emanuele Orlando, the Italian army's commander-in-chief Armando Diaz, and US ambassador Nelson Page (Rossini 101).

31 La Guardia's political program included the breaking of bankers' financial stronghold, work-relief programs for the unemployed, the end of corruption and racketeering, the replacement of patronage with merit-based civil service, and the modernization of transportation and parks. For information on La Guardia's career in New York see Ronald Bayor's volume *Fiorello La Guardia*.

32 The 20,000-seat stadium was funded by the YMCA and completed on 26 May 1919. The Inter-Allied Games were held between 22 June and 6 July 1919, under the aegis of the International Olympic Committee.

33 The expansion of the game in Italy after the victory against France is confirmed by the institution of its first championship and the publication of Arturo Balestrieri's first manual of basketball in the fall of 1919. More information on the Italy-France game and the impact of basketball in post-war Italy can be found in the 2015 volume by Mario Arceri, *La leggenda del basket*.

34 A good source to reconstruct the work of American propaganda in Italy is Nigro's 1999 volume *The New Diplomacy in Italy*.

35 Separate peace treaties with Germany, Austria, and Hungary were signed in 1921, under Harding's administration.

36 "Like many native-stock reformers, Speranza sought instead to impose upon southern Italian immigrants and their children a version of 'true' Americanism as he understood it. This Americanism, defined as the melting pot ideal, was supposedly comprehensible to all nationalities, races, and classes, but it was middle class in spirit and practice" (Salerno 134).

Epilogue

1 Futurism first appeared in the United States in the critical reviews by André Tridon in 1912 and 1913, and Futurist works by Balla and Severini were first displayed at the San Francisco World's Fair of 1915 (Hand 337–42). In the 1920s the movement gained some traction through the

work of Italian American artist Joseph Stella and the New York journal *Futurist Aristocracy* (launched by Nanni Leone Castelli in 1923), but Futurist art did not match either the local community's idea of *Italianità* or America's well-established association of Italian art with past heritage.

2 Depero's "paintings failed to sell and his commercial enterprise in the city, the Futurist house, did not survive longer than a couple of months […] After the Wall Street crash, he and his wife Rosetta offered free Italian food to attract potential clients to his studio. Rosetta cooked homemade ravioli and Fortunato fermented grapes in his bedroom to produce wine – an illegal but lucrative activity during Prohibition" (Bedarida).

3 Covello founded Il Circolo italiano (The Italian Circle) at DeWitt Clinton High School in 1914 and created the first department of Italian there in 1922. In 1934 he founded the Benjamin Franklin High School in East Harlem, extending his philosophy of education to the broader community (Carnevale 145).

4 As Carnevale points out, Covello aimed to build "an imagined, unified, pan-Italian-American community out of disparate, local, linguistic, and cultural groups" and at the same time to "weave Italian Americans into the fabric of American life" (137).

5 In the 1930s the general public in France was convinced "that the United States was fundamentally no different than a totalitarian state; that it obeyed the same collective, if not collectivist, logic; that it was even more totally totalitarian than its 'rivals' in Europe" (Roger 395).

6 For a broader study on the impact of Americanism in Germany in the 1920s, see Mary Nolan's 1994 volume *Visions of Modernity*.

7 "Unlike other production industries, the European film studios never recovered their vitality after the war, and everywhere except Germany succumbed to the scale and dynamism of the Hollywood oligopoly, which controlled production, distribution, and exhibition over an ever-widening horizon" (Ellwood 118).

8 Real academic legitimation of American culture came after the war, first with translations by Fernanda Pivano and then with the 1954 establishment of Agostino Lombardo as Italy's first professor of Anglo-American literature at the University of Rome (Boitani).

9 Pavese's "Essay on Americanism" first appeared in *L'Unità* on 3 August 1947 (with the title "In giro per l'America" ["Around America"]) and was republished later with the title "Saggio sull'Americanismo" in the 1951 volume *La letteratura americana e altri saggi* (*American Literature and Other Essays*). In the essay Pavese describes the emergence of Americanism in Italy in the 1930s in these terms:

Verso il 1930, quando il Fascismo cominciava a essere 'la speranza del mondo' accadde ad alcuni giovani italiani di scoprire nei suoi libri l'America, una America pensosa e barbarica, felice e rissosa, dissoluta, feconda, greve di tutto il passato del mondo, e insieme giovane, innocente. Per qualche anno questi giovani lessero tradussero e scrissero con una gioia di scoperta e di rivolta che indignò la cultura ufficiale, ma il successo fu tale che costrinse il regime a tollerare per salvare la faccia. Si scherza? Eravamo il Paese della risorta romanità dove perfino i geometri studiavano il latino, il paese dei guerrieri e dei santi, il paese del Genio per grazia di Dio, e questi nuovi scalzacani, questi mercanti coloniali, questi villani miliardari osavano darci una lezione di gusto facendosi leggere, discutere e ammirare? Il regime tollerò a denti stretti […] Menò qualche botta, ma senza concludere […] Per molta gente l'incontro con Caldwell, Steinbeck, Saroyan, e perfino col vecchio Lewis, aperse il primo spiraglio di libertà, il primo sospetto che non tutto nella cultura del mondo finisse coi fasci. (Pavese, "In giro per l'America")

[By 1930, when Fascism began to be 'the hope of the world,' it happened that some young Italians discovered America in their books, a thoughtful and barbaric America, happy and quarrelsome, dissolute, fruitful, heavy with all of the past of the world and, at the same time, young, innocent. For a few years, these young people read, translated, and wrote with a joy of discovery and revolt that outraged the official culture, but the success was such that it forced the regime to tolerate it in order to save face. Are we kidding? We were the country of the resurrected Roman world, where even surveyors studied Latin, the country of warriors and saints, the country of genius by the grace of God, and these new cobblers, these colonial merchants, these billionaire villains dared to give us a lesson in taste, causing themselves to be read, discussed, and admired? The regime tolerated it with clenched teeth […] It struck a few blows, but without achieving anything […]. For many people, the encounter with Caldwell, Steinbeck, Saroyan, and even with old Lewis let in the first glimmer of freedom, the first suspicion that not everything in the culture of the world ended with the Fascists.]

10 "If you look up the word 'Americanism' in a pre-World War II British, German, French, or Italian dictionary, you will find that besides describing words or expressions characteristic of American English, the term was used to refer to an inordinate admiration of the United States […] The situation changed after the war, when in most dictionaries the old meaning of the term 'Americanism' fell from first or second place to third or fourth place, and the new term 'anti-Americanism' made its appearance" (Mariani 54).

11 Case studies on Americanization in other areas or periods of time include Richard Kuisel's *Seducing the French* (1993) and *The French Way* (2012); Reinhold Wagnleitner's *Coca-Colonization and the Cold War* (1994); and Richard Pells's *Not Like Us* (1997).

12 "There is a lot of rhetoric surrounding these issues. There is a purely
   economic rhetoric, mainly on the American side, which presents the
   issue as solely one of free markets and consumer choice. And there is a
   culturalist rhetoric, mainly on the European side, which talks of cultural
   identities, of language as the soul of a nation, of the right to national
   self-expression, of resistance to alien cultural hegemony, and so on"
   (Nowell-Smith 2).
13 Roger points out that "the first use of the term 'anti-Americanism'
   catalogued by lexicographers dates back to 1948; by the early 1950s, it
   was a part of ordinary political language." In the late nineteenth century
   an equivalent of the not-yet-existing term *anti-Americanism* would be the
   word *yankism* or *Yankeeism* (Roger xiv).
14 Studies on anti-Americanism in the post–Second World War era include
   Stephen Haseler's *The Varieties of Anti-Americanism* (1985); Lacorne,
   Rupnik, and Toinet's *The Rise and Fall of Anti-Americanism* (1990); and
   Paul Hollander's *Anti-Americanism* (1992). In the Italian context, the most
   influential texts are Massimo Teodori's *Maledetti americani* (2002) and
   Sergio Fabbrini's *L'America e i suoi critici* (2005).

Works Cited

Abdill, Edward. "The Universal Brotherhood of Humanity." *Quest*, vol. 96, no. 5, Sept.–Oct. 2008, pp. 177–9.

Accornero, Cristina. "Il taylorismo e gli sviluppi dell'igiene industriale." *Treccani Enciclopedia*, https://www.treccani.it/enciclopedia/il-taylorismo-e-gli-sviluppi-dell-igiene-industriale_%28Il-Contributo-italiano-alla-storia-del-Pensiero:-Tecnica%29/. Accessed 28 June 2021.

Adamo, Sergia. "Dancing for the World: Articulating the National and the Global in the Ballo Excelsior's Kitsch Imagination." *Moving Bodies, Displaying Nations: National Cultures, Race and Gender in World Expositions; Nineteenth to Twenty-First Century*, edited by Guido Abbattista, Edizioni Università di Trieste, 2014, pp. 143–72.

Alatri, Giovanna. "Maria Montessori e Maria Maraini Guerrieri Gonzaga." *Annali di storia dell'educazione e delle istituzioni scolastiche*, vol. 25, 2018.

Alcott, Louisa May. *Da un Natale all'altro.* Translated by Ciro and Michelina Trabalza, Carrabba, 1908.

– *Da un Natale all'altro.* Translated by Ciro and Michelina Trabalza, Carrabba, 1911.

Allison, Raphael, "Walt Whitman, William James, and Pragmatist Aesthetics." *Walt Whitman Quarterly Review*, vol. 20, no. 1, 2002, pp. 19–29, https://doi.org/10.13008/2153-3695.1693.

"The American City at Pisa." *Red Cross Bulletin* (Italy ed.), 20 July 1918.

Anbinder, Tyler. *Nativism and Slavery: The Northern Know Nothings and the Politics of the 1850s.* Oxford UP, 1992. https://doi.org/10.1093/oso/9780195072334.001.0001.

Anderson, Benedict. *Imagined Communities: Reflections on the Origins and Spread of Nationalism.* Verso, 1983.

Arbìb, Edoardo.*Cinquant'anni di storia parlamentare del regno d'Italia.* Tip. della Camera dei Deputati, 1898–1907. 4 vols.

Arceri, Mario. *La leggenda del basket.* Baldini e Castoldi, 2015.

Association Montessori Internationale (AMI) – Canada. https://www.ami
-canada.com. Accessed 23 Aug. 2022.

Bacon, Francis. *New Atlantis and the Great Instauration*. Translated by Jerry
Weinberger, Wiley Blackwell, 2017.

Badger, Reid. *The Great American Fair: The World's Columbian Exposition &
American Culture*. Nelson Hall, 1979.

Bagnoli, Paolo, editor. *Giovanni Papini: L'uomo impossibile*. Sansoni, 1982.

Baldacci, Luigi. Introduzione. *Opere: Dal "Leonardo" al Futurismo*, by Giovanni
Papini, edited by Luigi Baldacci, Mondadori, 1977, pp. xi–xxxvi.

Balestrieri, Arturo. *Il giuoco del basket ball (palla al cesto) del dottore Luther Halsey
Gulick (inventore)*. Società editoriale italiana, 1919.

Barbata Jackson, Jessica. *Dixie's Italians: Sicilians, Race, and Citizenship in the Jim
Crow Gulf South*. Louisiana State UP, 2020.

Barlow, Joel. *The Columbiad: A Poem*. 1807.

Barone, Marianna. *Massoneria, istituzioni ed elite politiche: Nella storia di
Filadelfia di Calabria (1783–1920)*. Di Nicolò edizioni, 2019.

Barry, Gearóld. "Demobilization." *International Encyclopedia of the First
World War, 1914–1918*, https://encyclopedia.1914-1918-online.net/article
/demobilization. Accessed 24 Aug. 2022.

Barzini, Luigi, Sr. "Un incontro con Wright." *Corriere della sera*, 4 Oct. 1908.

Baudelaire, Charles. "L'art romantique: Suivi de Fusées." *Mon coeur mis à nu et
Pauvre Belgique*. Julliard, 1966.

– *The Painter of Modern Life and Other Essays*. Translated by Jonathan Mayne,
Phaidon P, 1964.

Bayor, Ronald H. *Fiorello La Guardia: Ethnicity, Reform, and Urban Development*.
2nd ed., Wiley, 2018. https://doi.org/10.1002/9781119374794.

Bedarida, Raffaele. "'Bombs against the Skyscrapers': Depero's Strange Love
Affair with New York, 1928–1949." *Italian Modern Art*, no. 1, Jan. 2019,
https://www.italianmodernart.org/journal/articles/bombs-against-the
-skyscrapers-deperos-strange-love-affair-with-new-york-1928-1949/.

Belasco, David. *The Girl of the Golden West*. 1905. Grosset & Dunlap, 1911.

Benjamin, Walter. *The Work of Art in the Age of Its Technological Reproducibility
and Other Writings on Media*. Belknap P of Harvard UP, 2008.

Berenson, Bernard. *Central Italian Painters of the Renaissance*. Putnam, 1907.

– *The Drawings of the Florentine Painters*. Murray, 1903.

– *The Florentine Painters of the Renaissance*. G.P. Putnam's Sons, 1909.

– *Lorenzo Lotto; An Essay in Constructive Art Criticism*. G. Bell & Sons, 1901.

– *Venetian Painters of the Renaissance: With an Index to Their Works*. Putnam,
1910.

Berg, A. Scott. *Wilson*. Simon & Schuster, 2013.

Berghaus, Günter. *Italian Futurist Theatre*. Clarendon P, 1998. https://doi
.org/10.1093/oso/9780198158981.001.0001.

Beria, Chiara. "La 'Rassegna settimanale' e la cultura europea."*Il verismo italiano fra naturalismo francese e cultura europea*, edited by Romano Luperini, Manni, 2007, pp. 119–49.

Bernardini, Caterina. "The Longest Day: Dino Campana and Walt Whitman; Across Italy and South America." *Walt Whitman Quarterly Review*, vol. 33, no. 1, summer 2005, pp. 4–20, https://doi.org/10.13008/0737-0679.2179.

Bevilacqua, Piero, et al., editors. *Storia dell'emigrazione italiana:Arrivi*. Donzelli, 2002.

Bhabha, Homi. "The Third Space." *Identity: Community, Culture, Difference*, edited by J. Rutherford, Lawrence & Wishart, pp. 207–21.

Bigazzi, Duccio. "Modelli e pratiche organizzative nell'industrializzazione italiana." *L'industria*, vol. 15 of *Storia d'Italia: Annali* , Einaudi, 1999, pp. 897–994.

Bisi Albini, Sofia. "Il trionfo di una donna: Maria Montessori." *Vita femminile italiana*, vol. 4, no. 5, May 1910, pp. 482–5.

Bohn, Willard. "The Poetics of Flight: Futurist 'Aeropoesia.'" *MLN*, vol. 121, no. 1, Jan. 2006, pp. 207–24, https://doi.org/10.1353/mln.2006.0028.

Boitani, Piero. "Agostino Lombardo." *Treccani: Enciclopedia italiana*, https://www.treccani.it/enciclopedia/agostino-lombardo_%28Enciclopedia-Italiana%29. Accessed 5 Oct. 2022.

Bonghi, Ruggero. *Lettere critiche di Ruggero Bonghi:Perché la letteratura italiana non sia popolare in Italia* F. Colombo, 1856.

Bonomelli, Geremia. *La chiesa e i tempi nuovi*. Cremona, 1906.

Bonsaver, Guido. *America in Italian Culture: The Rise of a New Model of Modernity, 1861–1943*. Oxford UP, 2023.

Borges, Jorge Luis. Prologue. *El espejo que huye*, by Giovanni Papini, Biblioteca de Babel, 1987.

– "Veinticinco de agosto." *La Memoria de Shakespeare*. Alianza Editorial, 2008.

Bottaro, Mario. *Genova 1892 e le celebrazioni colombiane*. Francesco Pirella Editore, 1984.

Bowser, Eileen. *The Transformation of Cinema, 1907–1915*. U of California P, 1994.

Brands, Henry William. *TR: The Last Romantic*. Basic Books, 1997.

Brodsky, Alyn. *The Great Mayor: Fiorello La Guardia and the Making of the City of New York*. St Martin's P, 2003.

Brunetière, Ferdinand. "Après une visite au Vatican." *Revue des deux mondes*, vol. 65, 1 Jan. 1895, p. 127.

Buffalo Bill Museum. "Did Buffalo Bill Visit Your Town? A Comprehensive Country/State Listing of William "Buffalo Bill" Cody's Tour Destinations." *Buffalo Bill*, rev. 2010. *Internet Archive*, https://web.archive.org/web/20210512120305/www.buffalobill.org/PDFs/Buffalo_Bill_Visits.pdf. Accessed 5 June 2021.

Buffon, Comte de (George-Louis Leclerc). *Histoire naturelle, générale et particulière, avec la description du Cabinet du Roi.* Imprimerie royale, 1749–1804. 36 vols.

Bugiardini, Sergio. "L'associazionismo negli USA." Bevilacqua et al., pp. 551–78.

Burg, David. *Chicago's White City of 1893.* UP of Kentucky, 1976.

Burns, Eric. *The Smoke of the Gods: A Social History of Tobacco.* Temple UP, 2007.

Busenghin, Maria Luciana. *Alice Hallgarten Franchetti: Un modello di donna e di imprenditrice nell'Italia tra '800 e '900.* Editrice Pliniana, 2013.

Bussoni, Mario. *Buffalo Bill in Italia: L'epopea del Wild West Show.* Mattioli 1885, 2011.

Buzzi, Paolo. *Aeroplani: Canti alati con il proclama futurista.* Lampi di stampa, 2009.

– "A Geo Chavez." *Versi liberi.* Treves, 1913.

"Cadorna Removed as Head of Italian Forces." *Washington Herald*, 10 Nov. 1917, p. 1.

Calvino, Italo. "Autobiografia di uno spettatore." *La strada di San Giovanni*, Mondadori, 1990, pp. 43–71.

Camboni, Marina. "Giovanni Papini e Walt Whitman tra Pragmatismo, Nietzsche e Futurismo." *Novecento Transnazionale: Letterature, Arti e Culture*, vol. 2, 2018, pp. 26–41.

Camera Work. A Photographic Quarterly. Directed by Alfred Stieglitz. New York: 1903–17. Periodical.

Campana, Dino. *Canti orfici.* Ali ribelli, 2019.

Caprara, Giovanni. *L'avventura della scienza: Sfide, invenzioni e scoperte nelle pagine del Corriere della Sera.* Fondazione Corriere della sera, Rizzoli, 2009.

Capuana, Luigi. *Gli "Americani" di Ràbbato.* Remo Sandron, 1912.

– "Il domatore di aquile." *La voluttà di creare: Novelle.* Treves, 1911, pp. 274–90.

– *Mondo occulto.* Edited by Simona Cigliana, Edizioni del prisma, 1995.

Carducci, Giosuè. *Giambi ed epodi.* Bologna, 1882.

Carlson, Robert. *The Americanization Syndrome: A Quest for Conformity.* St Martin's P, 1987.

Carnevale, Nancy, *A New Language, A New World: Italian Immigrants in the United States, 1890–1945.* U of Illinois P, 2009.

Carosso, Vincent, and Rose Carosso, editors. *The Morgans: Private International Bankers, 1854–1913.* Harvard UP, 1987.

Cecchi, Emilio. *America amara.* Sansoni, 1939.

Cecchin, Giovanni. *Hemingway: Americani e volontariato in Italia nella grande guerra.* Collezione Princeton, 1999.

Censimento degli italiani all'estero (31 dicembre 1871). Stamperia reale, 1874.

Chavinier-Réla, Sabine. "Inter-Allied Games." *International Encyclopedia of the First World War, 1914–1918*, https://encyclopedia.1914-1918-online.net /article/inter-allied_games. Accessed 19 Aug. 2022.

Chinard, Gilbert. *Thomas Jefferson: The Apostle of Americanism*. Floating P, 2011.

Choate, Mark, *The Making of Italy Abroad*. Harvard UP, 2008.

Cinel, Dino. *The National Integration of Italian Return Migration, 1870–1929*. Cambridge UP, 1991, https://doi.org/10.1017/CBO9780511584800.

Cingolani, Stefano. "L'amico americano." *Il foglio*, 16 July 2018. https://www.ilfoglio.it/economia/2018/07/16/news/lamico-americano-205810. Accessed 17 July 2024.

Clementi, Andreina. "La 'grande emigrazione': Dalle origini alla chiusura degli sbocchi americani." Bevilacqua et al., pp. 187–212.

Colella, Paul. "Reflex Action and the Pragmatism of Giovanni Papini." *Journal of Speculative Philosophy*, vol. 19, no. 3, 2005, pp. 187–215, https://doi.org/10.1353/jsp.2005.0018.

Colucci, Michele, and Stefano Gallo, editors. *L'emigrazione italiana: Storia e documenti*. Brescia, 2015.

Conan Doyle, Arthur. *History of Spiritualism*. Cassel, 1926. 2 vols.

Confessore, Ornella. *L'americanismo cattolico in Italia*. Studium, 1984.

Connell, William J. "Darker Aspects of Italian American Prehistory." *Anti-Italianism: Essays on a Prejudice*, edited by William Connell and Fred Gardaphé, Palgrave Macmillan, 2010, pp. 11–22, https://doi.org/10.1057/9780230115323_2.

Cook, David. "Edwin S. Porter | American Director." *Encyclopedia Britannica*, https://www.britannica.com/biography/Edwin-S-Porter. Accessed 7 July 2021.

Cooper, John Milton. *Pivotal Decades: The United States, 1900–1920*. Norton, 1990.

Coppa, Frank. "Commercio estero e politica doganale nell'Italia liberale." *L'industrializzazione in Italia (1861–1900)*, edited by Giorgio Mori, Il Mulino, 1977, pp. 161–70.

Corriere della sera. "Alla vigilia della guerra." 28–9 Mar. 1898, p. 1.

– "Aspettando." 28–29 Apr. 1898, p. 1.

– "L'attualità all'estero. Spagna e Stati Uniti." 17–18 Mar. 1898, p. 1.

– "La caccia." 21–22 May 1898, p. 1.

– "Una cagnara." 10–11 Aug. 1892, p. 1.

– "Domani." 7–8 Sept. 1892, p. 1.

– "Due pastori." 22–23 May 1898, p. 1.

– "Europa contro America." 21–22 Apr. 1898, p. 1.

– "L'inevitabile." 23–24 Apr. 1898, p. 1.

– "Intermezzo." 13–14 May 1898, p. 1.

– "L'Italia e il Papa nei contatti internazionali." 22–23 Feb. 1899, p. 1.

– "Nota sul delitto anarchico." 8–9 Sept. 1901, p. 1.

– "Le nuove migrazioni dei popoli." 22–23 Dec. 1888, p. 1.

– "L'onore." 21–22 July 1898, p. 1.

– "Perché ritarda?" 27–28 June 1898, p. 1.

– "La prima conseguenza della guerra." 6–7 May 1898, p. 1.
– "La sorpresa." 18–19 May 1898, p. 1.
– "Il suicidio." 8–9 July 1898, p. 1.
– "La trappola." 29–30 May 1898, p. 1.
– "La visita del re." 3–4 Aug. 1892, p. 1.
– "La visita di Zola a Genova." 29–30 Sept. 1892, p. 1.
Costantini, Paolo. "L'esposizione internazionale di fotografia artistica." *Torino 1902: Le arti decorative internazionali del nuovo secolo*, edited by Rossana Bossaglia et al., Fabbri, 1994, pp. 95–105.
– *La fotografia artistica, 1904–1917: Visione italiana e modernità*. Bollati Boringhieri, 1990.
Cotillo, Salvatore. *Italy during the World War*. Christopher Publishing House, 1921.
Cottini, Luca. *The Art of Objects: The Birth of Italian Industrial Culture, 1878–1928*. U of Toronto P, 2018, https://doi.org/10.3138/9781487516109.
– "Buffalo Bill and the Italian Myth of the American West." *Italy and the USA: Cultural Change through Language and Narrative*, edited by Guido Bonsaver et al., Legenda, 2019, pp. 89–102, https://doi.org/10.2307/j.ctv16kkzj9.11.
Covello, Leonard. *The Heart Is the Teacher*. McGraw Hill, 1958.
Crévecoeur, Hector St. John de. *Letters from an American Farmer*. Fox, Duffield, 1904.
Curami, Andrea. "La nascita dell'industria aeronautica."*L'aeronautica italiana: Una storia del Novecento*, edited by Paolo Ferrari, FrancoAngeli, 2004, pp. 13–42.
Cutolo, Francesco. "Battle of Monte Grappa." *International Encyclopedia of the First World War, 1914–1918*, https://encyclopedia.1914-1918-online.net /article/monte_grappa_battle_of. Accessed 24 Aug. 2022.
Dall'Osso, Claudia. *Voglia d'America: Il mito americano in Italia tra Otto e Novecento*. Donzelli, 2007.
D'Annunzio, Gabriele. *Forse che sì forse che no: Prose di Romanzi*, vol. 2. Edited by Annamaria Andreoli and Niva Lorenzini, Mondadori, 1989, pp. 519–887.
– *Notturno*. Zanichelli, 2011.
– *La sagra di Quarto: Orazione di Gabriele D'Annunzio*. Stabilimento Cromo-Tipografico, 1915.
– *Saluto a Francesco Baracca*. Editoriale aeronautica, 1938.
Davison, Henry. *The American Red Cross in the Great War*. Macmillan, 1919, https://doi.org/10.5479/sil.36822.39088001526805.
De Amicis, Edmondo. "Il cinematografo cerebrale." *Ultime pagine di Edmondo De Amicis III, Il cinematografo cerebrale (bozzetti umoristici e letterari)*, Fratelli Treves, 1909.
– *Cuore*. Mondadori, 1984.
– "Gli emigranti," in *Poesie*. 1882.
– *On Blue Waters*. Putnam & Sons, 1897.

– *Sull'oceano*. Garzanti, 1996. Originally published by Treves, 1888.

De Grazia, Victoria. *Irresistible Empire: America's Advance through Twentieth-Century Europe*. Harvard UP, 2005, https://doi.org/10.4159/9780674031180.

De Sanctis, Sante, editor. *Atti del V congresso internazionale di psicologia tenuto in Roma dal 26 al 30 aprile 1905*. Forzani, 1905.

Deschamps, Benedicte. "La stampa dell'emigrazione." Bevilacqua et al., pp. 313–34.

Devoto, Fernando. "In Argentina." Bevilacqua et al., pp. 25–54.

Di Peio, Giovanni. "Edoardo Arbìb – Dizionario biografico degli italiani." *Treccani*, https://www.treccani.it/enciclopedia/edoardo-arbib_(Dizionario -Biografico). Accessed 16 Apr. 2021.

La dolce vita. Directed by Federico Fellini, Riama Films / Pathé Consortium / Gray Films, 1959.

Domański, Jacek. "23 September 1910 – Jorge Chávez Flies through the Pennine Alps." *After Burner: The Aviation Magazine*, 23 Sept. 2023. https://afterburner.com.pl/23-september-1910-jorge-chavez-flies -through-the-pennine-alps.

Dorsey, Leroy. *We Are All Americans, Pure and Simple: Theodore Roosevelt and the Myth of Americanism*. U of Alabama P, 2007.

Dorsey, Leroy, and Rachel M. Harlow. "We Want Americans Pure and Simple": Theodore Roosevelt and the Myth of Americanism." *Rhetoric and Public Affairs*, vol. 6, no. 1, spring 2003, pp. 55–78, https://doi.org/10.1353 /rap.2003.0027.

Dos Passos, John. "Diary, Jan. 1, 1918." *The Fourteenth Chronicle: Letters and Diaries of John Dos Passos*, Townsend Ludington, 1973, pp. 115–16.

Dulles, Foster Rhea. *The American Red Cross*. Harper and Brothers, 1950.

Elliott, Walter. *The Life of Father Hecker*. 1891.

– *Vie du Père Hecker*. Translated by Félix Klein, Lecoffre, 1897.

Ellwood, David. *The Shock of America: Europe and the Challenge of the Century*. Oxford UP, 2012, https://doi.org/10.1093/acprof:oso/9780198228790 .001.0001.

Esposizione internazionale di fotografia artistica, Torino, 1902: Catalogo ufficiale. Tip. Roux e Viarengo, 1902.

Fabbri, Gualtiero. *Al cinematografo*. Edited by Raffaelli Sergio, Persiani, 2012, pp. 11–79.

Fabbrini, Sergio. *L'America e i suoi critici: Vizi e virtù dell'iperpotenza americana*. Il mulino, 2005.

Fenoglio, Beppe. *Una questione privata*. Einaudi, 1963.

Ferrero, Guglielmo. *Fra i due mondi*. Treves, 1913.

Ferri, Enrico. "Discussione alla Camera dei deputati – 22 giugno 1909." *Bollettino dell'emigrazione*. Ministero degli Affari Esteri, Tipografia Manuzio, 1909, pp. 1231–80.

Fiorentino, Daniele, editor. *Gli Stati Uniti e l'Italia alla fine del XIX secolo.* Gangemi, 2010.

Fogazzaro, Antonio. *Ascensioni umane.* Baldini Castoldi, 1899.

– *Piccolo mondo antico.* Newton, 2007.

– *Il santo.* Città armoniosa, 1991.

Foraker, Sheila. "Achille La Guardia. Bandmaster of the 11th U.S. Infantry." *Territorial Brass,* https://territorialbrass.com/LaGuardia. Accessed 23 Aug. 2022.

Fotografia artistica: Rivista internazionale illustrata. Directed by Annibale Cominetti. Turin, 1904–17. Periodical.

Franchetti, Alberto. *Cristoforo Colombo.* Performance at Teatro Carlo Felice Genoa, 6 Oct. 1892.

Franchetti, Leopoldo, and Sydney Sonnino. *La Sicilia nel 1876.* 1877.

Franzina, Emilio. "Conclusione a mo' di premessa: Partenze e arrivi." Bevilacqua et al., pp. 601–39.

– *Dall'arcadia in America: Attività letteraria ed emigrazione transoceanica in Italia (1850–1940).* Edizioni della fondazione Giovanni Agnelli, 1996.

Freud, Sigmund. *The Case of Dora.* W.W. Norton, 1952.

– *The Interpretation of Dreams.* Edited by William Jenkins, Macat International, 2016.

– *Jensen's "Gradiva" and Other Works.* Vintage, 2001.

– *Jokes and Their Relation to the Unconscious.* Vintage, 2001.

– *Psychopathology of Everyday Life.* Dover Publications, 2003.

– *Studies on Hysteria.* Penguin, 1974.

– *Three Essays on Sexuality.* Verso, 2016.

Friedman, Max Paul. *Rethinking Anti-Americanism: The History of an Exceptional Concept in American Foreign Relations.* Cambridge UP, 2012, https://doi .org/10.1017/CBO9781139029421.

Gabaccia, Donna. "Class, Exile, and Nationalism at Home and Abroad: The Italian Risorgimento." *Italian Workers of the World: Labor Migration and the Formation of Multiethnic States,* edited by Donna Gabaccia and Fraser Ottanelli, U of Illinois P, 2001, pp. 21–40.

Gardini, Carlo *Gli Stati Uniti: Ricordi.* Zanichelli, 1887.

Garroni, Maria Susanna. "Prospettive americane sugli immigrati italiani e la loro terra d'origine tra il 1870 e il 1914: Per un percorso di ricerca." *Gli Stati Uniti e l'Italia alla fine del XIX secolo,* edited by Daniele Fiorentino, Gangemi, 2010, pp. 101–16.

Gassert, Philipp. "'Without Concessions to Marxist or Communist Thought': Fordism in Germany, 1923–1939." *Transatlantic Images and Perceptions: Germany and America since 1776,* edited by David E. Barclay and Elisabeth Glaser-Schmidt, Cambridge UP, 1997, pp. 217–42, https://doi.org/10.1017 /CBO9781139052504.011.

Gelatt, Roland. *The Fabulous Phonograph: 1877–1977*. MacMillan Publishing, 1977.

Gelernter, David. *Americanism: The Fourth Great Western Religion*. Doubleday, 2007.

Gentile, Emilio. "Impending Modernity: Fascism and the Ambivalent Image of the United States." *Journal of Contemporary History*, vol. 28, no. 1, Jan. 1993, p. 7–29, https://doi.org/10.1177/002200949302800102.

Giacosa, Giuseppe. *Impressioni d'America*. Milan, 1898.

– "Gli Italiani a New York ed a Chicago."*Nuova Antologia*, vol. 15, 16 Aug. 1892, pp. 618–40.

Giannetti, Renato. "Il progresso tecnologico." *Storia d'Italia: Annali; L'industria*, vol. 15, Einaudi, 1999, pp. 387–440.

Giannini, Federico, and Ilaria Baratta. "Quando i migranti eravamo noi: Gli artisti che raccontarono l'emigrazione italiana di fine Ottocento." *Finestre sull'arte*, 28 July 2019, https://www.finestresullarte.info/opere-e-artisti /quando-i-migranti-eravamo-noi-emigrazione-italiana-nelle-opere-degli -artisti.

Gibson, Mary. "Biology or Environment? Race and Southern 'Deviancy' in the Writings of Italian Criminologists, 1880–1920." *Italy's 'Southern Question': Orientalism in One Country*, edited by Jane Schneider, Berg, 1998, pp. 99–115, https://doi.org/10.4324/9781003085768-6.

Gilbo, Patrick.*The American Red Cross: The First Century; An Illustrated History of the First Century of the American Red Cross, 1881–1981*. Harper and Row, 1981.

Gino Speranza Papers. *New York Public Library, Archives and Manuscripts*, https://archives.nypl.org/mss/2844. Accessed 23 Aug. 2022.

Giorgio S. *I due fratelli ovvero il ritorno dell'emigrato*. Potenza, 1897.

Goldoni, Carlo. *La locandiera*. Zanichelli, 2011.

Gozzano, Guido. "Alle soglie." *Tutte le poesie*, edited by Marziano Guglielminetti, Mondadori, 1980.

Gramsci, Antonio. *Americanismo e fordismo*. Universale Economica, 1950.

– *Prison Notebooks*. Columbia UP, 2011.

Gray, Charlotte. *Reluctant Genius: The Passionate Life and Inventive Mind of Alexander Graham Bell*. Phyllis Bruce Books, 2006.

The Great Train Robbery. Directed by Edwin Porter, Edison Manufacturing, 1903.

Grego Assagioli, Roberto. "Il nuovo pensiero americano: Il 'New Thought.'" *Leonardo*, Apr.–June 1907, pp. 201–12.

Grieveson, Lee. *The Silent Cinema Reader*. Routledge, 2004.

Griffin, Charles Eldridge. *Four Years in Europe with Buffalo Bill*. U of Nebraska P, 2010.

Guénon, René. *Theosophy: History of a Pseudo-Religion*. Translated by Alvin Moore, Jr., et al., Sophia Perennis, 2001.

Guglielmo, Thomas. "Toward Essentialism, Toward Difference: Gino Speranza and Conceptions of Race and Italian-American Racial Identity, 1900–1925." *Mid-America*, vol. 81, 1999, pp. 169–213.

Guidotti, Giovanni. *Ebe: Romanzo politico*. Palermo, 1895.

Halfeld, Adolf. *Amerika und der Amerikanismus: Kritische Betrachtungen eines Deutschen und Europäers*. E. Diederichs, 1928.

Hand, John Oliver. "Futurism in America: 1909–1914." *Art Journal*, vol. 41, no. 4, winter 1981, pp. 337–42, https://doi.org/10.1080/00043249.1981.10792498.

Hansen, Jonathan. "True Americanism: Progressive Era Intellectuals and the Problem of Liberal Nationalism." *Americanism: New Perspectives on the History of an Ideal*, edited by Michael Kazin and Joseph McCartin, U of North Carolina P, 2008, pp. 73–89, https://doi.org/10.5149/9780807869710_kazin.6.

Haseler, Stephen. *The Varieties of Anti-Americanism: Reflex and Response*. Ethics and Public Policy Center, 1985.

Hawthorne, Nathaniel. *The Marble Faun*. Oxford UP, 2020.

Hemingway, Ernest. *A Farewell to Arms*. Scribner, 1929.

Hirsch, Robert. *Seizing the Light: A History of Photography*. McGraw-Hill, 2000.

Hirshler, Erica. "'Gondola Days': American Painters in Venice." *The Lure of Italy: American Artists and the Italian Experience, 1760–1914*, by Theodore Stebbins, Museum of Fine Arts, 1992, pp. 112–28.

"History of JP Morgan Chase in Italy." *JP Morgan Chase & Co*, https://www.jpmorganchase.com/news-stories/italy-history. Accessed 5 June 2021.

"History of the Museum." *Museo teatrale alla Scala*, https://www.museoscala.org/en/history/museum/the-history-of-the-museum.html. Accessed 17 July 2024.

Hollander, Paul. *Anti-Americanism: Critiques at Home and Abroad, 1965–1990*. Oxford UP, 1992.

Houdini, Harry. *A Magician among the Spirits*. 1924. Cambridge UP, 2011, https://doi.org/10.1017/CBO9780511910586.

Immigration Act of 1882. *Immigration History*, https://immigrationhistory.org/item/1882-immigration-act. Accessed 31 Mar. 2021.

Incisa di Camerana, Ludovico. "La diplomazia." Bevilacqua et al., pp. 457–80.

Invernizio, Carolina. *I drammi degli emigrati*. Salani, 1910.

Ireland, John. *The Church and Modern Society: Lectures and Addresses*. D.H. McBride, 1897.

Irving, Washington. *A History of the Life and Voyages of Christopher Columbus*. 1828.

Irwin, Elisabeth. "The Story of a Transplanted Industry: Lace Workers of the Italian Quarter of New York." *Craftsman*, vol. 12, no. 4, July 1907, pp. 404–9.

Irwin, Julia. "The American Red Cross in Italy during the Great War." *Journal of the Gilded Age and Progressive Era*. vol. 8, no. 3, July 2009, pp. 407–39, https://doi.org/10.1017/S1537781400001328.

Italy: Handbook for Travellers. Vol 1, *Northern Italy and Corsica*. Vol. 2, *Central Italy and Rome*. Vol. 3, *Southern Italy, Sicily, and the Excursions to the Lipari Islands, Tunis, Sardinia, Malta, and Athens*. 1st ed., Baedeker, 1867. Following printed editions: 1869, 1872, 1873, 1875, and 1876 in Coblenz; 1880, 1883, 1886, 1890, 1893, 1896, 1900, and 1903.

James, Henry. *Italian Hours*. Grove P, 1909.

James, William. "La concezione della coscienza." *Leonardo*, June–Aug. 1905, pp. 77–81.

– "Le energie degli uomini." *Leonardo*, vol. 5, Feb. 1907, pp. 1–25.

– "G. Papini and the Pragmatist Movement in Italy." *Journal of Philosophy, Psychology and Scientific Methods*, vol. 3, no. 13, 21 June 1906, pp. 337–41, https://doi.org/10.2307/2011869.

– *The Letters of William James*. Vol. 2, Longmans, Green, 1920, https://doi.org/10.1037/11011-000.

– *Pragmatism: Popular Lectures on Philosophy*. Longmans, Green, 1907.

"Justice Cotillo Dead Here at 53." *New York Times*, 28 July 1939, p. 11.

Kane, John. "Ambivalent Anti-Americanism." *The Rise of Anti-Americanism*, edited by Brendon O'Connor and Martin Griffiths, Routledge, 2006, pp. 48–67.

Kasson, Joy. *Buffalo Bill's Wild West: Celebrity, Memory, and Popular History*. Hill and Wang, 2000.

Kazin, Michael, and Joseph A. McCartin. Introduction. *Americanism: New Perspectives on the History of an Ideal*, edited by Michael Kazin and Joseph A. McCartin, U of North Carolina P, 2008, pp. 1–22, https://doi.org/10.5149/9780807869710_kazin.3.

Kramer, Rita. *Maria Montessori: A Biography*. Basil Blackwell, 1976.

Kuisel, Richard F. *The French Way: How France Embraced and Rejected American Values and Power*. Princeton UP, 2012, https://doi.org/10.23943/princeton/9780691151816.001.0001.

– *Seducing the French: The Dilemma of Americanization*. U of California P, 1993, https://doi.org/10.1525/9780520918412.

Lacorne, Denis, and Jacques Rupnik et al., editors. *The Rise and Fall of Anti-Americanism: A Century of French Perception*. St Martin's P, 1990.

La Guardia, Fiorello. *The Making of an Insurgent: An Autobiography*. Capricorn, 1948.

La Guardia Gluck, Gemma. *Fiorello's Sister: Gemma La Guardia Gluck's Story*. Edited by Rochelle G. Saidel, Syracuse UP, 2007.

Le Bon, Gustave. *Psychologie des foules*. Presses Universitaires de France, 1947.

Leo XIII. "Apostolic Letter to Satolli." *Public Opinion*, vol. 19, no. 9, 7 Nov. 1895, p. 592.

– *Papal Encyclicals Online*, https://www.papalencyclicals.net/category/leo13. Accessed 13 Dec. 2018. (*Aeterni patris; In amplissimo; Longiqua oceani; Magni gaudii nostri; Non poteva; Quam aerumnosa; Quarto abeunte saeculo; Rerum novarum; Testem benevolentiae nostrae*.)

Leonardo: Rivista d'idee. G. Spinelli, January 1903–August 1907. Periodical.

Leopardi, Giacomo. *Operette morali*. Edited by Giorgio Ficara, Mondadori, 1993.

Licht, Fred. "American Artists in Twentieth Century Italy." *The Lure of Italy: American Artists and the Italian Experience, 1760–1914*, by Theodore Stebbins, Museum of Fine Arts, 1992, pp. 129–45.

Livingstone, Arthur. "Gino Speranza: The Evolution of an American." *The Diary of Gino Speranza, Italy, 1915–1919*, by Gino Speranza, edited by Florence Colgate, Columbia UP, 1941, pp. ix–xxvii, https://doi.org/10.7312/sper93312-001.

Lombroso, Cesare. "Il pericolo nero in Francia." *Nuova antologia*, no. 36, 1 Sept. 1901, pp. 139–50.

– *Ricerche sui fenomeni ipnotici e spiritici*. UTET, 1909.

– *L'uomo delinquente*. Hoepli, 1876.

Lomonaco, Alfonso. *Da Palermo a New Orleans: Note di viaggio*. Loescher, 1897.

Luconi, Stefano. "The Lynching of Southern Europeans in the Southern United States: The Plight of Italian Immigrants in Dixie." *The U.S. South and Europe: Transatlantic Relations in the Nineteenth and Twentieth Centuries*, edited by C.A. van Minnen and M. Berg, UP of Kentucky, 2013, pp. 125–43.

Luti, Giorgio, editor. *La nascita della modernità: Leonardo 1903–1907*. Vallecchi, 2002.

Maccheroni, A.M. *Come conobbi Maria Montessori*. Edizioni vita dell'infanzia, 1956.

Maddalena, Giovanni, and Giovanni Tuzet, editors. *The Italian Pragmatists: Between Allies and Enemies*. Brill Rodopi, 2021, https://doi.org/10.1163/9789004440876.

Magnani, Ilaria. "I migranti nella letteratura italiana: Dall'assenza all'equivalenza." *Zibaldone: Estudios italianos*, vol. 3, no. 1, Jan. 2015, pp. 260–70.

Maignen, Charles. "Le père Hecker, est-il un saint?" *Études sur l'Américanisme*. Desclée, Lefebvre, 1898.

Mancuso, Franco. *"Volare necesse est": Gabriele D'Annunzio nella storia del volo*. Ianieri Editore, 2013.

Mangiafico, Luciano. "Before Serving in Congress and as a Three-Time Mayor of New York, the Colorful Fiorello LaGuardia Spent Nearly Five Years in the U.S. Foreign Service." *American Foreign Service Association*,

https://afsa.org/our-man-fiume-fiorello-laguardia's-short-diplomatic
-career. Accessed 19 Aug. 2022.

Mangoni, Luisa. *Civiltà della crisi: Cultura e politica in Italia tra otto e novecento.*
Viella, 2013.

— *Una crisi fine secolo: La cultura italiana e la Francia tra otto e novecento.* Einaudi,
1985.

Manzoni, Alessandro. *I promessi sposi.* Edited by Salvatore Nigro, Mondadori,
2002.

Manzotti, Luigi. *Excelsior.* Music by Romualdo Marenco. Performance at
Teatro La Scala, Milan, 11 Jan. 1881.

Marazzi, Antonio. *Emigrati: Studio e racconto.* Fratelli Dumolard, 1880–1.

Mariani, Giorgio. "What We Talk about When We Talk about Anti-
Americanism: An Italian Perspective." *Global Perspectives on the United
States: Pro-Americanism, Anti-Americanism, and the Discourses Between,* edited
by Jane Desmond and Virginia Dominguez, U of Illinois P, 2017, pp. 46–60,
https://doi.org/10.5406/illinois/9780252040832.003.0004.

Marinetti, Filippo Tommaso. *L'aeropoema del golfo della Spezia.* Milan, 1935.

— *Teoria e invenzione futurista.* Edited by Luciano De Maria, Mondadori, 1968.

Marinetti, Filippo Tommaso, et al. *Primo dizionario aereo italiano.* Morresi,
1929.

Martelli, Sebastiano. "Dal vecchio mondo al sogno americano: Realtà
e immaginario dell'emigrazione nella letteratura italiana." *Storia
dell'emigrazione italiana: Partenze,* edited by Piero Bevilacqua et al., Donzelli,
2001, pp. 434–88.

Matticoli, Francesco Paolo. *Maria: Scene americane.* 1881.

McCain, Rea. "Walt Whitman in Italy." *Italica,* vol. 20, no. 1, Mar. 1943,
pp. 4–16, https://doi.org/10.2307/476681.

McCauley, Elizabeth Anne. *Isabella Stewart Gardner and the Palazzo Barbaro
Circle.* Isabella Stewart Gardner Museum, 2004.

McGrath Morris, James. *The Ambulance Drivers: Hemingway and Dos Passos and
a Friendship Made and Lost in War.* Da Capo P, 2017.

Melville, Herman. *At the Hostelry and Naples at the Time of Bomba.* Istituto
universitario orientale, 1989.

Messina, Maria. "La Mérica." *Piccoli Gorghi,* Sellerio, 1988, pp. 99–114.

Metropolis. Directed by Fritz Lang, UFA, 1927.

Moe, Nelson. "The Emergence of the Southern Question in Villari, Franchetti,
and Sonnino." *Italy's 'Southern Question': Orientalism in One Country,* edited
by Jane Schneider, Berg, 1998, pp. 51–76, https://doi.org/10.4324
/9781003085768-4.

Molinari, Augusta. "Porti, trasporti, compagnie." *Storia dell'emigrazione
italiana: Partenze,* edited by Piero Bevilacqua et al., Donzelli, 2001,
pp. 237–56.

Monsagrati, Giuseppe. "Un mondo che cambia: Gli americani e l'Italia di fine ottocento." *Gli Stati Uniti e l'Italia alla fine del XIX secolo*, edited by Daniele Fiorentino, Gangemi, 2010, pp. 75–100.

Montessori, Maria. *Il metodo della pedagogia scientifica applicato all'educazione infantile nelle Case dei Bambini*. Tipografia della Casa Editrice S. Lapi, 1909.

– *The Montessori Method: Scientific Pedagogy as Applied to Child Education in the Children's Houses*. Translated by Anne E. George, Frederick A. Stokes, 1912, https://doi.org/10.1037/13054-000.

Montevecchi, Luisa. "Fonti per la storia dell'emigrazione italiana in Africa, Asia e Oceania negli archivi di personalità nell'Archivio Centrale dello Stato." *L'emigrazione italiana, 1870–1970: Atti dei colloqui di Roma. 19–20 settembre 1989; 29–31 ottobre 1990; 28–30 ottobre 1991; 28–30 ottobre 1993*, Ministero per i beni e le attività culturali. Direzione generale per gli archivi, 2002, pp. 603–22.

More, Thomas. *Utopia*. Translated by Paul Turner, Penguin, 2003.

Morris, Edmund. *Theodore Rex*. Random House, 2001.

Mosso, Angelo. *La democrazia nella religione e nella scienza: Studi sull'America*. Treves, 1908.

Muson, Howard. "Fiorello La Guardia: From Congressman to WWI Hero in the Air." *History Net*, 18 Sept. 2020, https://www.historynet.com/the-life-of -fiorello-la-guardia-new-york-mayor-and-wwi-hero/.

New York Times. "Entertain Dr. Montessori." 7 Dec. 1913, p. 17.

– "J.P. Morgan Returns Ascoli Cope to Italy." 4 Nov. 1904, p. 1.

– "Waiting for the Homecoming of Colonel Roosevelt." 3 Apr. 1910, p. 14.

Niccoli, Riccardo. *Book of Flight: From the Flying Machines of Leonardo da Vinci to the Conquest of Space*. Friedman/Fairfax Publishers, 2002.

Nigro, Louis John. *The New Diplomacy in Italy: American Propaganda and U.S.-Italian Relations, 1917–1919*. Peter Lang, 1999.

Nolan, Mary. *Visions of Modernity: American Business and the Modernization of Germany*. Oxford UP, 1994, https://doi.org/10.1093/oso/9780195070217 .001.0001.

Nowell-Smith, Geoffrey. Introduction. *Hollywood and Europe: Economics, Culture, National Identity, 1945–95*, edited by Geoffrey Nowell-Smith and Steven Ricci, BFI Publishing, 1998, pp. 1–18.

Nugent, Walter. *Crossings: The Great Transatlantic Migrations (1870–1914)*. Indiana UP, 1992.

"Ocean Crossings: The Mauretania." *National Museum of American History*, https://americanhistory.si.edu/collections/nmah_1342703. Accessed 7 June 2024.

O'Connor, Brendon. "The Anti-American Tradition: A History in Four Phases." *The Rise of Anti-Americanism*, edited by Brendon O'Connor and Martin Griffiths, Routledge, 2006, pp. 11–24.

Odorico, Odorico. "Alla conquista dell'aria: Dirigibile o aeroplano?" *Corriere della sera*, 16 June 1908.

Ojetti, Ugo. "Accademia navale ad Annapolis." *Corriere della sera*, 27–8 Aug. 1898.

– *L'America e l'avvenire*. Treves, 1905.

– *L'America vittoriosa*. Treves, 1899.

– "Boston e la guerra." *Corriere della sera*, 31 Aug.–1 Sept. 1898.

– "Le cateratte del Niagara." *Corriere della sera*, 23–24 Sept. 1898.

– "Epilogo." *Corriere della sera*, 18–19 Aug. 1898.

– "La grande America e il piccolo mondo." *Corriere della sera*, 3 Oct. 1904.

– "Giudizi e pregiudizi sull'America." *Corriere della sera*, 28 June 1904.

– "Intervista a McKinley." *Corriere della sera*, 29–30 July 1898.

– "John Ireland." *Corriere della sera*, 19–20 Aug. 1898.

– "Lettere dall'America." *Corriere della sera*, 19–20 July 1898.

– "Pellegrinaggio a Mont Vernon." *Corriere della sera*, 16–17 Aug. 1898.

– "Quando gli uomini voleranno." *Corriere della sera*, 18 June 1908.

– "Ritorno dalla flotta da Santiago." *Corriere della sera*, 22–23 Oct. 1898.

– "Su Chicago." *Corriere della sera*, 26–27 Sept. 1898.

– "L'università di Harvard." *Corriere della sera*, 8–9 Sept. 1898.

– "Visita a Baltimora a Gibbons." *Corriere della sera*, 21–22 Aug. 1898.

Olivetti, Camillo. *Lettere americane*. Einaudi, 1968.

Ostuni, Maria Rosaria. "Leggi e politiche di governo nell'Italia liberale e fascista." *Storia dell'emigrazione italiana: Partenze*, edited by Piero Bevilacqua et al., Donzelli, 2001, pp. 309–22.

Pacomio, Fra. "L'America, il Vaticano e la missione di Monsignor Satolli." *Corriere della sera*, 8–9 Feb. 1893.

– "Che cosa diventerebbe il papato in mano agli americani?" *Corriere della sera*, 28–29 June 1892.

– "Note Vaticane." *Corriere della sera*, 15–16 Dec. 1888.

– "Note Vaticane." *Corriere della sera*, 4–5 Mar. 1889.

Page, Thomas Nelson. *Italy and the World War*. Chapman and Hall, 1921.

Panunzio, Constantine. *The Soul of an Immigrant*. Macmillan, 1921.

Papini, Giovanni. *Il crepuscolo dei filosofi*. Vallecchi, 1921.

– "La filosofia del cinematografo." *La Stampa*, 18 May 1907.

– "Franche spiegazioni (a proposito di rinascenza spirituale e occultismo)." *Leonardo*, Apr.–June 1907, pp. 129–43.

– *Il pilota cieco*. Riccardo Ricciardi Editore, 1907.

– *Sul pragmatismo: Opere; Dal "Leonardo" al Futurismo*, by Giovanni Papini, edited by Luigi Baldacci, Mondadori, 1977.

– *Lo trágico cotidiano y el piloto ciego*. La España moderna, 1908.

– *Il tragico quotidiano*. Lumachi, 1906.

– "Uomo-Dio." *Leonardo*, Feb. 1906, pp. 6–15.

– *Un uomo finito.* Libreria della Voce, 1913.

– "Walt Whitman." *La nuova antologia,* Jan. 1908, pp. 1–16.

Pascarella, Cesare. *La scoperta de l'America.* Enrico Voghera, 1895.

Pascoli, Giovanni. "Chavez." *Tutte le poesie,* Mondadori, 1958, pp. 793–6.

– "Italy." *Tutte le poesie,* Mondadori, 1958, pp. 309–30.

Pasi, Marco. "Antonio Fogazzaro e la Teosofia: Una ricognizione sulla base di nuovi documenti inediti." *La ricerca della totalità: Riflessa in una biblioteca dedicata alla storia delle religioni, alla filosofia e, soprattutto, all'esoterismo,* vol. 3, edited by Hans Thomas Hakl, Scientia Nova, 2017, pp. 231–65.

Patriarca, Silvana. "How Many Italies? Representing the South in Official Statistics."*Italy's 'Southern Question': Orientalism in One Country,* edited by Jane Schneider, Berg Publishers. 1998, pp. 77–97, https://doi.org /10.4324/9781003085768-5.

Pavese, Cesare. "In giro per l'America," *L'unità,* 3 Aug. 1947, p. 3.

– *La letteratura americana e altri saggi.* Einaudi, 1951.

Pazzini, Claudia. *Coltivare l'immaginario: Letture e albi illustrati dei bambini di Palazzo Sorbello.* Fondazione Ranieri di Sorbello, 2019.

– *Maria Montessori tra Romeyne Ranieri di Sorbello e Alice Franchetti: Dall'imprenditoria femminile modernista alla creazione del Metodo.* Fefè editore, 2021.

Pells, Richard. *Not Like Us: How Europeans Have Loved, Hated and Transformed American Culture since World War II.* Basic Books, 1997.

Perotti, Antonio. "La società italiana di fronte alle prime migrazioni di massa: Il contributo di Mons. Scalabrini e dei suoi primi collaboratori alla tutela degli emigrante." *La società italiana di fronte alle prime migrazioni di massa,* edited by Cordasco Francesco. Arno P, 1975, pp. 3–196.

Pierantoni, A. "I linciaggi negli Stati Uniti e la emigrazione italiana." *Italia Coloniale,* vol. 6, 1904, p. 51.

Pirandello, Luigi. "L'altro figlio." *Novelle per un anno.* Newton & Compton, 1994, pp. 508–18.

– "Dal naso al cielo." *Novelle per un anno.* Newton & Compton, 1994, pp. 687–93.

– *Il fu Mattia Pascal.* Mondadori, 1988.

– "Rinunzia." *Saggi e interventi,* edited by Ferdinando Taviani, Mondadori, 2006, pp. 126–9.

– "La veste lunga." *Novelle per un anno.* Newton & Compton, 1994, pp. 334–40.

Pius X. *Pascendi Dominici Gregis: Sugli errori del modernismo.* Edizioni Cantagalli, 2007.

Poe, Edgar Allan. *Collected Works of Edgar Allan Poe.* Belknap P of Harvard UP, 1969–78.

Poggioli-Kaftan, Giordana. "The 'Third Space' in Luigi Capuana's *Gli Americani di Ràbbato.*" *Studi d'italianistica nell'Africa Australe,* vol. 31, no. 2, 2018, pp. 29–51.

Porpora, Geneviève. *Le industrie femminili italiane: Una rete culturale per lo sviluppo economico territoriale*. Morlacchi, 2002.

Pozzetta, George E.. "Gino C. Speranza: Reform and the Immigrant." *Reform and Reformers in the Progressive Era*, edited by David R. Colburn and George E. Pozzetta, Greenwood P, 1983, pp. 47–70.

Praino, Rodrigo. "Once upon a Time, the President Rode into Italy on a Sea of Love." *IItaly*, 9 June 2008, http://www.iitaly.org/magazine/focus/facts -stories/article/once-upon-time-president-rode-italy-sea-love. Accessed 13 Sept. 2023.

A Primer of Theosophy. Rajput P, 1909.

"Programma sintetico." *Leonardo*, vol. 1, 4 January 1903, p. 1.

Puccini, Giacomo. *Giacomo Puccini's "La Fanciulla del West,"* edited by Burton Fisher, Opera Journeys Publishing, 2013.

Raffaelli, Sergio. "Un pioniere." *Al cinematografo*, by Gualtiero Fabbri, edited by Raffaelli Sergio, Persiani, 2012, pp. 81–101.

Randall, Annie, and Rosalind Gray Davis, editors. *Puccini and the Girl: History and Reception of "The Girl of the Golden West."* U of Chicago P, 2005.

Ranieri, Ruggero. "Artistic Philanthropy and Women's Emancipation in Early Twentieth-Century Italy, in the Life and the Work of Romeyne Robert and Carolina Amari." Textile Society of America Symposium Proceedings, 2020. *Digital Commons – University of Nebraska*, https://digitalcommons.unl .edu/tsaconf/1192. Accessed 25 Aug. 2022.

– "Romeyne Robert: From Female Entrepreneurship to Cultural Diplomacy." *YouTube*, uploaded by Italian Innovators, 1 June 2022, https://www .youtube.com/watch?v=SLblW7IVki4.

Reghini, Arturo. "Il punto di vista dell'occultismo." *Leonardo*, April–June 1907, pp. 144–56.

Repplier, Agnes. "Americanism." *The Atlantic*, March 1916, https://www .theatlantic.com/magazine/archive/1916/03/americanism/305935. Accessed 19 Sept. 2022.

Reuter, Frank. *Catholic Influence on American Colonial Policies, 1898–1904*. U of Texas P, 1967.

Riis, Jacob. *The Making of an American*. Macmillan, 1901.

Rivista fono-cinematografica e degli automatici, istrumenti pneumatici e affini. Directed by Gualtiero Fabbri. Turin, 1907–8. Periodical.

Rocchetti, Lucio. *Brevetti di invenzione sul doppio fondo fotografico, sul colorito istantaneo e sulla vernice preservativa Sistema Crozat: Tecnica e diffusione tra i fotografi italiani nel 1870*. Gangemi Editore, 2016.

Roger, Philippe. *The American Enemy: The History of French Anti-Americanism*. U of Chicago P, 2005.

Romboli, Floriano. "L'arte 'impersonale' e l'opera romanzesca di Luigi Capuana."*Il verismo italiano fra naturalismo francese e cultura europea*, edited by Romano Luperini, Manni, 2007, pp. 83–117.

Rondina, Francesco Saverio. *L'emigrante italiano: Racconto estratto dalla Civiltà Cattolica, riveduto e corretto dall'autore*. Befani, 1892.

Roosevelt, Theodore. "Americanism." 1915. *What So Proudly We Hail*, Great Hearts Institute, https://whatsoproudlywehail.org/curriculum/the -american-calendar/americanism. Accessed 15 Sept. 2022.

– *The Foes of Our Own Household*. George H. Doran, 1917.

– *The Rough Riders*. Charles Scribner's Sons, 1899.

– "What 'Americanism' Means." *The Forum*, Apr. 1894, pp. 196–206. *Teaching American History*, https://teachingamericanhistory.org/document/true -americanism-the-forum-magazine. Accessed 30 Sept. 2022.

– *The Winning of the West*. U of Nebraska P, 2015.

Roselly de Lorgues, Antoine. *Christophe Colomb: Histoire de sa vie et de ses voyages d'après des documents authentiques tirés d'Espagne et d'Italie*. Didier et cie, libraires-éditeurs, 1856.

Rossi, Adolfo. *Un italiano in America*. La cisalpina, 1899.

– *Nel paese dei dollari (tre anni a New York)*. Max Kantorowicz Edit. (Tip. Degli Operai), 1893.

Rossi, Egisto. *Gli Stati Uniti e la concorrenza americana: Studi di agricoltura, industria e commercio*. G. Barbera, 1884.

Rossini, Daniela. *Woodrow Wilson and the American Myth in Italy: Culture, Diplomacy, and War Propaganda*. Harvard UP, 2008.

Rydell, Robert W, and Rob Kroes, editors. *Buffalo Bill in Bologna: The Americanization of the World, 1869–1922*. U of Chicago P, 2005, https://doi .org/10.7208/chicago/9780226732343.001.0001.

Sacchetti, Enzo. "Ricordi giornalistici." *Gazzetta letteraria*, vol. 24, no. 13, Milano Torino, 31 Mar. 1900.

Sagala, Sandra. *Buffalo Bill on Stage*. U of New Mexico P, 2008.

Salerno, Aldo. "America for Americans Only: Gino Speranza and the Immigrant Experience." *Italian Americana*, vol. 14, no. 2, summer 1996, pp. 133–47.

Salgari, Emilio. *La scotennatrice*. Sonzogno, 1909.

– *Le selve ardenti*. Sonzogno, 1910.

– *Sulle frontiere del West*. 1908. Fabbri, 2002.

Salvemini, Gaetano. "La camicia di Nesso." *L'unità*, 3 May 1919.

– *Dal patto di Londra alla Pace di Roma: Documenti della politica che non fu fatta*. Piero Gobetti, 1925.

Salvetti, Patrizia. *Corda e sapone: Storie di linciaggi degli italiani negli Stati Uniti*. Donzelli, 2003.

Salzano, Achille. *Verso l'Ignoto, il romanzo dell'emigrante*. Tip. Gennaro Errico e Figli, 1903.

Samuels, Peggy. *Teddy Roosevelt at San Juan: The Making of a President*. Texas A&M UP, 1997.

Sanfilippo, Matteo. "Breve storia del cattolicesimo dei migranti – Cristiani d'Italia." *Treccani*, https://www.treccani.it/enciclopedia/breve-storia-del -cattolicesimo-degli-emigranti_%28Cristiani-d%27Italia%29. Accessed 25 Mar. 2021.

– "Chiesa, ordini religiosi, ed emigrazione." *Storia dell'emigrazione italiana: Partenze*, edited by Piero Bevilacqua et al., Donzelli, 2001, pp. 127–42.

– "La chiesa cattolica." Bevilacqua et al., pp. 481–8.

Sassoon, Donald. *The Culture of the Europeans: From 1800 to the Present*. Harper P, 2006.

Scalabrini, Giovanni Battista. *Il disegno di legge sull'emigrazione italiana: Osservazioni e proposte di Mons. Giovanni Battista Scalabrini, Vescovo di Piacenza. La società italiana di fronte alle prime migrazioni di massa*, edited by Francesco Cordasco, Arno P, 1975, pp 233–57. Originally published by Tipografia dell'Amico del Popolo, 1888.

– *L'emigrazione italiana in America: Osservazioni di un vescovo. La società italiana di fronte alle prime migrazioni di massa*, edited by Francesco Cordasco, Arno P, 1975, pp 201–30. Originally published by Tipografia dell'Amico del Popolo, 1887.

Schneider, Jane. "The Dynamics of Neo-Orientalism in Italy (1848–1995)." *Italy's 'Southern Question': Orientalism in One Country*, edited by Schneider, Berg Publishers, 1998, pp. 1–26, https://doi.org/10.4324/9781003085768-1.

Semplice. "La città di New York." *Corriere della sera*, 6–7 May 1893, p. 1.

– "L'esposizione di Chicago." *Corriere della sera*, 18–19 May 1893, p. 1.

– "Filadelfia." *Corriere della sera*, 25–26 July 1893, p. 1.

– "Hartford." *Corriere della sera*, 2–3 Aug. 1893, p. 1.

– "L'Italia agli Stati Uniti." *Corriere della sera*, 18–19 Aug. 1893, p. 1.

– "Un po' di politica." *Corriere della sera*, 8–9 May 1893, p. 1.

– "La Rabida a Chicago." *Corriere della sera*, 8–9 July 1893, p. 1.

– "Sull'esposizione di Chicago." *Corriere della sera*, 23–24 Apr. 1893, p. 1.

– "La vita in America." *Corriere della sera*, 2–3 May 1893, p. 1.

Shalhope, Robert. "Anticipating Americanism: An Individual Perspective on Republicanism in the Early Republic." *Americanism: New Perspectives on the History of an Ideal*, edited by Michael Kazin and Joseph McCartin, U of North Carolina P, 2008, pp. 53–72, https://doi.org/10.5149 /9780807869710_kazin.5.

Sorbello, Giuseppe. "Luigi Capuana e l'immaginario scientifico di fine secolo: I raggi x, la telepatia e la fotografia del pensiero." *Dalla Sicilia a Mompracem e altro: Studi per Mario Tropea*, edited by Giuseppe Sorbello and Giuseppe Traina, Edizioni Lussografica, 2015, pp. 547–61.

Soresina, Marco. "Italian Emigration Policy during the Great Migration Age, 1888–1919." *Journal of Modern Italian Studies*, vol. 21, no. 5, 2016, pp. 723–46, https://doi.org/10.1080/1354571X.2016.1242260.

Speranza, Gino. *The Diary of Gino Speranza, Italy, 1915–1919*. Edited by
Florence Colgate Speranza, Columbia UP, 1941, https://doi.org/10.7312
/sper93312.
– *Race or Nation? A Conflict of Divided Loyalties*. Arno P, 1975.
Staiti, Claudio. "The Ocean Is Bridged: The Italian Great War in the Diary of
Gino C. Speranza (1915–1919)." *Journal of Mediterranean Knowledge*, vol. 6,
no. 1, 2021, pp. 9–33.
Stead, William Thomas. *The Americanization of the World*. H. Markley, 1901.
Svevo, Italo. *La coscienza di Zeno*. Edited by Giovanna Joli, UTET, 1990.
Taylor, Frederick Winslow. *The Principles of Scientific Management*. Routledge/
Thoemmes P, 1993.
Tenneriello, Susan. *Spectacle Culture and American Identity, 1815–1940*. Palgrave
Macmillan, 2013, https://doi.org/10.1057/9781137360625.
Teodori, Massimo. *Maledetti americani: Destra, sinistra e cattolici; Storia del
pregiudizio antiamericano*. Mondadori, 2002.
"Teosofia in Italia." *Società Teosofica italiana*, https://www.teosofica.org/it
/societa-teosofica/origine-e-storia/teosofia-in-italia/,29. Accessed 28 June
2021.
Teti, Vito. "Emigrazione, alimentazione, culture popolari." *Storia
dell'emigrazione italiana: Partenze*, edited by Piero Bevilacqua et al., Donzelli,
2001, pp. 575–600.
Tocqueville, Alexis de. *De la démocratie en Amérique*. Charles Gosselin,
1835–40.
Tomes, Nancy. *The Gospel of Germs: Men, Women, and the Microbe in American
Life*. Harvard UP, 1999.
Toninelli, Pierangelo. "La questione energetica." *Storia d'Italia: Annali;
L'industria*, vol. 15, Einaudi, 1999, pp. 351–84.
Tosti, Gustavo. "Review. Angelo Mosso's *La democrazia nella religione e nella
scienza*." *Science*, New Series, vol. 14, no. 347, 23 Aug. 1901, pp. 293–5,
https://doi.org/10.1126/science.14.347.293.
Tozier, Josephine. "An Educational Wonder-Worker: The Methods of Maria
Montessori." *McClure Magazine*, vol. 37, May 1911, pp. 3–19.
– "The Revolutionary Educational Work of Maria Montessori as Carried Out
in Her Own Schools." *McClure Magazine*, vol. 38, Dec. 1911, pp. 123–37.
Trask, David. *The War with Spain in 1898*. Macmillan, 1981.
Traxel, David. *1898: The Birth of the American Century*. Vintage Books, 1999.
Trento, Angelo. "In Brasile." Bevilacqua, et al., pp. 3–24.
Tuchman, Barbara. *The Zimmermann Telegram*. Ballantine Books, 1985.
Twain, Mark. *The Innocents Abroad*. Oxford UP, 1996.
Umbro, Apollonio, editor. *Futurist Manifestos*. MFA Publications, 2001.
Valoroso, Antonella, and Ruggero Ranieri, editors. *Uguccione Ranieri di
Sorbello: Un intellettuale tra due mondi*. Morlacchi, 2019.

Vecoli, Rudolph. "Negli Stati Uniti." Bevilacqua, et al., pp. 55–88.

Villari, Pasquale. *Lettere meridionali*. Tipografia dell'opinione, 1875.

Viscusi, Robert. Introduction to the American Edition. *Italoamericana: The Literature of the Great Migration, 1880–1943*, edited by Francesco Durante, Fordham UP, 2014, pp. xv–xxx, https://doi.org/10.2307/j.ctt13x0432.5.

Vitali, Luigi. "Le idee di un vescovo cattolico americano." *Rassegna nazionale*, 16 Dec. 1894, pp. 809–25.

Vittorini, Elio. *Americana: Raccolta di narratori*. Bompiani, 1941.

Wagnleitner, Reinhold. *Coca-Colonization and the Cold War*. U of North Carolina P, 1994.

Watt, Mary Alexandra. *Dante, Columbus, and the Prophetic Tradition: Spiritual Imperialism in the Italian Imagination*. Routledge, 2017, https://doi .org/10.4324/9781315232959.

Wells, Herbert George. *The Future in America*. St Martin's P, 1987.

Whitman, Walt. *Foglie d'erba*. Translated by Luigi Gamberale, Milano-Palermo-Napoli, Remo Sandron editore, 1907.

"Wild West: 1906 Program Milano, Italy." *Library Center of the West*, http:// library.centerofthewest.org/digital/collection/BBOA/id/1635. Accessed 16 May 2017.

Wilson, Woodrow. "President Woodrow Wilson's Fourteen Points (1918)." *National Archives*, https://www.archives.gov/milestone-documents /president-woodrow-wilsons-14-points. Accessed 25 Aug. 2022.

"World War One and the American Red Cross." *American Red Cross*, https:// www.redcross.org/content/dam/redcross/National/history-wwi.pdf. Accessed 19 Aug. 2022.

Wylie, Winifred. "Montessori and the Theosophical Society." *Quest*, vol. 96, no. 2, March–April 2008, pp. 53–5.

Yarrow, Clarence. "The Forging of Fascist Doctrine." *Journal of the History of Ideas*, vol. 3, no. 2, Apr. 1942, pp. 159–81, https://doi.org/10.2307/2707175.

Zangwill, Israel. *The Melting Pot*. Performance, 5 Oct. 1908, Washington, DC.

Zeiler, Thomas. "Basepaths to Empire: Race and the Spalding World Baseball Tour."*Journal of the Gilded Age and Progressive Era*, vol. 6, no. 2, Apr. 2007, pp. 179–207, https://doi.org/10.1017/S1537781400001997.

Index